Prague Notebook

PRAGUE NOTEBOOK

The Strangled Revolution

by Michel Salomon

Translated from the French
by Helen Eustis

Little, Brown and Company
Boston–Toronto

Published simultaneously in Canada
by Little, Brown & Company (Canada) Limited

PRINTED IN THE UNITED STATES OF AMERICA

Author's Note

This book does not set out to be anything more than a journalist's account of what he saw and heard during Prague's "thaw." It is the record of one of those lost opportunities which are milestones in our postwar history. Probably it is the most serious, the one for which we will entertain the most acute regrets, and also the one whose failure will seem to us the most unreasonable, because the conditions for success seemed so signally united in it.

When I conceived the idea for this work, not only had I no suspicion of the tragic outcome of the thaw, but I was motivated by an optimism which now seems ridiculous.

What excited me in observing the process of democratization from its beginnings was the "realization of the un-realizable," to use an expression of one of my friends, one of the architects of the "renaissance" in Slovakia, which was that unprecedented transition from totalitarian oppression to something which was not yet clearly discernible but which, without any doubt, was a new form of democratic life. And this through a phenomenon equally without precedent.

What was surprising about the whole business was not so much the pacifist, utterly nonviolent character of the transition from dictatorship to democracy on the one hand, or the scrupulous respect for the rules of "socialist legality" on the other (Novotny was overthrown by a shift of majority like a popular bourgeois prime minister), as the role played by public opinion.

The "quiet revolution" was first and foremost the result of an overwhelming popular consensus, to the extent that the Czechs and the Slovaks could make their voices heard, could loosen the gag which had muzzled them for twenty years. Thanks to those voices, a handful of inexperienced men, often disarmingly naïve, were able to triumph over the formidable power of a totalitarian state — police, army, and omnipresent machine — by simple virtue of words, of persuasion.

So I decided to study from their beginnings the internal mechanisms of the different means by which the comprehensive transition from centralism would be effected.

The "powers that be" at that time were new and without arrogance. The men whom I interviewed in turn interviewed me. They carried on dialogues with the newspapers, with the man in the street. Prague, more than the Paris of May, was the forum of all debates, one of the high places of political thought. The future of Europe, perhaps its unity, would depend on the solutions the Czechs found for the major and minor problems which exist in all popular democracies, indeed in all the free world.

What mechanism for the control of power could be substituted simultaneously for an obsolete parliamentarianism and an authoritarian communist centralism? How could justice be made congruous with liberty and economic socialism, with the necessary spirit of enterprise and competition? How were the press, radio, and television to be protected simultaneously against censorship and the distortions of the "market"? How could one reconcile antagonistic "nationalities," conflicting generations, or variant social classes that a "class struggle" had crushed together, in the end leaving the "workers" no better off than the former "bourgeois"?

This book is made up of two parts.

In the first we shall review, from the fall of the dictator Novotny to the Soviet invasion, the history of those eight months which nearly succeeded in giving a human countenance to a communist state. The continual alteration of crazy hopes and bitter disappointments left the witness with the taste of ashes in his mouth. It is easier to be a spectator of clear-cut catastrophe than to watch hope encouraged and stifled by turns.

In the second part, we shall recall the far-reaching reasons which gave birth to the new course of action; some of these arose as long ago as Munich and the Prague coup of 1948. The collapse of the economy, the revolt of the intellectuals and the Slovaks, and the ever painful memory of Stalinist excesses — the factors whose combined effect was to unleash the process of democratization — will be analyzed.

I would here like to thank but leave unnamed, for reasons easily understood, all those men and women who, in Prague and Bratislava, helped me with my work and who believed, for a moment, that the time for free dialogue had come.

I dedicate this book to them.

Contents

Author's Note   v

I. A CZECHOSLOVAKIAN SPRING: NOTES ON EIGHT MONTHS
   OF DEMOCRATIC SOCIALISM

1. Prelude: Death of a Regime . . . June–December 1967   3

   Prague 1967 — Anton Novotny — The Writers' Congress
   (June) — Footnote: Hendrych — Dissension (September)
   — Footnote: A Discreet Inquiry — Rebellion (October) —
   The Month of Conspiracies — Revolt (December) — Ap-
   pendix: The Disease of Power

2. Interlude: Democratic Socialism Aborning . . . January–
   March 1968   51

   The Red Tsar of Hradschin — His Partisans — His Friend
   Sejna (January) — The Opposition and Its Watchdog — The
   People (February) — Their Man Dubcek — Novotny's Death
   Knell (March)

3. Five Months: A Lifetime . . . March 22–August 22,
   1968   78

   Heatwave — Spring Cleaning (April) — The Party and Its
   Policy — The Parade (May) — The Program — The Quarrel — Delusion — The Spirit of Munich (June) — The

Contents

Czechoslovakian Case — Appendix: Two Thousand Words — Letter from the Five — Prague's Reply

4. Toward the End . . . July 18–August 22, 1968   **132**

Voices of Unanimity (July) — A War of Nerves — The Last Chance — The Appeal — One Moment in Time — The Last Days (August) — Appendix: The Citizens' Appeal — Bratislava Communiqué — Tass Communiqué

5. Invasion . . . August 20–26, 1968   **175**

Midnight at Ruzyne Airport — Betrayal and Confusion — The Reports of Ambassador Chervonenko — A Journey to Moscow — The Curtain Falls — Appendix: Proclamation by the Government of Czechoslovakia to All Czechoslovakian People — Proclamation of the Special Meeting of the Fourteenth Congress of the Czechoslovakian Communist Party to the Citizens of Czechoslovakia — The Protocol from Moscow — The November Resolution of the Central Committee

II. HERITAGE AND HOPE: NOTES ON THE PRISONS, THE PEOPLES, AND THE PROBLEMS OF THE FUTURE

1. Nightmare   **211**

Ruzyne — Kolodeje — "Report on the Violations" — *Deportation Journal* — Jachimov — Reading the Statistics — Remember . . . — The Shadow of the Terror

2. Revolt   **232**

The Intellectuals' Bridge — Pen and Sword — Operation Sparrow — Boomerang — The Communist Revolt — A Socialist Victory — Caesar the Magnificent — Guard in a Cemetery

3. A Lion by the Tail   **254**

A Marriage of Reason — The Separation — Charter of Kosice — Bratislava — Prague — Model for Conciliation

4. Debacle: A Conversation with an Economist   **274**

The Face of the Victim — The Facts: Ota Sik Speaks Out — The Conversation with Eugen Loebl

5. Reflection: Conversations with a Philosopher   302

The Magic Lantern — A Marxist but Not a Communist —
The System and Its Myths — Winter, Spring, and Summer
1968 — A Digression — Antithesis to Summer — A Prospectus for Autumn — Perspective

Epilogue   333

March–April 1969 — May 1969 — Conclusion

Index   351

I.

A Czechoslovakian Spring

Notes on Eight Months
of Democratic Socialism

1.

Prelude: Death of a Regime
... June–December 1967

Prague 1967 — Anton Novotny — The Writers' Congress
(June) — Footnote: Hendrych — Dissension (September) —
Footnote: A Discreet Inquiry — Rebellion (October) — The
Month of Conspiracies — Revolt (December) — Appendix:
The Disease of Power

[Prague 1967]

From what point in time can the beginning of the "quiet revolution" in Czechoslovakia be dated? From a congress of writers in the spring of 1967? From a student demonstration a few months later? The Czechs often speak of the "victorious January" of 1968, derisively borrowing the official terminology which christened the date of the Prague coup, the take-over of power by the Communist party in 1948, "victorious February." In fact, a long sequence of events preceded the successive explosions which transformed the severest communist rule in Central Europe into that "democratic socialism" whose advent threatened to upset the political chessboard of Europe and perhaps of the world.

Prague in 1967 was the empire of Novotny at its zenith. The marvelous baroque city which was literally crumbling to

3

ruins — that spring a number of pedestrians were injured and two little girls killed by falling cornices — mirrored a country worn to the bone, crowded with police and informers, soiled with posters and primitive slogans, appearing to the Western eye as merely a shadow theater. But in this country where Trnka's marionettes were elevated to the stature of the Japanese No drama, one had to learn to interpret the characters of this theater.

[Anton Novotny]

I tried to get to know Anton Novotny, the last Stalinist caesar of the Czechoslovakian Republic. A little while after his fall, I went to Novotny's home, a big gray ugly villa on residential Smichov Hill. I rang the doorbell and rang again. A curtain moved, but no one came to open the door. Hilare, a neighbor of the fallen dictator, told me: "He won't let you in. He lets in no one except his old friend the ambassador of the U.S.S.R."

This neighbor, a young painter, invited me into his home: "I was here when Novotny brought his belongings back to his villa after he lost his job. He brought a whole library home in his black Tatra; he moved it himself, hugging his books to his heart." The painter laughed. "In all Czech memory nobody's ever seen him read one. But perhaps he was trying to understand how writers, those wretched scribblers he scorned so much, could have dislodged him from his throne."

Anton Novotny, the president of the Socialist Republic of Czechoslovakia and the secretary-general of the Communist party, ruled in Prague for fourteen years. With his sad face, thin lips, and square chin, Novotny was the perfect bureaucratic robot, the apparatchik. He succeeded the violent, full-blooded Klement Gottwald as a pale understudy. This former metalworker had none of the plebeian energy of his predecessor. He was not even an actor of any importance in the country's Shakespearean drama at the time of the great trials. His discretion and his unbelievable servility to Moscow had alone served him.

In 1967 Anton Novotny was the only sachem of the satellite countries who combined in his rule party leadership with the presidency of the Republic. This last title was surrounded by a prestige greater in the homeland of Masaryk than anywhere else in the East. Vain, obsessed with pomp and protocol, Novotny spent his time on the left bank of the Vltava at Hradschin, the presidential château set in the handsome architectural jewel of Mala Strana, the pride of the old city. He left the operation of the machine to his supporters, among whom Hendrych was his *éminence grise*.

Son of a workman, Anton was born in Prague in 1904. He joined the ranks of the Communist party at the age of seventeen, but he did not win a responsible post until the eve of Munich. He was thirty-five years old when he became the secretary of Hodonin, a little town in Moravia. A year later, when the party was made illegal, Novotny was a member of the C.P. of Prague, before being arrested by the Gestapo in 1941 and sent to the concentration camp at Mauthausen for four years. (An unpleasant controversy erupted in May 1968 during the appeal proceedings of Rudolf Barak, Novotny's former minister of the interior.[1] Barak stated to the court that he possessed evidence that Novotny was an informer for the Nazis in the concentration camp. His lawyer stated on Barak's behalf that Novotny had been classed as a war criminal by the Netherlands government. However, the Russian tanks entered Prague before the "evidence" of Novotny's former companion was produced. In any case, the Commission of the Second World War in the Netherlands was willing neither to confirm nor to deny this serious charge.)

Prelude: Death of a Regime

Until September 1951, when he was again a party functionary in Prague, Novotny was simply in the rank and file. Later,
to make Novotny a figure at Gottwald's side, photography experts would have to retouch the group photographs of the
"victorious February." The Slansky trial (1951–1952), which
decimated the ranks of party headquarters, provided a place
for Anton in the Politburo. He was vice-premier, member of
the government, and, in 1953, first secretary of the Central
Committee. His political capital: he enjoyed the limitless confidence of the Russians, of Khrushchev in particular. In November 1957 after Antonin Zapotocky's death, Novotny was
elected president of the Republic, at the direct pressure of
Moscow.

Morose, gruff, speaking in clichés, totally lacking any humor,
Novotny was hated with a touching unanimity that gave rise to
a folklore of jokes as funny as they were inexhaustible. But this
dull and hardworking bureaucrat, this model pupil of Stalinism, had a Janus face.

Ladislav Mnacko, the celebrated Slovakian author, had given
some thought to the dictator in writing his book on Novotny's
regime, *The Taste for Power*, and was to tell me: "This man so
long-faced in public was capable of roaring with laughter in
private. This puritan, who fired secretaries caught wearing mini-
skirts in the corridors of the presidential palace, had a mistress.
But it was probably the best-kept secret in the Republic. The
truth is that power terrified him. He didn't feel he had either
the intelligence or the strength of character to assume the
crushing burdens of secretary-general of the party and presi-
dent-dictator."

To strangers he appeared to be the most charming and con-
siderate of hosts. Yet Guy Mollet and François Mitterrand,
secretary-general and deputy respectively of the Federation of
the Democratic Left and Socialists, remembered their amaze-
ment in 1966 at the brutal frankness with which Novotny

spoke to them of the position of his country and its relationship with Moscow. Pacing up and down his presidential salon at Hradschin, he would burst into curses against the Soviet exploitation of his country, creating such uneasiness among his guests that they at times thought he was up to some devious provocation.

The French minister of foreign affairs, Maurice Couve de Murville, on an official trip to Prague in the summer of 1966 wished during a visit of protocol to propose a "treaty of friendship" similar to the one which linked Czechoslovakia to the U.S.S.R. Before his own stunned ministers and a hypnotized Couve de Murville, tipsy on Tokay and Crimean champagne, Novotny went so far as to ignore the Warsaw Pact and NATO. An hour later he had lost all recollection of his unlikely proposal of a treaty between members of rival alliances.

Blundering, stubborn, mistrustful, alternately amazingly sly and disarmingly naïve, Novotny in 1967 ruled over a country which had touched bottom and which as the hardest of the three countries in the famous iron triangle, East Germany, Poland, and Czechoslovakia, seemed to have a granite immobility. But in reality, beneath this surface immobility the three factors which were to lead to the fall of Novotny and the beginning of the quiet revolution — economic unrest, the discontent of the intellectuals, and, last but not least, the restlessness of the Slovaks — had been fermenting for a long time, since the 1956 Twentieth Congress of the Soviet C.P., in fact, which had tried to exorcise the Stalinist demons.

The crushing of Budapest in 1956 had been only an intermediate tragedy. "It showed us how far one could go," one of the planners of the quiet revolution said to me, "and, in light of the U.S.S.R.'s subsequent loss of prestige and of the predicament of international communism, just how far the Soviets could afford to go — if a new crisis comparable to that of 1956

7

were to break out." My interlocutor was not a very good prophet.

The two swallows which announced the Czechoslovakian spring took flight from the very heart of the Communist party in 1963 in the form of two commissions of experts — one a group of thirty-six historians under the direction of Gustav Husak, vice-president of the Council of Ministers; the other an assemblage of economists under the aegis of Ota Sik,[2] who was later vice-premier in the Dubcek team. Novotny did not believe for an instant that those gentle scholars to whom he opened the party archives for the first time would constitute a danger to his regime. On the contrary, they were to surround it with that halo of "scientific" prestige to which he was partial. He wanted to be the equal of the U.S.S.R. in his "establishment" of conformist academicians. But the red tsar of Hradschin did not know the history of his own country very well nor the close bonds which, from the beginning of time, had united an old and cultivated people with its intellectual elite. The two commissions began to bring forth from the party archives, a veritable Pandora's box, the very facts, figures, and statistics which would furnish the debate with the arsenal of arguments it lacked.

[The Writers' Congress (June)]

On June 2, in the grand ballroom of the Lucerna, the Writers' Congress opened in a turbulent atmosphere. Kafka had known this dingy, hollow, three-story pleasure palace whose entrance opened on one of those singular covered passageways which permit those who know Prague to cross the center of the city without getting wet on a rainy day. This Writers' Congress was to be the first open eruption against the Novotny regime.

According to police reports, Novotny did not at first attach much importance to the lucubrations of the "chatterboxes." His attitude is conceivable simply because the Congress was initially unbelievably confused, particularly by the misunderstanding which from the beginning separated the Czech and the Slovak delegations. For several years the Slovak writers had enjoyed a privileged role, thanks to the tolerant politics of the secretary-general of the Slovak C.P., Alexander Dubcek, and could not understand the bad temper of the Czechs who had undergone a Draconian repression for the preceding few months. The Prague writers were dismayed by their colleagues from Bratislava, whom they accused of egoism, if not treason. (Mnacko himself impulsively collected signatures for a petition in favor of Novotny, whom several weeks later he was to attack violently.)

This Congress was dominated by an extraordinary series of lectures by a young writer of proletarian origins, Ludvik Vaculik, then forty-one years old and a party member. His contribution, greeted by a long ovation, was the fiercest attack against neo-Stalinist dogmatism ever heard from either side of the iron curtain and a vibrant plea for free and democratic socialism (see appendix in this chapter). This speech marked, in the view of a number of qualified observers, the birth of the "new direction," or at least its transition from romantic dreams to a clear doctrinal formulation. It is not surprising that this same Vaculik was to be the originator of that other explosive document called "Two Thousand Words" (see appendix in chapter 3).

This ungainly fellow with wild hair, a fierce timidity, and the look of a countryman despised speaking in public. He was to tell me: "It had to come out. I considered every word for years. Finding the truth again in things and words was painful and dazzling after so many distortions and lies. I had to rediscover the simplest words and what they meant. What is justice, what is liberty, what is socialism? I never exactly knew what socialism was; it's a complicated business. But at least I do know what it isn't."

Anton Liehm, one of the founders of the *Literarni Noviny* (*Literary News*), the writers' weekly, was on the rostrum of the Writers' Congress and described the explosion of fury of Jiri Hendrych, the ideological commissar of the Communist party. From the first day, Hendrych had followed the development of the debates with growing rage. The members of the Congress had protested with unaccustomed vigor against censorship, anti-Semitism inside the party, the pro-Arab policy of the government, and the despotism of the police. Pressure was mounting dangerously. After Pavel Kohout's speech, when he read from the rostrum Alexander Solzhenitsyn's famous secret letter against censorship, Hendrych exploded. According to Liehm: "This big man, fifty-two years old, who had had several heart attacks in the past, almost had another cardiac crisis. Standing there, he stammered with rage; his face was the color of an eggplant. Unable to restrain himself, he rushed out of the lecture hall, got tangled in the red draperies, and bumped violently into a window which he mistook for the door. Quite giddy, he leaned against the wall for a moment, refusing any help. Before finally leaving, he loosed this Parthian shot: 'You'll pay me for this, everything you're worth.' "

Hendrych immediately went to the Hradschin castle and asked Novotny to close the Congress. Hesitating, the sullen dictator counseled patience, and with his bureaucrat's habit of being meticulous to the point of caricature, demanded a "report": Who takes writers seriously? Let these chatterers talk themselves hoarse. He sent his *éminence grise* about his business.

[Footnote: Hendrych]

This did not help dissipate the uneasiness which had existed for some time between the two men. Such cavalier treatment persuaded Hendrych, already abnormally suspicious by nature, like all the *proeminenz* in a communist regime, that Novotny was preparing to deal him a low blow. Previously, in the first weeks of May, Novotny had solemnly summoned his colleague and, showing him a thick dossier, had said: "Pan Hendrych, I have enough here to hang you. I know from police reports that your daughter sleeps with the writer Jan Benes, an enemy of our Republic. Your daughter's escapades don't interest me, but the fact that she transmits documents concerning the security of the state is serious. These documents are addressed to Pavel Tigrid, a Paris émigré who is our worst enemy . . ." Then, good-naturedly, Novotny had forgiven and dismissed him. Hendrych later said, using the diminutive of Anton, President Novotny's first name, "Tonichke, you're not going to make another Barak out of me."

In fact, the writer Benes, a young man of thirty, was sentenced by a closed court in July to five years in prison. In a little apartment in the Latin quarter I asked Pavel Tigrid, the founder of the Czech-language review *Svedectvi (Evidence)*, what was at the bottom of this incident. Bursting into laughter, the journalist gave me his version:

"Hendrych's daughter had nothing to do with this story. Young Benes, who used to write down all his romances in a little notebook, did in fact know a Miss Hendrych from Brno. When the police were trying to make life hard for writers in any way they could, they pretended to know that this was the daughter of the formidable ideological commissar of the party. Examined in his prison cell, Benes admitted to anything. And then Novotny came into the game, believing, like a good Stalinist, that the faked dossier would give him a better hold on his colleague."

This little game was to cause Novotny's downfall several months later. While waiting, the tormented Hendrych swung between the desire to regain his master's confidence by a show of excessive zeal and the wish to get rid of him in order to save his own skin. This police farce would have decisive consequences in the genesis of the January revolution.

[Dissension (September)]

On the first of September 1967, Anton Novotny gave the "hardest" speech of his career before the students of the military academies. The intellectuals' agitation, which he had tolerated up to now, thereafter took on much greater importance. Before the young officers standing at attention in the historic court of the castle of Prague, the dictator fulminated: "Much pacifism, frivolity, and absence of scruples has poisoned the spirit of the people, both in information and in education. Liberalism is spreading, as is objectivism."

This dealt a killing blow to the timid and altogether academic discussions on economic management and the structures of the state, which Novotny himself had at one time encouraged among the historians grouped around Husak and the economists on Ota Sik's staff. But perhaps he was beginning to realize the dangers which accompanied even academic research into the truth. He continued:

"We have tolerated a number of opinions in the discussion about future means of development in the socialist society, and some people have interpreted this as a weakness of the Communist party, a weakness of the leadership of the state. As a result they have taken action . . . These are class enemies, former national socialists of the right,[3] champions of the clergy, and social democrats who once more are spreading the opinions against which the party fought after 1945. Democracy and liberty have their limits. It is no longer possible to tolerate the spread of opinions and of an ideology which is hostile to socialism and foreign to the Communist party."

He announced administrative measures — that is to say, police measures — and the replacement of personnel judged to be too soft, in order that "this conciliatory spirit, incubator of political compromise and inconsistency," should be eliminated.

The next day, at the meeting of the Politburo, Novotny asked the ten holders of supreme power in Czechoslovakia[4] to ratify his new hard line on the premise that "the class enemy has raised its head again." He demanded an immediate purge of party cadres to insure that important posts would be held only by communists who were uncontaminated by bourgeois ideas, were "100 percent sure." These demands plunged the Presidium into disorder. There is no doubt that the Presidium, with the exception of Dubcek and Cernik, was composed of the orthodox.

But even these men, closer to day-to-day reality than Novotny, with his dreams of grandeur under the carved ceilings of Hradschin, were aware of the repercussions a new turn of the screw would have in a country already discouraged, demoralized, and bled dry.

Novotny's demands precipitated ideological conflict, for they were contrary to the latest party line enunciated in February on the thirteenth anniversary of the Prague coup. The resolution that was passed declared that the class struggle was no longer the driving force of the revolution because, in effect, there were no longer any conflicting classes and, thus, no class enemies in the Republic; all the people without exception were to be considered "socialist" citizens, equal in rights and duties.

Ideological discussions, in all their Byzantine glory, are subjects for laughter in the West. In Eastern Europe an adjective or a misplaced comma in a communiqué can bring about the death of men or the ruin of an economic sector. Words can kill. In this September session, a little man broke the shocked silence of Novotny's Presidium audience. In a soft poised voice, the secretary-general of the Slovak C.P., Alexander Dubcek, said, "I don't agree with you, Comrade President Novotny; your analysis does not seem correct to me." [5]

Dubcek's interruption prompted a discussion which was animated but not heated. The discussion was stopped short in order that the "theses" for the October meeting of the Central Committee might be outlined. The proposals for the October meeting, prepared by the inevitable Hendrych and adopted unanimously, contained a bland phrase which passed unnoticed at the time: "We must take up the problem of pluralism in the high levels of the machine and of the party." This was a ritual phrase, repeated almost mechanically from year to year in the preparatory papers for the Central Committee conferences.

The Central Committee of one hundred and ten members, elected every four years by the congress of the C.P., had previously not played much of a part: according to the thesis of political centralism dear to Lenin, the Central Committee served as an echo chamber which simply ratified the decisions of the Presidium. The September session of the Central Committee was particularly lamentable. In the course of this plenum, held on September 27 and 28, Ivan Klima, Ludvik Vaculik, Pavel Kohout, and Anton Liehm were expelled. These four were writers accused of having held ideas which "nourished anticommunist propaganda" at the Writers' Congress. The future progressives raised no objections. Only two delegates of the Central Committee admitted to timid reservations on the decision to exclude the writers without having heard them: Vaclav Slavik, who was one of the secretaries of the Central Committee, and Frantisek Vodslon, an old man who had been the president of the Athletic Associations of Czechoslovakia. Novotny, who had dismissed Vodslon from his post two months earlier, said jokingly, "I know why Comrade Vodslon won't give us his vote."

Josef Smrkovsky told me, "We didn't want to open hostilities over a matter which seemed minor to us. We did not wish to expose our weapons too soon."

The progressives had begun to regroup their ranks and to count their numbers, but the assumption made later of a conspiracy between the two factions of party malcontents, the seething intellectuals and the Slovaks, seems contradicted by the facts. A cold putsch had not, at that time, been premeditated by the progressive elements. Nevertheless, the arguments and feverish transactions in both camps could not long escape the notice of Novotny's omnipresent police and military security, both of which were themselves infected by a virus of doubt, to be recognized several months later by the conservatives and their spearhead, Major General Jan Sejna.

At Vlkovice, a little town in Moravia, the party secretary of Brno, Josef Spacek, a forty-five-year-old engineer who was a big blond bespectacled fellow with a penchant for food, received Dubcek, Smrkovsky, and others in his country house. These men were preparing for the meeting of the Central Committee in October.

Like Cestmir Cisar, Spacek was a typical apparatchik of the second generation, that generation which had ceased to romanticize the working class and had reallied itself with Czech traditions of culture and democracy. Spacek was a scientist, if not a technocrat, who for a long time had passed for an eccentric; he was often teased about his mania for cross-indexing and filing all questions raised in the course of party meetings. This placid man who both enjoyed solid friendships among the intellectuals and entertained the affections and respect of the workers in Brno was to be the strategist of the revolution of which Dubcek was already the tactician.

The chief weapon of the revolutionaries was to be that harmless little phrase about pluralism of functions. This little phrase, lost in the mass of documents presenting theses for debate, had not been placed there by chance. For the Communist party had been in a crisis — a crisis of recruitment. Youth had turned its back. Cell meetings, business meetings — those dreary orations of hot air which are the only form of political life in the communist world — were attended to by a handful of "veterans," survivors of the workers' militia, covered with tin insignia, who rehashed their exploits of February 1948 like old soldiers. Times had changed; it was no longer necessary to have a party card to receive professional recognition. The era of hairdresser-factory-managers had ended; in the face of economic ruin, competence was actually humbly sought, even in the ranks of "enemies of the regime." [6]

[Footnote: A Discreet Inquiry]

Concerned by the aging of party members and militants, the Presidium had in 1966 directed that a discreet inquiry be made by a team of sociologists and statisticians into six hundred Communist organizations — factory cells, women's groups, athletic groups, philatelic groups, and the like. This sampling was expected to give a complete "chart" of the state of health of the C.P. throughout the country. The conclusions of the probe were disastrous, for it revealed a crisis whose gravity no one had even imagined. "The party has almost no moral or political influence on our youth or on the activist elements in the nation," the report concluded, without rhetorical euphemism.

The party stood isolated in the midst of a population whose hostility was veiled by indifferent disdain. Cut off from the masses, its dictatorship was no longer that of one class but of the caste of apparatchiks. Novotny's reaction was that of the perfectly orthodox Stalinist: if things were going badly, it was because the party was not strict enough. This report, more than the agitation of the writers at the May Congress, decided the terms of his speech to the army cadets on the first of September. The iron hand would rule again.

In asking for ratification of this hard line in the September Presidium, Novotny had given Dubcek his chance to intervene. The protocol in this session of the Presidium is still secret, but a witness to this historic session — which took place, as usual, in a large room in the forbidding building of the "Nabrezi Kijevske Brigade," beside the Vltava headquarters of the Central Committee and the former ministry of transportation of the first Republic — described to me the tenor of this first passage at arms. Dubcek, basing his speech on the report of the sociologists and statisticians, said in substance: the party is getting old, the party is dying; to win back the people's confidence, we must elaborate precisely a program which will be attractive to all, especially to youth; we must divide responsibility clearly between the party and the government. It was on this occasion that he used for the first time the phrase which became his slogan: "We must give socialism back its human face."

My witness went on to say, "We still did not know what was going to happen, did not realize the intensity of the personal and political conflict between these two men . . . With the exception of Cernik, who showed Dubcek a discreet sympathy, the other members of the Presidium, devoted and longstanding friends of Novotny's, scarcely seemed to take the matter seriously."

Nevertheless they were all impressed by the secret document

17

of more than a thousand pages which had been passed out among them. This document revealed the results of the sociologists' inquiry into the condition of the party. It disclosed not only disastrous figures (in more than 50 percent of the party organizations there were no militants under thirty; at Psarov, in Moravia, the cell of one important business had to be dissolved for lack of members; and so on) but also quoted deliberately insulting observations made by militants and local party members about Novotny. He, with somewhat forced humor, had underlined with red pencil in his copy the words "Novotny is an ass, an idiot, incapable of leading the party and the government. . . ." He made this pitiful comment, typical of Novotnyan humor: "See how far class enemies bore from within . . ."

The Presidium's September session ended with the usual vote of confidence in Novotny. The Dubcek incident seemed to have been shelved.

[Rebellion (October)]

On October 30 the plenum of the Central Committee opened with the usual decorum, ritual, and routine in the vast Spanish room of the Hradschin palace (a masterpiece of Gothic art where tourneys were held in the Middle Ages and an inclined ramp, still in existence, had given the knights access to the stage). The hundred and ten delegates listened quietly to the reading of the Presidium theses and to the conclusions of the sociologists' and statisticians' report. They were too well aware of the situation of the party in their regions and districts to be much surprised by the latter.

The session promised to be dreary. From black plastic briefcases stamped with the party emblem the delegates drew out an agenda proposing discussion of "Situation and Role of the

Party in the Republic" and "related subjects." They arranged around themselves the pages of their contributions to the debates, prepared and approved in advance, as was proper.

Discussion of the "related subjects" touched off the first incident. Dubcek reproached Novotny and Hendrych for replacing with others certain documents that had been submitted to the Central Committee and approved by the Presidium. Dubcek particularly questioned the substitution of those relating to Slovakian issues, specifically "investments." Excited, but very much in command of himself, Dubcek attacked the problem of Slovakia's development; this being the eternal complaint of the Bratislavan delegates, his audience barely listened. Since 1918, in any and every assembly, the Czechs had sullenly and resignedly endured the recriminations, not always legitimate, of their sister nation. During the course of Dubcek's speech, however, the delegates became more attentive. "We are in a period of class resurgence, not of class struggle. . . . What threatens us as much as counterrevolutionary forces are the conservative forces within our own party, the dogmatists," he said. Without citing Novotny by name, Dubcek declared that the leadership of the party "had no idea of the new phase into which the party was entering, nor any concept of how to adapt and guide it." Passing from the general to the particular, never raising his voice, Dubcek went on to say that the party leader was no doubt a good Communist, devoted and faithful, but nevertheless incapable of understanding the times: "He can no longer help socialism, make it move forward; he acts as a brake on socialism, for his leadership is sterile." He inveighed against the Presidium's theses, attributing the responsibility for the crisis to the local and regional organizations: "History demonstrates that if the masses are passive, their leaders have erred." It was for the Central Committee rather than their supporters to determine the proper course. Dubcek ended his speech, which had lasted twenty minutes, with a demand for the establishment of a program of action which would be made public and would include constructive propositions for the resolution of the national (that is, Slovak) question.

Dubcek's proposals called forth a violent response from Martin Vaculik, secretary of the Presidium and leader of the C.P. of Prague. With the wild-haired look of an art student, this former party chief of Brno, only recently arrived in the capital, was of ambiguous stature; he passed as a progressive in Moravia but had since become the hardest of partisans of the conservative coterie.[7] He falsely declared that Dubcek held views contrary to those formulated by the Presidium and denounced him for the crime of lèse majesté, which consisted of "personal attacks on our revered comrade Anton Novotny from the podium of the Central Committee. This must not happen again."

From that moment the session became unruly. The Slovakian clique reacted with vigor. Forty-five-year-old Maria Sedlakova, a small dark roly-poly woman with high cheekbones in a very Slavic face, interrupted furiously.[8] For the first time in the history of the Czechoslovakian Communist party and of the whole Communist world — if one excepts the dramatic arguments in the Bolshevik Central Committee which ended in 1920 with Lenin's dissolving of all "fractional groups" — the atmosphere of the Central Committee resembled that of a bourgeois parliament in a period of crisis. In the boos and bravos — the latter were the more numerous — the "Slovak Passionaria" undertook the defense of "Comrade Dubcek whom I know, who has no personal interests in this affair, and who is an honest man."

When the secretary of the session asked her to be brief because a plane awaited Comrade Novotny (who had to go to Moscow for the anniversary celebration of the October revolution), Sedlakova retorted by accusing Novotny of always convening sessions of the Central Committee in haste so that the delegates would not have time to discuss seriously the problems under consideration. She then criticized herself for having voted to exclude the writers during the September session. She pointed out that only at the end of an exhausting day of argument had Novotny declared that the Writers' Congress was controlled by radio from abroad, organized by Paris émigrés, and paid for by German film-producers (sic) and American spies. Why had he not brought this up at the beginning? She turned toward a frowning Novotny, who consulted cards and whispered with Hendrych, to ask him for evidence. She objected to the Presidium's statement on the theses proposed to the Central Committee that "a place should be found in the bosom of the party for artists and writers." Did not America, England, and France, where the party was not in power, have writers and artists? It was time to stop patronizing the intellectuals. The party did not have to give them anything at all; they were creators, workers of the mind, who must themselves regulate the quality of their work, must win the public by their talents alone. In her opinion, there could be no justification whatsoever for denying writers the right to explain and protest.[9] Her voice rose. She accused Novotny of baseness in his pretense that Comrade Vodslon had taken up the defense of the writers in revenge, and she cited the Oriental fable in which a cadi said to a witness with a harelip, "How can you say straight words when you have a twisted mouth?"

"Our party is responsible for everything, including the distribution of toilet paper," Sedlakova went on, amid laughter. "We have spent a day on four unhappy writers but we have concerned ourselves not at all with a national catastrophe." In the last days of October, the rising Danube had inundated hundreds of square kilometers of the Slovakian plain. Before leaving the podium, she loosed a parting shot: "Lying and demagoguery are neither communism nor a method of government. We have been elected not to love and congratulate one another, but to seek the truth and the solutions to specific problems."

Following Sedlakova, Dr. Frantisek Kriegel spoke out. A veteran, sixty-year-old Kriegel had maintained simultaneously and with dedicated fervor for thirty years the careers of brilliant doctor and responsible communist. At the age of retirement, this tranquil veteran of the International Brigades was still on duty at his hospital from early dawn and he passed his nights at party headquarters. President of the National Front (the cover organization which united around the C.P. the vestiges of the bourgeois parties authorized after 1948), his Jewish origins made Kriegel, after Prague's thaw, the object of fierce anti-Semitic campaigns of the Polish press.[10] To the Central Committee he declared briefly that he offered his support to Dubcek and asked that a secret ballot be taken immediately. His proposal, denied, seems to have been premature, for the ten orators succeeding him were divided between Dubcek and Novotny — a clear majority favored the latter.

In an atmosphere which remained charged, the secretariat of the Presidium asked for an adjournment of the session, which was to reconvene in December. In spite of the unusual excitement, the second day of the October session of the Central Committee ended on a note of ceremonious unanimity; the delegates, feting the fiftieth anniversary of October,[11] put on a good face for the group photographs which would be in the papers, papers which up to January 25 were imperturbably to neglect any allusion to the upheavals disrupting the party and government leadership. During the month of November, daily exhausting meetings of the Politburo followed one after another.

[The Month of Conspiracies]

Alois Svoboda, invited to be editor-in-chief of *Politika,* a new
political weekly of the Communist party which was to appear
in October 1968, confided in me: "At that time, neither Novotny nor Dubcek had a clear idea of the relations between the
conservatives and the progressives. The Central Committee's
debates had been vehement but confused. Dubcek felt he was
expressing the popular discontent, but he did not know to
what extent the army, secret police, workers' militia, and various parts of the machine shared in it."

Alexander Dubcek and his friends were not to discover until
after the coup the virtues of democracy, of a freely informed
public opinion, and they remained militants too much disciplined to conceive of that sacrilege which in communist regimes was the revelation of differences of opinion at the top of
the party hierarchy. The Presidium must always appear to be a
monolithic assembly of high priests, smilingly infallible before
its worshiping masses. Even Yugoslavia, the most liberal of
communist regimes, did not escape this axiom; its Milovan Djilas was made a scapegoat not for holding heretical ideas on the
"new class" but for publishing the "fractional dissensions" at
the heart of the headquarters of the Communist League.
During the entire month of November the upper echelons of
the party were boiling. Throughout this month of "conspiracies," the malcontents of the regime sought out one another —
with great caution, for the police of the regime were on the
lookout. Novotny had every reason to believe himself protected from surprise. At the Presidium, among the ten members and the four secretaries, Dubcek's avowed partisans numbered only one incumbent, Cernik, and one secretary, Kolder.[12]
No one outside the narrow circle of those involved had the
smallest suspicion of the events to come. Western journalists

23

posted in Prague or Vienna sent practically nothing to their papers.[13]

The demonstration of City University students during this month came as a surprise. A student present at the demonstration told me about it later in the glacial university dining room on Strahov Hill:

"There was nothing epic about what happened. One evening, for the third time in a week, we had an electrical blackout. Since there had also been heating failures during the winter, we were exasperated. Someone suggested we demonstrate in the street. Everybody went out, making a lot of noise. It was an opportunity for the boys to find girls, which was usually forbidden after midnight. It turned into a party. We laughed, we danced, we played the guitar. Nobody thought of politics. Then someone yelled: 'Let's get candles and go demonstrate.' We formed a procession and marched, symbolic candles in hand, shouting: 'We want light!' and 'We want work!' Near the presidential palace, on the Hradschin, we ran into some police. They immediately charged fiercely into us, knocking down and trampling young girls, hitting us over the head with their rubber truncheons. For the first time several voices cried 'Fascists,' and 'Democracy,' and we began to fight back, throwing anything we could find at the cops, starting with the paving stones of Neruda Street."

This relatively minor incident had considerable political consequences. The progressive movement found itself significantly reinforced in both the Presidium and the Central Committee. The Czech writers' excitement, hitherto restrained, now overflowed as the students swept into the street. Mr. Cutka, a high functionary of the Central Committee,[14] told me of the emotion which possessed the political cadres: "For the first time in the history of the second Republic, children born and raised under the regime and subject to no other influence

than that of socialist education were beaten by the police and
chanted slogans hostile to the government and to the party."

[Revolt (December)]

Several days after the December meeting of the Central Committee, Novotny, hard pressed and at bay, committed that supreme blunder which was finally to cause his downfall: he ap-
pealed to his Soviet protectors. The unexpected arrival of
Leonid Brezhnev in Prague on Friday, December 9, 1967, was
announced by Novotny to the Presidium as a routine visit. He
had telephoned Comrade Brezhnev about several practical
problems, Novotny stated, and had asked if he should go to
Moscow, but Comrade Brezhnev preferred to come to Prague.

No one was deceived, and the unhappy Brezhnev, his plane
barely landed, was attacked on all sides by the members of the
Politburo. He was indignant to learn that he had been invited
without the knowledge of the Presidium, as he had believed
himself summoned by the collective. He was extremely angry
with Novotny and had to be held by the coattails to keep from
taking the next plane back to Moscow. Brezhnev refused to
"preside" at a session of the Politburo, dryly reminding Novotny that he was a *foreign* chief of state on a visit. He agreed
to attend a dinner of the members of the Presidium but had
not cooled off by evening, particularly because his "man-to-
man" interviews with the two rival groups had thrown no light
on the fundamental reasons for the crisis, which appeared to
him as a new episode in the perennial rivalry of Czech and
Slovak. "This is your business" he finally declared to Novotny
and took a plane back to Moscow after a forty-eight-hour stay.

The three sessions of the Politburo following the departure
of the Soviet leader were stormy. The Dubcek clan was no

longer a minority but did not yet have a firm majority. The plenum of the Central Committee reopened on December 19, after having been adjourned for a week, with a Presidium which appeared divided into two groups of equal importance. The confusion and upheaval of the October session repeated itself even more emphatically; the plenum, planned to last forty-eight hours, went on for three days. The debates centered on the question of the pluralism of Novotny's powers (he was at the same time president of the Republic and secretary-general of the party). They ended only with a picturesque revolt of the women delegates. The political secretary of the National Front, Ladislova Bessarova, shouted, amid the applause of the other women present: "We're all fed up with these endless discussions. Nearly eighty comrades still want to speak. If they do, we'll still be here in January. How will we make Christmas cakes for our families? Later with quiet minds we can make decisions on Comrade Novotny's pluralism of functions. I propose that we entrust this matter to the Presidium until the next plenum."

Late on the gray morning of Thursday, December 21, it was decided not to continue the debates beyond that evening. Just before the end of the morning session, Anton Novotny made an unexpected confession. He apologized for the very hard words he had used against Dubcek during the October session, spoke of his physical fatigue, assured the assembly of his sympathy for the Slovaks, and stated that, contrary to malicious rumors, the Presidium was solid and united. So rigidly must the dogma of unanimity be preserved before the theoretical trustees of communist power, the members of the Central Committee, that Alexander Dubcek and his friends dared not protest. They joined halfheartedly the ovation which greeted Novotny's peroration. But change was imminent in that echo chamber called the Central Committee. The session resumed that afternoon in a recaptured atmosphere of boredom and se-

renity; the secretaries proceeded to read interminable reports
on the reform of economic planning, the next meeting of sister
parties in Budapest, and so on. Novotny, taking his turn at the
podium, told of his trip to Moscow. Scarcely had he finished
when old Frantisek Vodslon, that obscure member of the
Central Committee who had already played wet blanket in
October, rudely challenged the rostrum:

"Your self-criticism this morning, Comrade President," he
said, addressing himself to Novotny, "seemed to me false,
without sincerity; Comrades, you take us for idiots. We should
be told what is really happening in the Presidium. If it is true
that it is divided into two equal parties, how can it function?
How can you work, lead the party? Why must we, members of
the Central Committee, always learn from other sources what
is going on? The quarrels of the Presidium are known to all
those interested in the internal life of the party. Even the foreign journalists know more than we, members of the Central
Committee. It is time for the comrades of the Presidium to tell
us the truth. It is time that we think of the public, of our
active members. It is time to act, if we want to keep the trust
of the country."

The paralysis of the Presidium was unquestionably an open
secret, but the assembly was stupefied to witness a man who
refused any longer to play the game.

Ota Sik followed Vodslon. He was sick; an ambulance had
brought him directly from the hospital to Hradschin. At forty-
nine, this round-faced academic, habitually affable and smiling,
this former Mauthausen deportee, was considered one of the
most brilliant economists of Eastern Europe, equal to a Lang
or a Lieberman. Feverish, his features gaunt from fatigue, Ota
Sik pronounced a veritable indictment à la Fouquier-Tinville
against Novotny. He declared that economic reform was inconceivable without major political changes. And these
changes could not be made as long as Novotny was in power.

27

He must step down and cede his place to a new secretary-general. And he named Dubcek, Smrkovsky, and Kriegel — to their consternation.

A witness to this session, a member of the Central Committee, assured me later that Ota Sik's tempestuous zeal almost ruined "months and perhaps years of patient efforts by Dubcek and his friends. I believed Sik had gone crazy. He spoke as if he were a backbencher of the opposition in the House of Commons. Or as if he intended to rescue Novotny. The scandal was so great that if the president of the meeting, Lastovicka, had not been so stupid Novotny would have received a vote of confidence from 90 percent of those present."

During his summation Ota Sik succeeded in rousing laughter. Jozef Lenart, president of the Council, interrupted to remark that the end of the duality of powers would make the position of Comrade Walter Ulbricht, first secretary and chief of state, very uncomfortable. Sik replied: "If Comrade Ulbricht needs Comrade Novotny to survive, things must be going very badly for him indeed!"

One of Ota Sik's concrete suggestions for breaking the deadlock roused real interest. He proposed in effect "to elect an ad hoc committee within the Central Committee which would submit the names of two candidates for the post of first secretary as is done for new candidacies for the renewal of the Presidium."

This proposal reopened the controversy between partisans and adversaries of Novotny. However, the promise made to the ladies to finish the session before night had to be kept. The plenum of the Central Committee suspended work on December 21. It had been decided that the Presidium would gather the representatives of the party's regional federations to study the issue of "the duality of powers." No doubt this decision made an impression on the majority of the delegates; it did not assume, however, the urgency which Ota Sik had imparted. The ebullient economist saw his proposal diluted to suit a Presidium packed with elements representing "the provinces," assumed to be more conservative than Prague. Novotny had every reason to be optimistic. His proposal to resume the plenary session in January was adopted unanimously. Comrade Bessarova could go home to roast her traditional goose and cook her Christmas cakes in peace.

And on December 22 a great Western daily could publish: "The Central Committee has settled the leadership crisis of the Czechoslovakian party. By every indication, Mr. Novotny has succeeded in surmounting the serious crisis which threatened to put an end to the functions he has performed for fourteen years."

Notes for Chapter 1

1. Barak was minister of the interior 1953–1961 and member of the Presidium of the Central Committee from 1954 until February 9, 1962, the date of his arrest, when he was condemned behind closed doors by a military court to fifteen years in prison for embezzlement and double-dealing abroad with "public funds." After his early release in May 1968, Barak declared that these "funds" were only intended to supply resources for Czechoslovakian espionage in foreign countries. He implicitly confirmed that his removal was due to Novotny's fear of being the victim of the young technocrats and economic planners by whom he liked to be surrounded. These very elements, of whom Ota Sik was one, were to play a fundamental role in the birth of the thaw.

2. The Economic Commission had been established by Novotny at Khrushchev's suggestion. Khrushchev had been most impressed by Kennedy's methods of working, especially by his brain trusts, and wished to adapt them to his empire. In a general way, Novotny in turn was fascinated by the truculent personality of the Ukrainian. But he never succeeded in establishing a rapport as warm and intimate as was his relationship with the team of Brezhnev and Kosygin.

3. The Centrist Socialism party of President Eduard Benes.

4. The Presidium which grew out of the Thirteenth Congress in June 1966 was composed of Oldrich Cernik, Dubcek, Drahomir Kolder, Jaromir Dolansky, Hendrych, Michal Chudik, Bohuslav Lastovicka, Jozef Lenart, Novotny, and Otakar Simunek.

5. Although this was the first open conflict between Novotny and Dubcek, Novotny's antipathy for Dubcek was an open secret in the party. Novotny reproached Dubcek less for his progressivism, only timidly revealed, than for his Slovak "nationalism." In 1965, after the nomination of Alexander Dubcek as secretary-general of the Communist party of Slovakia, the Prague press was forbidden to give him that title for six months. During his official trips to Slovakia, Novotny obstinately refused, despite the demands of protocol and simple courtesy, to permit Dubcek to accompany him. It was Dubcek's associate in the general secretariat of the Slovak C.P., Vasil Bilak, who traveled with Novotny then.

6. Dr. K., a doctor in a large hospital in Prague and a member of the Populist Party (Christian), told me his story. He had been imprisoned for several years. On his release, he could find work only as a nurse. In the 1960's, this excellent practitioner was authorized to re-

turn to hospital service. He was then pressed to take out a party card and was promised the directorship of the hospital. After several years of stubborn resistance, he was offered the position unconditionally.

7. Nothing is simple in communist regimes. Martin Vaculik's rule at Brno made the Moravian capital the center of the intellectual rebellion against the regime. At the opening of a satirical play, *The Dragon Is a Dragon*, which was forbidden everywhere in Czechoslovakia and which presented a grim picture of trials and apparatchiks, he said laughingly to his appalled entourage, "You recognize yourselves, gentlemen." The same man, as part of the Prague party machine, became a violent Novotnyan. On the telephone he explained himself with resigned good humor: "I am a political man who must pay for his mistaken choices. I bet on the wrong horse." At forty-three, he seemed to have ended his meteoric career in the obscure headquarters of a petty party employee. However, during the Soviet invasion, his patriotism and courage returned to Vaculik the confidence of the people of Prague.

8. She was, in fact, the editor-in-chief of the daily *Pravda* of Bratislava.

9. On October 8, *Literarni Noviny*, the organ of the Writers' Union, was taken away from them and put under the control of the party machine.

10. Novotny and his friends were to their credit never to use anti-Semitism in their exchanges with the progressives. This unhappy privilege was reserved to the Poland of Wladyslaw Gomulka, whose official press was to brand conspirators Kriegel, Ota Sik, and Eduard Goldstuecker as Zionists.

11. Again for the first time in twenty years, without the final traditional celebration.

12. After the thaw, Kolder, plainly outstripped by events, had to take an increasingly conservative position. The militants of his fief, the mining town of Ostrava, did not return him to office in June 1968.

13. During the whole of November, *Le Monde*, whose correspondent in Central Europe, Michel Tatu, was probably the best-informed Western journalist, published not more than twenty lines, on November 2, 1967, on the session of the Central Committee in October, and one article on November 28, on the uprising of the students of Strahov.

14. Political secretary to Cestmir Cisar, he was to be the first party functionary arrested by the Soviets after the invasion.

Appendix

The Disease of Power . . . June 2, 1967

Ludvik Vaculik speaks to the fourth Writers' Congress.

I wish to express certain things which you already know; I have a few suggestions to make. According to the letter of resolution, the goal of the socialist regime is to make possible the reintegration of man, whose status as citizen must be guaranteed. "Citizen" — there is a term whose past is glorious and revolutionary. This term designates a person who cannot be governed without, in some clever manner, giving him the impression that he is governing himself. To create this impression among the governed is the end product of a specialized and absorbing labor: politics. In reality, the idea of a citizen governing himself has always been a myth.

Marxist criticism led to the illumination of relationships which up to that time had not been explored, relationships between political power and ownership of means of production. This discovery, and the interpretation of the history of humanity as the history of class struggle, prepared the socialist revolution, from which was expected the solution to a problem as old as the world, the problem of power. Although the social revolution has succeeded in our country, the problem of power continues. It seems that power, no matter who holds it, is subject to its own laws of development and conduct. Power is a specifically human phenomenon, dependent on the fact that in every group of persons someone must take command, that even in a society composed only of noble minds, someone must sum up the results of discussion and define the necessary formulations. Power is a uniquely human predicament. It includes those who lead and those who are led, and it is unhealthy for both groups.

The millenary experience of humanity has pushed man to seek and to find certain rules for the control of power, a sort of regulation of circulation. Such is the significance of formal democracy, with all its mechanisms of retroaction, its control buttons, and its time limits. However, the interests of those persons who take power — through possession of capital, force of arms, advantageous family connections, monopoly of production, and so on — interfere with the clearly defined mechanism of government. The rules then no longer protect against the disease of power, and a slightly falsified interpretation of such a situation can induce individuals to pretend that the very rules of formal democracy cause the disease. These rules are not in themselves either capitalistic or socialistic; they do not determine what must be done, but only define the manner in which decisions should be made. These rules are a human invention and in essence make things more difficult. They favor the governed but also save those who govern from the firing squad when their government falls.

This formal system of democracy does not provide an extremely solid government but does give rise to the conviction that the next government may be better than the last. Thus, the government falls, but the citizen survives. And vice versa, when the government remains in power forever, or for a long period of time, the citizen falls. How does he fall? I will not give pleasure to our enemies by saying that he is shot down by a firing squad. This fate is reserved for only a few dozens or hundreds of citizens. However, our enemies know that the fate of these few is enough, because then the entire nation falls prey to fear, political indifference and polite resignation, little everyday worries and bad dreams — in a word, the nation falls into a new kind of vassalage, which it is impossible to explain to any observer.

I believe that citizens no longer exist in our country. To support this conviction, I have arguments founded on my long experience working in the press and radio, to which I can add this: this Congress has not met when the members of our organization decided to meet but when the master, having examined the issues, has graciously given his consent. In exchange, he expects, as he has become accustomed to do over hundreds of years, that we will show veneration for his dynasty. I suggest that we shall not show it. I suggest that we examine the text of the resolution which was proposed to us and that we remove from it anything that smells of the vassal. In a country which developed its culture by criticizing its rulers, writers ought not to forget this tradition and this education. I suggest that every man who speaks at this tribunal propose his own solutions to the problems which are troubling him. Let us play the game of being citizens, since we have permission to play it and to use this playing field. And let us act for three whole days as if we were adults, in our majority. I speak as citizen of a state which I shall never deny but in which I cannot live with satisfaction.

I am thinking of my affairs as a citizen, but I am in a delicate position for I am also a member of the Communist party and am not permitted to discuss party affairs — in any case, I do not wish to do so. But in our country the situation is such that there remains practically nothing which is not a party matter, nothing which we can discuss. What should I do when these two — my party and my government — have done everything possible to entangle their affairs? In my opinion, this confusion is a drawback to both. It makes very difficult the position of the citizens met together here. The party members are obliged to refrain from discussing crucial aspects of the principal questions before nonmembers, and the nonmembers have no access to the only places where one can seriously discuss these crucial problems. Thus party members and those who are not members are limited in their fundamental civil liberty: that of speaking to one another as equals.

What I will say may be in contradiction with Article 20 of the constitution. However, I am disciplined; I restrain myself to my field of action as citizen, and I shall only address my remarks to the government. In cases where this term "government" does not apply, and only in these cases, I will speak of "circles of leadership." This older and more proven nomenclature, in spite of its apparent imprecision, is more exact than many others. Since time immemorial, it has designated those who really lead, whatever the function they exert on the democratic scene, those whose power has its origin behind the scenes, whether in riches, influence, monopoly, or possession of arms. This denomination also covers the government backstage, the urgent messages sent by special courier in the middle of the night, the treaties and laws adopted before having been submitted to parliament. After the last war, the state was restored as a political body whose sole objective was to organize socialism. One of the postulates of the new regime was unity among those who were led and those who led — in fact, their identity, for the people and the government are one.

Now I would like to return to my reflections on the nature of power. Its development and its mode of exercise are subject to laws which cannot be changed, neither for the person nor for the class in power, for these laws are those which apply to human behavior in a certain situation. These laws govern those who are in power.

The first characteristic of power is the struggle to continue to exist. Power reproduces itself, in increasingly precise forms. It becomes more and more homogeneous, eliminating any foreign element to the point where all its units are interchangeable; eventually a cell situated on the periphery of power can replace its center; individual cells can be permutated without damaging consequences, without preventing the power apparatus from functioning correctly. Power is not especially conceived to react to changes in environment, attitudes, the composition of the population, and so on; rather, it is always conceived to suit a certain type of action — to form an environment serving its own designs. Uniformity permits the machine always to apply the same simple process. Thus power becomes more independent and, by a new law of its nature, it does not ask for support but leans upon itself, while the center leans on the periphery, and vice versa. Each unit is absolutely able to rely upon the other; each is also necessary to every other, since they form a circle. No part can be eliminated; no part can be liberated. Internal disagreements and disgraces are corrected from within.

Hence evolves a new phase which I call "dynastization." At a favorable moment, the regime calls together the legislative assembly and charges it with consecrating its independent position in a constitution. From that point, the regime acts in accordance with the constitution, however it is composed. And, because no undesirable subject is placed on the agenda for ten, twenty, or fifty years, because, according to the constitution, nobody else can do this or call another legislative assembly, a dynasty is founded by means of the constitution. It is a dynasty of a new historical type; it preserves an important democratic principle: those who wish can board the moving train. This dynasty cannot become extinct for lack of a male or a female heir.

From our point of view, most interesting is an internal law of power: the regime prefers people whose internal structure is analogous to its own. But because their numbers are too few, it must manufacture others according to its needs. It is *natural* that those most suitable to serve the regime are those who themselves covet power, those who by nature are obedient, those who have no scruples, those whose desire for riches, profit, and advantages knows no moral limits. One can condition people who have large families, people who, once humiliated, now voluntarily accept an occasion to affirm newly acquired pride, and people who were born to a certain pattern; different types of moral absolutists can be equally useful, as can disinterested enthusiasts, like myself, who are badly informed. Essentially outmoded means are used to condition people: Physical or psychological temptation, threats, compromising situations, denunciations, unjustified accusations which they try to refute by demonstrating their loyalty. People can also be purposely pushed into bad company from which they may then be rescued. Or mistrust can be sown everywhere. Trust knows several levels: most people are not considered absolutely trustworthy. Information too has its levels of quality: on pink paper, green, or yellow, or on ordinary newsprint.

I have spoken about the character of power in a very general sense: I do not necessarily even have in mind a socialist state. Socialism for me signifies scientific exploration. And the scientific theory of socialism cannot do without a psychology of power, any more than it can do without a philosophy, a political economy, or a sociology. It requires a psychology of power, and this profits from the understanding acquired from individual psychology and group psychology, psychoanalysis and psychopathology.

I leave aside the question of character of the ruling class, for this question appears as an element in the problem of power in general. But specifically in our country we have witnessed the selection of people according to their usefulness to the regime. The trust of the regime was accorded to the obedient, to those who did not make trouble, to those who asked no questions beyond those which the regime itself asked. At each stage of selection, the common man, that silent and vague example of general obedience, was the most likely to be chosen; those endowed with personal charm, those who expressed their thoughts, disappeared from the political scene. The alliance of the two words "politician" and "thinker" lost all significance; the word "movement" rang hollow and dead. The structure on which rested material existence and the culture belonging to local communities, factories, and workshops was destroyed. No longer was anything bearing the mark of an individual hand authorized: the word "studio" was preserved only in rare cases; directors of schools were turned out if they tried to put into effect personal methods of education; cultural and athletic clubs and well-known societies of long standing were dissolved. All those institutions which represented for some people the historical continuity of their city, their region, or their state were banished.

Bejamin Klicka, in his work *Wild Daja*, said: "Be sure to remember that your competence is an insult to your superior; pretend to be stupid as a doornail, if you want to live long and be happy in this land of ours." This quotation is forty years old and was written in the society which preceded the social revolution. I think that it did not acquire its full value in our country until after this revolution, for everyone has since been able to verify for himself just how true it is.

You may have noticed that all of us, Czechs and Slovaks, have a tendency to think that in our various occupations we are led by men less competent than ourselves. But we do nothing but complain each time that we meet one another. This is odious in the long run, for incompetents, those good for absolutely nothing, and people of limited intelligence complain as bitterly as those who have reason to do so. The former, too, say that they ought not to do this, that they are not authorized to do that. A dangerous and false unanimity is created between people who do not in any way resemble one another. However different our motives, we are all united by the most wretched bond one could imagine — our common aversions. Practical people have found areas in which they can be active; those who are not practical wear a martyr's crown. In literature, depression, nihilism, and spiritual decay are in style. Snobs give themselves over to orgies. Intelligent people become stupid. From time to time, the instinct of self-preservation does reappear; people want to kick over the traces. But when they raise their eyes and see what is above them and then lower their eyes and see people ready to crush them in order to take their places, they wonder: "My God, for whom are we doing all this?" Let us remember that those who have succeeded best in the last twenty years are those who offer the least resistance to all the demoralizing influences distilled by power.

Those who have scruples of conscience do not find any support in the regime, any recourse in the laws which, according to their texts, ought to support them. According to the letter of the law, it would seem that a code of rights and duties really existed in our country. I have observed, in my work on newspapers and on radio, that in fact the citizen rarely invokes his constitutional rights because anyone on the periphery of power can place conditions on the exercise of these rights, conditions which are not included in the constitution and which, in all decency, could not be inscribed there.

I have read and reread the constitution recently and arrived at the conclusion that it is badly written, and, perhaps because of this, it does not command the respect of citizens and authorities. In style the constitution is grandiloquent, but in con-

tent vague. To cite an example concerning the field of work
and thought of our own Union, Article 16 says: "The entire
cultural policy of Czechoslovakia, the advancement of knowledge, education, and teaching, shall be conducted in the scientific perspective of Marxism-Leninism and in strict relation to
the life and work of the people." Setting aside the fact that
every good educator will consider it understood that "education" implies a relationship between life and work, it does not
appear clearly what office, or perhaps what court, should decide whether or not an opinion is scientific. This inadequacy is
augmented in that "science" implies a movement and change
of opinion resulting from the progress of knowledge, and this
adaptation is contrary to the immutable and unequivocal nature of the concepts expressed in any legal rule. This contradiction in terms can be overcome if "vision of the scientific
world" represents only a simple collection of words. Otherwise,
it could provide occasion to question whether our state is to be
considered in a doctrinaire rather than a scientific fashion. And
it is surely the second possibility which our legislators envis-
aged.

Another example connected with my subject, Article 28,
says: "In accord with the interests of the workers, freedom of
expression is guaranteed for all citizens in all branches of the
life of the society, more especially freedom of speech and freedom of the press." In my opinion, these liberties are in themselves *in the interest* of the workers and I consider this passage
superfluous and even the direct cause of error, because the
interpretation of the interest of the workers is left to each individual. I think that if a specialist judged as necessary the use of
this formulation, he would judge as equally necessary specifica-
tion of what does and what does not represent the interest of
the workers. I also think that a legislator of foresight would
avoid citing examples and would insist on giving statistics. Personally, I would prefer a succinct formulation whose validity

could not be placed in question. Only a short and clear formulation gives to rules the authority of a proverb that is accepted as law, valid in all cases; for when this is true, awareness of good and evil is so universal that it becomes almost useless to go before the courts.

The prolix languages and devious ideas of the constitution make it awkward to apply. The supreme legal norm becomes a program and an expression of good intentions, rather than a guarantee of the rights of citizens. Moreover, in my opinion, the constitution should have the same function as any other legal norm and, as it is the supreme norm, no other norm of an inferior level — no ordinance, statute, decree, or arrest — should supersede its validity or obscure its sense.

I have expressed my point of view on the character, the development, and the behavior of all regimes and have tried to show that the mechanism of control, intended to watch over the regime's evolution, is lacking in our country, so much so that the citizen loses self-respect and objectively also loses his status as citizen. When this state of affairs lasts as long as it has lasted in our country, it is only normal that it should take root in everybody's mind, especially in the minds of the younger generation and in its philosophy of life. The latter has learned neither from its studies nor from experience that there is a certain continuity in human efforts to realize a democracy nearer to perfection. If this state of things should last much longer (and if the normal human defense reactions do not operate) the character of our nation will change in the next generation. A cultural community possessing a certain power of resistance will be replaced by an anonymous mass that will be easily dominated and child's play to govern. If we allow this to happen, our millenary resistance will have been in vain.

Persuaded that none among us was born to be dominated and only dominated, I propose that the Writers' Union, perhaps in cooperation with the Journalists' Union and other similar associations, take the initiative in asking the Czechoslovakian Academy of Sciences for its expert advice on the constitution. If it should prove necessary, the Union could launch a movement for the revision of the constitution by recommending, for example, that its members be present at electoral meetings during the next campaign to raise these problems and to see to it that the elected deputies are aware of them. Perhaps each of us should see his own deputy before this campaign and ask him to develop this theme before the National Assembly.

As I speak here, I have not at all that feeling of liberty that a man should have when he says what he wants to say. I have rather the sensation that I am exploiting, and in a cowardly way, a sort of armistice between the citizen and the regime, that I am breaking the truce, the "summer vacation," which has been granted to writers and artists. How long it will last I don't know — until winter, or perhaps only until tomorrow. All the same, I do not believe that the citizen and the powers can function as one, that the governed and the government can sing the same tune. I do not even believe that art and power can ever feel at ease together. They never will be; they cannot be; they are different; they don't go together. What is possible, and what gives us hope for the success of our efforts, is that the two partners may become aware of the situation and work out decent rules for their mutual contacts.

I am going to tell you about an incident of which I have often thought during these last two days. As a member of the editorial committee of *Literarni Listy*, I was present last March at a meeting of the ideological department of the Central Committee of the party. The meeting did not take a favorable turn for us. I had a seat exactly opposite the secretary of the Central Committee, Comrade Jiri Hendrych, and so I was able to observe the features of this man who is older than myself. When I was a child, I was told to bow to people like him, much older than myself. The face of this man who, up to that time, had seemed to me more an institution than an individual revealed his personal, professional, and other worries, exactly as does my own, and he had been obliged to master them much longer than I have.

I was not very brilliant at that meeting. I wanted to speak absolutely frankly, but I was afraid. I spent the time concealing my true self; I thought that they would misunderstand my motives. They murmured something in my ear; I gave up, more and more overcome by a feeling of despair. I felt myself humiliated and the result was that I lost my calm.

Returning to my home, a totally new idea came to my mind in thinking of the conference, a quite disturbing feeling which divided everything into two camps: "us" and "them." I felt as if I were swept by a wind from the unknown, felt that I was beginning to understand the human distress caused by a certain situation which was not expressible with the aid of those concepts so often used in our country, those of "class point of view," "opposition," and the like. These concepts were terms of battle. Naturally, I had, even if it was only temporarily, to get hold of myself, and I told myself that the anguish of political men was part of the game. That was the way it was, because they wanted it so. But this experience gave me a new sensation; it made me think of power as a human situation.

I conclude this digression and return to where I left off. Writers are human beings, and leadership circles are also composed of human beings. Writers do not want anarchy; they too would like to live in attractive cities, have nice apartments, and hope for the same things for others. They hope for prosperous industries and flourishing trade, and this is impossible without the organized activities of the government. Art cannot be indifferent to the government, for to govern is continually to make direct and indirect decisions; administrative acts engage man's life, his well-being, and his deceptions — everything he thinks, everything that cannot be dictated to him. Power's field of action encroaches upon that of art, especially in the areas in which it is impossible to separate the two and in which decisions must be made, one way or another. Art cannot abandon its critiques of government because governments, whatever their nature, whatever their customs, are the products of the culture of their nations.

Our government pleases artists when it congratulates them, for example, for having designed a beautiful pavilion for the New York World's Fair. The government is surely happy to do this, though such statements also have a political aspect. And perhaps their intentions are honest. But it remains no less true that artists are not obliged to be happy with the government. Such a pavilion, which in a certain sense benefits from the right of cultural extraterritoriality, simply shows what these same creators could, if they were allowed, do in their own country. So I must wonder if we do not all labor under a delusion that we build beautiful pavilions representing our culture, when we know that our best work will find no taker, that we make all things only by the grace of God, that we are moving toward a reckoning whose date we do not know. All that our culture has evolved, all the good things that men have done or created in our country, all the good products, the beautiful buildings, the good ideas from our laboratories or institutes, all this has gone on for years in spite of our leadership. Literally in spite of them. But I do not want to be unjust; I am convinced that even with the best-intentioned leaders, all betterment of style of government must be paid for dearly, demands must be sacrificed, and that even if its advantages are obvious, all progress must be earned by open resistance.

Then where shall we go, in what direction? I see only barriers. For years, not once have I said to myself, when reading one of their speeches, "Such a splendid idea has never come to the mind of anyone!" On the contrary, I have often said to myself lugubriously, "So what — everybody knows that!" And most often I have asked myself how, in the midst of all this, I can save my own ideas, how I can trick them, since I can't persuade them, because I never see them. I see and I hear that power retreats only when it strikes an obstacle too strong for it. No argument convinces it. Only failure, repeated failure when it wants to do things the old way, sways power. Failure costs us all money and wears on our nerves. I see a permanent wish and also a permanent danger: the bad old days can return. For what does it mean that we have the Union, the *Litfund*,[1] publishing houses, and periodicals? We are threatened that they will be taken away if we don't behave ourselves. If I admit that this is their right, I am saying as my sister often used to say: He hath given; He taketh away. But are they really masters of all? What do they leave to the discretion of others? Nothing? Then we need not exist. But they ought to say so. Then it would be perfectly clear that fundamentally a handful of people decide on the existence or nonexistence of all that should be done, thought, or felt. This then — not works exhibited somewhere — shows the position of culture in our country.

/

Lastly, we have often heard it said that the circle of leadership recognizes a certain degree of autonomy in culture's own domain. But culture should not feel troubled, they say, if it is blamed when it ventures into the political arena. They accuse us of breaking our own rule: each type of work should be done by its specialists. It is true that politics should also be carried on by specialists. But how do we know, in any sure way, who the specialists are? I do not know and I choose to describe my doubts in an imaginative way. A doctor is certainly a specialist.

He is more capable than we of making a diagnosis; he can give us appropriate care, but he certainly cannot say better than we can how we feel under the effect of his treatment. Only a very incompetent doctor would perform a complicated operation on us without our having given him authorization. Autonomy of art and culture? This is no more than a slogan and a frequently used tactic. Today one thing is valid, tomorrow something else: it seems to change, but one needn't be an expert to see that it is the same thing running from the same barrel by two different taps.

Just as I do not feel very secure in a politico-cultural situation in which the regime can obviously cause evolution to the point of conflict, so I do not feel secure as a citizen outside this room, outside this playing field. Nothing is happening to me, and nothing has happened to me. That sort of thing doesn't go on any more. Should I be grateful? I don't think so; I'm afraid. I do not see any certain guarantee. It is true that justice is better administered by the courts, but the judges themselves have no strong and solid guarantee. I see that the work done by the public ministry is better, but have the magistrates of the public ministry guarantees, and do they feel secure? If you wish, I would be happy to interview some of them about it for the papers. Do you believe that such interviews could be published? I would not be afraid to interview the attorney-general himself, to ask him why the unjustly condemned and rehabilitated men do not quite simply regain their previous rights, why national committees show reserve in returning to them their apartments or houses — but this would not be published. Why is nothing ever really forgiven them? Why have they not the advantages of the politically persecuted? Why do we haggle with them over money? Why can't tailors go to Vienna for three years and painters go to Paris for thirty without being considered criminals?

Our parliament evidently acts on the principle *nullum*

crimen sine lege, no crime without law. This implies that it can furnish the state with as many criminals as it pleases. Why aren't people who don't want to live in our country not authorized to go to the devil, and why don't they leave, these people who no longer hope to see democratic reforms which have not yet begun?

It is true that some new and better laws have passed and that others are under examination. It is also true that the new law on the press has greatly cleared the air. They are also preparing to modify laws concerning other public liberties — the right of assembly and the right of association. The project is under study at the ministry of the interior, but an article which should have appeared on this subject in *Literarni Listy* was confiscated. I see no guarantees.

What guarantees? I don't know. And here I stop, because there is a point at which I am in doubt: the circles of leadership themselves, the government and its members. Do they have guarantees of their own civil rights without which it is impossible to create, or even to carry out, a policy? Here I can only refer to the formula already used by others: millstones sometimes grind the very ones who set them turning.

The real cultural level reached by a nation is measured by the way in which the state organizes its actions. It is thus more a question of cultural level of policy than of good cultural policy.

When the policy of politicians is cultural, then writers, artists, scientists, and engineers are not required to weaken their minds by continually struggling for their right to work, their right to consideration, their professional rights, their right to assemble, their right to associate. They have no need to explain the precise character of their work. They are not obliged to compare themselves to other citizens, to workers, to peasants, to office workers, who have the same rights as they but have not the means of putting their thoughts through the filter of

47

censorship, and who do not know how to present them in artistic form, a picture, an aphorism, a poem, or a musical work. A noncultural policy arouses centers of struggle for freedom; nevertheless, such a regime feels offended when this is mentioned. The regime does not understand that liberty exists only where one has no need to mention it, and it takes offense at what people speak of and what they see. However, instead of changing what people see, the regime wants to change their eyes. And meanwhile we lose the only thing which justifies all this talk, the dream of a government which is identified with the citizens, the dream of a citizen who governs himself almost alone. Is that dream realizable?

We have arrived at some partial successes in the realization of this dream, which has been the goal of the nation from the beginning of history. One such success has been the achievement of an independent Czechoslovakia, a success brought about by popular progressive forces and politicians of progress; this success has not yet been mentioned in the text of the resolution, and I propose that it should be inscribed there. A way station was reached which, in spite of the inherent imperfections in the nature of the regime of this period, brought with it a high level of democracy which did not in the least prevent citizens from dreaming of a socialism which would not be realizable except in a second phase of the development of the state. The idea of a social state transformed itself, after the war, to a socialist program. The special conditions in which socialism was realized and the state of socialist theory at that time resulted in certain distortions in the course of its realization in our country. Certain events took place which were not explicable by the prevailing conditions in this country and which had their source neither in the character of the people nor in its history.

When we speak of this period and we seek reasons to explain why we have lost so much, morally and materially, why we are economically backward, the ruling circles say that it was necessary. Perhaps it was necessary to the spiritual development of the functions of the regime, which obliged all partisans of socialism to share this experience with them. It is indispensable to understand that, in the last twenty years, no human problem has been solved in our country, from the most elementary needs such as shelter, schools, and economic prosperity to the most beautiful needs of life which no nondemocratic system can fulfill — for example, the feeling of having worth in the society, the subordination of political decisions to ethical criteria, belief in the value of even subordinate work, the need for trust between men, education for all the people. I fear that we have not risen to the level of the world's development, and I have the impression that our Republic has lost its reputation. I suggest that we have not contributed to humanity any original idea or any new inspiration, that we have not even, for example, any ideas of our own on methods of production or on a safeguard from asphyxiation by the results of production, that we are following without struggle the dehumanized civilization of the American type, that we are repeating the mistakes of both East and West, that our society does not possess any organization charged with seeking a shorter way in the halting, miasmic development of modern life.

In saying this, I do not wish to say that we have lived in vain, that nothing of all this has any value. It has value. But the question is whether it is only advertising value. Even in such a case, the total consciousness of humanity would progress. But is it necessary to turn a country, which understands the dangers which its culture is running, into a guinea pig in order to teach this kind of lesson? I suggest that in our resolution we should state that progressive Czechoslovakian culture already knew this thirty years ago, or at least foresaw it.

I have recently met many people of extraordinary freshness, whether isolated or belonging to work or interest collectives.

Their resistance is remarkable; they demonstrate their escape from the influence of power; they follow the natural principles of honest men: to work hard, to be faithful to their work, not to betray, not to become poisoned. To these qualities, the classic summing up of the honest man, they added a new one — absence of a sense of distance between subordinates and superiors.

In conclusion, I would like to express what my whole account must have made clear, the knowledge that my criticism of the power in this state is not a criticism of socialism. I do not believe that the evolution which we have gone through was necessary and I do not identify this power with socialism, though it tried so to identify itself. It is not even certain that they are moving toward the same destiny. And those who exert the power — I exonerate them from this charge for a moment, and I appeal to them as individuals, with their own feelings and thoughts — if they come here and ask us if socialism is realizable, they must accept the answer as the expression of our good will and at the same time of our highest civic loyalty: "I do not know."

Notes for Appendix

1. *Litfund* ("literary funds"), the organization which distributes fellow-ships and subsidies to writers and artists.

2.

Interlude: Democratic Socialism Aborning ... January–March 1968

The Red Tsar of Hradschin — His Partisans — His Friend
Sejna (January) — The Opposition and Its Watchdog — The
People (February) — Their Man Dubcek — Novotny's Death
Knell (March)

[The Red Tsar of Hradschin]

The noxious charm of power is such that old men laden with
glory and honor will spoil rather than relinquish the last chapter of their biographies. Churchill, Adenauer, Ben Gurion, and
many others imposed humiliating and useless trials on democracy. Old dictators should be sentenced to the axe, so patient
are their ruses, so tenacious is their obstinacy. Anton Novotny
was not unaware that he was losing the reality of power for the
power of a gentle tyrant, confused and blundering, whose apparent stability was due less to the controls of his police than
to the lassitude of a people whom hope had deserted years
ago.

He was apparently resigned to the loss. His traditional
speech of January 1, delivered in a particularly mournful voice,
was a feeble echo of his autocritique in the Central Commit-

51

tee. Four months after his bellicose speech before the army cadets, Novotny pleaded for reform in all departments: "We are following the right path and should continue to follow it." He invited his audience to study the technical and cultural accomplishments of the West; he promised appropriate measures to assure the rapid development of Slovakia; and the like.

But this was only one trick more from the red tsar of Hradschin. He exploited the Christmas-cake truce to mobilize his partisans in Prague and Bohemia: workmen's militias, the police, the army. Intoxicated by his own propaganda, surrounded by flatterers and mediocre men reflecting his own mediocrity, Novotny believed himself to be dealing with a fractional minority, while Dubcek and his friends, perhaps in spite of themselves in the beginning, actually represented the general feeling of the entire country, of communists and noncommunists alike.

The Czechoslovakian crisis was to become less a political affair than a moral crisis. It was to be an immense upheaval of a proud little people who were culturally sophisticated, industrious, and disgusted with a regime which combined all the defects of popular democracies without any of their possible virtues. Milk cow of the socialist bloc, Czechoslovakia had permitted itself with unparalleled meekness to be colonized and domesticated by Moscow. Neither Janos Kadar nor Wladyslaw Gomulka, not even Walter Ulbricht or Nicolas Ceausescu, would have allowed themselves to be bled like Novotny, who refused nothing and would always give more on demand.

Thus, the recent war in the Near East was to cost more than five hundred million dollars in armaments and supplies furnished to the Arab countries on Moscow's orders, and the Republic would benefit not one heller. Czechoslovakia had been the victim of other "gifts" required by Moscow to the profit of Guinea, Indonesia, Cuba, and Vietnam.

The Czech people felt not only impoverished but debased and humiliated. Its workmen, like the French proletariat, were very civilized, *kulturny*; the party had never been able to root out their instinctively petit bourgeois behavior. The blatant "workers' " demagoguery imported from the U.S.S.R., did not impress them at all. I had noted previously that, compared to factories in other bloc countries, those of Czechoslovakia were noticeably bare of banners, portraits, and Stakhanovite slogans. Now there were almost none.

The Czechs are a lively minded, bantering people who do not swallow anything whole, and Prague, during the Stalinist darkness, was the source of the bitter jokes encountered in variously adapted versions from Pankow to Erivan. Prague used humor in self-defense against the grimness of a universe prophetically described by two of its most glorious sons, Kafka in *In the Penal Colony* and Capek in *War with the Newts*.

Above all, the Czechoslovakian people suffered a sharp sense of shame for the immorality that had fallen on their country. "He who does not steal robs his family": a veritable anthology of proverbs had evolved since "victorious February." The bitterness of these betrayed those carved earlier on wood panels or lovingly embroidered and hung over mantels, those proclaiming the domestic virtues of Czech families: order, cleanliness, discipline, honesty — in short, a specialized version of a German *Gemütlichkeit*.

Behind the monotonous façade of socialist order, the country was corrupt to the marrow. The worker stole tools and raw material and stretched his wages by moonlighting. In an economy of acute penury where a ball-point pen is a little treasure, the thick network of Tuzex stores, theoretically planned for tourists, furnished the regime's profiteers with all the luxuries of the West, from Gillette razor blades to foreign automobiles.

For a long time the Czechs and the Slovaks, though more or less accustomed to the form of the state, had wanted at least a communism that was decent. Dubcek's extraordinary popularity (that smiling little man, so modest and sincere, somewhat drab) arose because he reconciled the Czechoslovakians with their image. To me, Dubcek revealed himself to be much more than an honest man, but that was perhaps his primary quality, and instinctively the people opened their hearts to him during the first days of the crisis.

[His Partisans]

Before the session of the Central Committee, whose reopening he was trying to delay, Novotny made a count of his partisans. Theoretically he had all the trumps and could, like Gomulka in Poland, take command of the situation.

The writer Jan Prochazka, resuming his function as substitute member of the Central Committee after the Writers' Congress, said to me, speaking of this period: "The writers have heralded the general feelings of the times, for we expressed the discontent of the whole population and of many members of the C.P. itself at all levels. We found ourselves in basic agreement with the progressive elements of the majority of the workers. But the working class is not homogeneous and it is still possible to find reactionary tendencies there."

Fortunately for the progressives, the Czech worker, heir to social democracy, full of common sense and sickened by demagogy, did not lend himself to a solution à la polonaise; he could not be made to rise against the intellectuals. Anti-Semitism, which certain of Novotny's lieutenants tried to exploit, roused no heat in the miner or the metalworker.

Then, too, a conflict between generations, such as was to break out in France during May, was crippling the factories. The young created a deadlock in the aging party, many of whose members were veterans of the famous workers' militia.

In 1948, this militia of fifteen thousand men had carried off the Prague coup on the night of February 22. The aged and grumbling veterans, still constituting a potentially formidable force, were now disarmed by jeers.[1]

The police, informers, press censors, and the like had also aged greatly in twenty years. More delayed than anywhere else, de-Stalinization and the horrors subsequently revealed had to a certain extent demoralized the security services.

Jan Stern, one of the founders of *Prace*, the union newspaper, and among the men in the forefront of the liberation, told me that the censors "had in a certain sense become part of the newspaper: they were good functionaries who wanted above all to avoid trouble. They often came up to the editorial department, with a suspect piece in hand, to advise us to change a word, to modify a turn of phrase. Their idea was to say the same thing in a more 'astute' manner. They rejoiced, often noisily, in the subtlety or the ferocity of an attack against a regime that they were the first to be able to appreciate." Novotny's police empire managed to be like both Orwell's Big Brother and the Marx brothers. The rigors of the heroic years had given place to an amiable disorder.

Only the army could keep the Novotnyan dictatorship in power. The Czechs, who had not fought since Jan Hus and the battle of the White Mountain, were not exactly lightning bolts on the battlefield. Nevertheless, their army of 225,000 well-equipped men was, with the exception of the Polish army, the most important in the socialist bloc.[2] In case of an emergency, the active army could be reinforced by intensively trained reserves; Prague could line up 700,000 reservists immediately and could ultimately mobilize 2.5 million men of fighting age. An almost legendary fatalism ruled the relations between the Czechoslovakian chiefs of state and their army. In 1938, with a levy of a million men at his disposal, Eduard Benes had been in a position to offer the Nazis a more than symbolic resist-

55

ance; had he done so, the destiny of Europe and the world might have been decisively affected. But Benes hesitated. He even consulted Klement Gottwald, the leader of the Communist party and the chief power of the opposition. Munich came and went; the partition heralded world war.

In February 1948, Benes had again had at his disposal sufficient support to oppose the workers' militia. Although the army was divided, its anticommunist elements were by far the most numerous. But the tired old man, terrified by the specter of civil war, again hesitated, until again it was too late.

The same thing was to be true of Novotny. In December, at the end of the plenum's first session, he met with Miroslav Mamula, chief of the Central Committee's eighth section (army and security). These two gentlemen, bringing out their "index cards," established with maniacal care a list of 1,030 suspects. After the thaw, everyone in Prague boasted of being on this famous list, whose existence was never officially confirmed. Although it was at that time the subject of innumerable jokes, Mamula's list was to be put to use eight months later. While the "boss" succumbed to his mania for paperwork, the military prepared a series of measures in preparation for a putsch.

[His Friend Sejna (January)]

The minister of defense, General Bohumir Lomski, changed the date of the meeting of the Central Committee, initially planned for December 12, to coincide with an unexpected mobilization of Prague's reservists. An unusual amount of publicity was given by the press, radio, and television to a move which public opinion interpreted with alarm. After the thaw, Lomski tried to justify himself in a television statement to the effect that this partial mobilization and subsequent maneuvers around Prague were a routine affair. Pressed with questions by journalists, he admitted "that probably the date was unfortunately chosen," but he passed responsibility to his chief of general staff, Colonel General Vladimir Janko, who was also vice-minister of defense.

With the approach of Christmas, the military's preparations speeded up. At the principal regional military headquarters, commandants of units discussed the subject of an endangered socialist revolution. General Janko collected the commanders of the armored units to sound out their intentions, in the event that the "unity of the party should be in danger." The commanders hesitated. Finally, only one, the commander of the first armored unit stationed at Ceske-Budejovice in southern Bohemia, declared that he was ready to march on Prague in such an event.[3]

Major General Jan Sejna passed his Christmas holidays making "a tour of mess halls," gathering signatures of generals on a petition demanding support for Novotny in all his functions. The first to sign it were generals Janko and Rytir, head of counterespionage. Thereafter, Sejna had no difficulty in obtaining the approval of one hundred and eighteen others, with the exception of Lieutenant General Martin Dzur, future minister of war in the Cernik government.

The denunciatory document was intended to intimidate the members of the Central Committee, whose resumption of work Novotny had delayed in order to permit the readying of all possible means of intimidation.

On the morning of January 4, while the party plenum was opening, General Sejna called together the chiefs of the general staff. His associate, Commandant Moravec, submitted to them the resolution that had been signed by the generals. This confused text, written in the customary dogmatic style, called for cooperation of the army "shoulder to shoulder with the eager forces of the party under the direction of Comrade No-

57

votny." It represented a flat ultimatum to the Central Committee: "The Communists of the army demand that Comrade Novotny be supported in his functions as president of the Republic and as first secretary of the Central Committee. Comrade Novotny is our guarantee of revolutionary continuity." No one present could agree on the exact wording. After hours of argument, the exhausted Sejna closed the session by announcing a plenary session for the next day. This session would include, besides the military, a great part of the civil service.

A hundred people met on Friday, January 5, at 7:30 A.M. in the meeting hall of the third floor of the ministry of defense. Sejna held the floor for several hours. He was nervous to the point of hysteria, because unlike most of his audience he knew what was being plotted at that very moment in the Central Committee: the progressives were on the point of carrying the party. Novotny had sent him an S.O.S. The putsch would be now or never. Sejna read a revised version of his text. The army no longer insisted but asked . . . It was noon. Sejna asked for ratification of his text by a show of hands.

The single report on the affair of the putsch was an interview with General Dzur which appeared in the army newspaper *Obrana Lidu* of April 6, 1968.[4] The article gave the following details:

In the hour that followed, all those who took the floor were against sending this letter and most of the objections concerned its content. One would have thought that the meeting was going to be a failure for Sejna. He stood on the podium and listened. After each counterproposal he added a few dry and unequivocal words: the situation is serious, who is not for this project is against it. When Sejna left the podium, I took the floor:

"This letter is in contradiction to the theses of the

plenum of last October. We know nothing of the actual session of the Central Committee and we wish to become involved in it. Our representatives to the Central Committee have already informed us as clearly as possible that everything went on in a democratic fashion. Do you not therefore think that this letter is out of place, that in essence it expresses our lack of confidence in the Central Committee? I also have the impression that our meeting today is not in accord with the party bylaws."

Dzur was preaching in a desert. After his interruption, discussion continued, less on the matter than on the manner. Sejna read a new and third version of the letter, but the content was practically the same.

In Dzur's own words: "Time was passing and Sejna looked dizzy. General Janko was nervous; he demanded of Sejna (these two had always hated each other): 'Come on then, hurry up, let's vote. Who is for?' A forest of arms rose, some with heavy hesitation . . . All but one — all but mine."

The letter-ultimatum from Sejna was to be the victim of universal military bureaucracy. Just as German revolutionaries "never walked on the grass," a harsh remark attributed to Rosa Luxembourg, Sejna wanted to complete his putsch with all due respect to form. He transmitted his ultimatum through the proper channels to his superior, Lieutenant General Vaclav Prchlik, head of the political department of the army, so that the latter, whom Sejna thought had been won to his cause, could send it to the Central Committee. It was delayed, in a drawer, until the die was cast. It did not reach the Central Committee until after Dubcek was appointed first secretary of the party, and ironically it was to be the first document delivered into the hands of the new progressive leader.

The "Sejna petition" permitted General Prchlik to eliminate some weeks later several of the most compromised generals on the pretext of testing the political intelligence and the professional qualities of the superior officers. To General Rytir, who defended himself like a demon, swearing that he did not know the reason why a letter directed to Novotny had been delivered to Dubcek, Prchlik replied with wry humor: when the chief of a counterespionage service is ignorant of the events taking place several hundred meters from his offices, how can he learn what is going on at NATO?

In his interview in *Obrana Lidu,* Dzur made these comments on the lamentable end of Sejna's pseudoputsch:

The letter was delivered after it had been decided to separate the functions of president of the Republic and first secretary of the Central Committee. So it was in vain. But we learned after the coup that certain Communists in our plenary meeting had been aware of what was going on in the Central Committee. These were the very comrades who distinguished themselves as champions of the Sejna proposal: such seemed to them customary, thus attractive, that is to say (between ourselves) conservative. Their attitude: above all, don't change anything, hold onto the conquests of the past.

The business of the letter ricocheted back at them. These comrades all held important posts, were among the influential members of the army's military and political hierarchy. They could not pretend to have lacked information; only one conclusion was possible: they acted against the interests of progress, against the renaissance which was beginning.

Faithful to the rules of the game in the Dubcek era, Dzur spoke of this whole affair as if providence had put a stop to the malice of the enemies of progress. In fact, Dubcek's friends

inside the general staff and the ministry of defense were anything but inactive.

In the end, three factors contributed to the uncapping of
the affair: the vigilance of General Prchlik, who was to be established as the strong man of the progressive team and who
was won to its cause from the beginning; the indecision of
Novotny, who still hoped that the majority of the Central
Committee was his; and, above all, the cunning refusal of numerous subordinate elements of the police and army to continue to support their dictator.

Zdenka N., wife of a high functionary in the ministry of
foreign affairs, witnessed a comic incident in this resistance à la
Schweik. On January 2, her child felt abdominal pains; appen-
dicitis was diagnosed and Mrs. N. hurried to a hospital: "We
had to go to several hospitals before the child could be admitted. There were no free beds. A doctor told us that an abnormal number of officers from the Prague garrison had just
fallen sick."

[The Opposition and Its Watchdog]

The Central Committee's session January 3–5, which was to
set in motion the new course of action, was cloaked in absolute
secrecy. The atmosphere in Prague was heavy with contradictory rumors circulating among the people. Press, radio, and television were as bland as ever. Not until January 20 did the
news media explode with information.

The Central Committee sat during the day at the same time
as the Presidium, which continued to hold night sessions. At
the Central Committee's opening, a committee of experts appointed in December recommended the end of Novotny's duality of powers and the nomination of a new secretary general.
This nomination was the business of the Presidium and the

Presidium was deadlocked: the Politburo was still divided, five votes supporting Novotny and five demanding his resignation.

The Presidium's paralysis prompted a majority of the Central Committee to vacillate toward the hitherto minority group which wanted *immediate* change. Previously, a large number of delegates had thought that this question of duality could be attended to in the future, within the framework of the next party congress, perhaps in 1971. Naturally, this inclination was enthusiastically encouraged by Novotny's partisans, who would thus have had time to eliminate the opposition. It is probable that this group, so vague on the question of "delays," was at the bottom of Novotny's indecision about his friend Sejna's putsch.

One of the actors in the drama, Colonel B., who worked with General Prchlik to thwart the "plot," said to me later, "When you think about it, it's a crazy story. The country was on the verge of civil war. A brave lady persuaded Dubcek's friends to postpone the revolution until 'after the holidays.' The revolutionaries would quietly eat roast goose at home while the 'putschists' played bogeymen like extras at Barandov,[5] waiting for Novotny-Hamlet, tangled in indecision, to decide to do something. If I hadn't been a Marxist and atheist, I'd have thought that God protected Dubcek."

Providence also made Hendrych — Novotny's right arm and devil's advocate for ten years, depositary of all his secrets, and subtle connoisseur of the art of pulling strings — Dubcek's most precious ally. Alexander Dubcek, who had a somewhat romanticized reputation as an upright and generous man, had not become secretary-general of the Slovak C.P. without having been well initiated. But he stood as a choir boy beside the old apparatchik of Prague. Delicious paradox, the most conservative politician, the most dogmatic member of the Czech Communist party, the bugbear of intellectuals and liberals, victim of a "shaggy dog story" of the political police, would prove the prime mover of Novotny's downfall. Hendrych's attitude would confuse the party ranks to such an extent that authentic liberals would support Novotny while fierce conservatives sided with Dubcek. All would misunderstand Hendrych's role, because he was not playing politics at all; he was saving his skin and gratifying his vengeance. At the second nighttime session of the Presidium, Hendrych's aggressiveness broke up the Novotnyan bloc. Alexander Dubcek's nomination "by unanimous vote of the Presidium" was announced on the morning of January 5 at the plenum of the Central Committee.[6]

The Central Committee in turn accepted the resignation of its first secretary Anton Novotny and elected — "unanimously," of course — Alexander Dubcek to this post. Novotny remained president of the Republic.

Hendrych played his role of watchdog to the new secretary-general with unflagging devotion. When Dubcek, in accord with his character, was inclined to reconciliation, Hendrych, who knew "his" machine, literally had to push him to get rid of the most dangerous Novotnyans.

Cestmir Cisar, who succeeded Hendrych as the head of the important ideological committee of the party, told me with laughter that Hendrych could be seen enthusiastically destroying what he himself had built, to the great distress of Dubcek, who spoke to him of legality, democracy, and so on. Hendrych penetrated the offices of the ideological committee and spoke to the functionaries of the censorship committee, whom he himself had put in office: "You're no longer any use to our new direction." Snatching up their resignations, he hurried to Dubcek's house to announce, letters in hand, that Comrades X and Y no longer wished to hold their offices. These measures seemed to depress the new secretary-general.

[The People (February)]

During January and February the new power tried to consolidate itself while press, radio, and television, discovering the taste of freedom, exploded in a joyous frenzy.

Television was to play a part unequaled anywhere since the Joseph McCarthy affair in the United States. Like insects under the entomologist's lens, the Novotnyans came to justify themselves, exposing their faces to the cameras. Their expressions were more revealing than all their speeches. Ministers, stool pigeons, press censors, prison wardens, all were bombarded with vengeful questions from the journalists; all fought back a little, lost their footing, and ended by begging pardon for their mistakes.

Jiri Pelikan, forty-five years old, head of television (but also member of the Central Committee and president of the foreign affairs committee in the parliament) had long made TV a stronghold of progressivism. From time to time, one of his shows would escape the vigilance of the censors. In 1964, in a program called "The Curious Camera," he introduced a sequence on the problem of the children of the "bourgeois" who were cut off from all access to higher education. The sequence showed, among others, a young woman department-store clerk, a precocious mathematician, whose hometown party cell had expelled her from school because her father had formerly been a landowner. Pelikan, reminiscing, said: "That time I almost had to skip town with my whole crew. Novotny, who not only had watched the show but also had been deluged with complaints from party functionaries about it, accused us of criticizing the guiding role of the C.P."

Pelikan told me of a few other programs in which "we wished to express our concern and sometimes our anguish as communists at the crisis threatening us. In the end it was no

64

longer a struggle between conservatives and liberals but a desperate battle against stupidity. When the thaw came, we were like somnambulists. What we had held in for so many years exploded. And then I saw that censorship had left us with very rich archives. The true riches of our television were intact, stored reels of film crammed with talent and inventiveness."

My visits to Prague at this time were enlivened by an extraordinary festival atmosphere. Vaclavske Namesty (Wenceslas Square), the Champs Élysées of Prague, swarmed with people at every hour, day and night. There was the atmosphere of liberation, comparable to the May days in Paris, though less exclusively youthful and less violent. Strangers talked with each other; groups formed on the spur of the moment and argued until they were out of breath. When the papers came out, crowds stampeded the kiosks. Those gazettes, four small pages of badly printed grayish paper, poor but written with feverish joy by journalists rediscovering freedom of expression, were devoured. The *Rude Pravo* itself became readable; good Czech replaced its dreary Marxist clichés. When people were not poring over the newspapers, they were avidly listening to the radio or watching television. Tape recorders disappeared from the market; the insatiable ones would record radio programs at the same time that they were watching TV. The rest of the time, people were rushing all over town to improvised meetings which went on without interruption, addressed by enthusiastic and exhausted speakers who appeared not to have slept for weeks. It was a party, a permanent happening.

In the austere Central Committee building, young men selected from outside the machine made up the first brain trusts which imposed themselves on the Novotnyan machine. These were the first communists I was to see whose careful dress and nervous and hurried affability reminded me of the West. Everything was attacked at once in committees formed for the most part by university students. Things moved so quickly that the federation, which Slovak Vasil Bilak, member of the Presidium, called "unthinkable" on January 3, became two weeks later "indispensable," according to the conclusions of a committee preparing a program of action for the Communist party. Bilak was on this committee.

[Their Man Dubcek]

The role and personality of Dubcek took some time to emerge. Not only was the new secretary-general quite unknown in Prague; he was also a Slovak, and the average Czech's attitude toward Slovaks often reminded one of an innocent and worldly anti-Semitism: "I have nothing against them but . . ." or "Some of my best friends are Slovaks."

At the beginning of January, such celebration marked the fall of the dictator — Novotny's retention of the title president fooled no one — that his replacement, whoever he had been, would have enjoyed limitless overdraft of confidence. The information media which played such a decisive role in the thaw were to make Dubcek into a popular figure in spite of himself, for during these first weeks he made practically no statement, did not show himself in public, and saw no journalists.[7]

Alexander Dubcek had taken it into his head that first of all he would win over the machine, the sacrosanct machine of the party. Was he not an apparatchik himself, a pure product of this party machine? He was an "empirical" democrat of some kind, whose natural qualities of heart and mind would, from the beginning of his career, incline toward a more progressive form of communist power. In Bratislava, the only city where he was known, Edo Fris, editorial writer of the Slovakian *Pravda* told me: "He was always obsessed by what he called problems of socialist morals . . . 'This is humane . . . this is not humane . . .' were words often on his lips."

Dubcek's first public appearance took place on February 20. From the historic balcony of the old square where Gottwald had harangued the workers' militia of Prague, Dubcek in his turn spoke to these shock troops, spearhead of the revolution which he led by virtue of his function as secretary-general. Though timeworn, these troops, always equipped with heavy weapons and trucks, were ready for street fighting or rapid mobilization, were organized in every factory, in every city. They were believed to be under the thumb of Novotnyans and ready to boo, if not harm, Dubcek. The new party secretary obstinately refused any protection from the police or army. At the appointed hour the immense square was overflowing with militiamen; the citizens of Prague found themselves crowded back into the side streets. Some of the workers carried placards bearing the names of their factories — one could pick out the names of the Novotnyan "fortresses," the C.K.C. factory of Prague, the Kladno mines. Others were clad in leather jackets and their old red armbands of 1948. Dubcek seemed to be the only one in a business suit. In spite of the microphones his voice was so soft, so composed, that there were cries of "Louder! Louder!" from all sides. To these "hard cases" accustomed to Novotnyan protocol and "virile" slogans, Dubcek spoke in simple and moving language. He told them how beautiful their city was; he spoke to them of the difficulties of building a socialism which was "humane, just, and brotherly"; he closed his peroration with a pathetic "Help me . . ."

The applause, at first meager, burst into an immense ovation. If the prejudices of the hardest of the hard were overcome, the party was won. Dubcek in his later speeches, whether in the streets or on television, was to continue this custom, to ask for help from all and to thank the citizens effusively for their support and confidence. For the Czechs and the

Slovaks who had given their confidence to no one since 1938 and to whom no one had said thank you since 1948, Dubcek's words were new and moving. I saw people in the cafes blowing their noses loudly after one of Dubcek's speeches. Within a few weeks, this little man, a continual smile on his wrinkled face, and myopic eyes behind spectacles balanced on a long nose (which was the delight of caricaturists who, for the first time in a communist regime, could poke a little fun at their leaders), became the first political idol of the country since Thomas Masaryk.

Refusing to become the object of a personality cult, Dubcek would not authorize the public sale of his portrait. Nevertheless, I was often to see his photograph, cut from a newspaper, pasted up on the windshield of a taxi or in the showcases of a state store. Little by little, the public at large learned his un-dramatic family life.

Dubcek's home was still in Bratislava where he went, when he could, on the weekends. A little Fiat 600 with Anna Dub-cek, a young blond plump woman, at the wheel or the oldest of his three sons, a medical student (the other two were still in school) would be waiting for him there at the airfield. His prowess as a swimmer, his passion for football, his irreproach-able past as a courageous and devoted militant, were already familiar. His was a disarming personality, the picture of the perfect Communist. He would have been hateful if he had not also been convinced and sincere.

Three factors in Alexander Dubcek's past were to condition his political career: his intimate knowledge of the U.S.S.R., his valuable experience as party secretary in a small town, and his Slovak origin.

Dubcek was a pure product of communism. He had *never* traveled outside the iron curtain. His father, Steve Dubcek, who had emigrated to the United States before the first world war and was a member of the crypto-communist Socialist party of Illinois in 1917, returned to Slovakia with the firm intention of rejoining the great fatherland of workers. The birth of Alexander in 1921, in the village of Uhrovec, changed his plans.[8] A year later, Steve Dubcek with three hundred other idealists, Czech and Slovak, founded the cooperative farm of Interhelpo at Frunze in Soviet Asia. The young Alexander first went to school in Kirghiz. The Dubceks returned to their homeland in 1938 and settled in Trencin in western Slovakia. Alexander, seventeen years old, began work in a factory, while educating himself on his own. Dubcek had occasion to supplement some of the gaps in his education at the political school of the Central Committee of the Soviet Communist party in Moscow between 1955 and 1958. During these years he acquired a familiarity with the Soviet Union, its institutions, and the mentality of its people and its leaders which was to be unique in a foreign communist leader and probably Dubcek's most valuable trump card in the eight months of the thaw. Dubcek had seen the worst — forced collectivization, the murder of the kulaks, the gigantic crimes and errors of Stalin's empire — and the best. He would always feel half-Russian (his knowledge of the language was faultless) and no one could cast doubt on his sincere love and respect for the U.S.S.R.

Alexander Dubcek began his apprenticeship to power in 1953 when he became the secretary of the party at Banska Bystrica, a historic city in the heart of the Slovak country, in the marvelous Low Tatra Mountains, birthplace of the anti-German uprising in 1944. He had rejoined the ranks of the party at eighteen, when he was working in the Skoda factories in Dubnica, near Trencin. (He never left that area; after World War II, he worked in Trencin in a yeast factory.)

Neither great brilliance nor dramatic events characterized Dubcek's political career. Ten years after his appointment as secretary of the party in Bratislava, he became first secretary of the Slovak Communist party and a member of the Presidium and of parliament. Dubcek made Slovakia a proving ground for his empirical and singularly undogmatic communism. He was neither a weakling nor an innocent.

Mastery of the subtle workings of the machine in a district was important — other party secretaries during those last ten years had made their fiefs into oases of tolerance and relative intellectual liberty — but not sufficient. If Dubcek had not been a Slovak, he would not have been propelled into the seat of highest authority. The Prague thaw could not have come as quickly nor have developed as it did without the stimulus of the eternal Slovakian question which, from Masaryk to Novotny, haunted the sleep of the leaders of the Republic. Unlike Stalin, that Georgian who wished to be Russian, ultra-Russian, and yet who could never escape his southern accent or his grammatical errors, Dubcek was an unambiguous Slovak, loyal to his nationality. Espousing his people's grievances, he understood immediately that his battle against Novotny's tyrannical centralism could not be dissociated from the struggle of the Czechs and the Slovaks against other aspects of the dictatorship. The melding of the 1950s had proved that Stalinist dogmatism could, with threat of the gallows, associate the claims of the Slovakian autonomists with other aspects of counterrevolution. Only a process of democratization of the system could ensure the Slovaks their local rights. This was a progressive discovery for the young Dubcek. He struggled courageously against the Nazis in 1944; he was wounded twice in the mountains and his brother Julius died at his side. During the whole of his career he never ceased to hound the central powers for more investments in the eastern provinces. Dubcek's cell in Trencin was the first to shake Novotny's authority. At Bratislava, writers and journalists enjoyed a liberty unknown elsewhere. The alliance between Dubcek and the intellectuals which made the quiet revolution possible dated from that time.

Western public opinion initially saw Dubcek as a "centrist," a clever opportunist rather than a real reformer of the system. The Slovak party leader seemed worlds removed from those brilliant scholars whom television reportage and interviews had made familiar to Paris, London, and New York. Intellectuals like Eduard Goldstuecker (the brilliant Kafka scholar), Ivan Svitak (the philosopher), and other eloquent, polyglot men already known in the West seemed to be "snatching" from a party which was losing momentum the future liberties of the nation. Between January and July of 1968, until the eve of the "verbal terrorism" of the U.S.S.R. and its allies against the Czechoslovakian experiment, the silent, discreet Dubcek would be held responsible for breaking up the happy marriage, so long postponed, between socialism and "bourgeois liberties." The gravity of Moscow's threat to Prague was not understood.

In fact, this worker's son, this worker become party man who spoke no foreign language save Russian, although not an "intellectual" by profession, had an innate taste for culture. He had surrounded himself since his political beginnings with journalists, writers, teachers; in January he had only to choose among them to form his famous brain trusts. Again, a fundamental trait of the Czech and Slovak people was demonstrated: the conflict with Moscow appeared as much cultural as political.

The support — apparent support, at least — of the workers' militia reassured Dubcek. He was going to try gently, by persuasion, to win over to his policy as many cadres of the machine as possible. In accord with this attempt Dubcek was slow to change personnel, even in the most tainted administrations, like the army; he executed a hesitation waltz, one step forward, one step back, which continued to irritate public opinion to the eve of the Soviet aggression. Dubcek seemed to want simultaneously to reassure the people of the continuation of the process of democratization and liberalization and to sway the most obstinate primates of the machine in both Prague and Moscow. Thus the editor-in-chief of *Rude Pravo*, Oldrich Svestka, ultraconservative member of the Presidium, retained his position though disowned by nearly all his editors; they refused to speak to him "except for business purposes" and polemicized fiercely against him in the columns of other papers.

[Novotny's Death Knell (March)]

Anton Novotny received many people in his presidential palace. His partisans were still numerous within all party and government machinery; there was no guarantee that Dubcek could maintain his precarious majority in the Central Committee and in parliament. The authority of the Presidium had been shaken a little since December when its differences had been publicized; the game of democracy could easily turn against its promoters. Moreover, the first manifestations of bad temper were appearing in the Moscow and Warsaw press.

Over this uncertain situation the Sejna affair burst like a clap of thunder. Another gift of providence, the affair was to give Dubcek three more months of respite. General Sejna had managed somewhat to sink into obscurity after his blundering attempt at putsch between Christmas and Saint Sylvester's. Theoretically, a charge was outstanding against him with the attorney-general of the army, but the latter, like millions of other functionaries in the country, not knowing if the "new direction" had really triumphed, took refuge in prudent delay. While awaiting a summons which would not arrive until the day after his flight, Sejna was free as a bird. He kept his titles, his uniform, and even his orderly and his army vehicle.

Those who knew Jan Sejna, general of the Czechoslovakian army, deputy of the Litomerice province, member of the Presidium of the National Assembly, secretary of the Central Committee of the C.P. while at the ministry of national defense, cannot help a feeling of sympathy for him. Some thought that he was the most beautiful creation of Czech humor since Schweik, while others found him a rough diamond or the most charming of companions.

On February 27, 1968, General Sejna, out of uniform, at the wheel of a brand new Skoda MB, and accompanied by his son and a young girl — introduced as his daughter but in fact his mistress — arrived at a frontier station on the Hungarian border. He finally entered the United States via Yugoslavia and Italy.

The man who exhibited a brand new diplomatic passport and confided to a stationmaster, respectfully standing at attention, that he was leaving on an "important mission" abroad, was theoretically under a warrant for arrest — a warrant not to be found in the offices of the military administration until after he had left. Novotny's clan, the president at its head, had managed to the end to cover for this adventurer who would go directly to the headquarters of the C.I.A. The details of his incredible exploits are particularly fascinating; they could not illustrate better the state of corruption in a "model" regime of the socialist bloc on the eve of the new direction.

Sejna, squat, jolly, his red face always alight, was forty-one years old at the time of his escape. A confidant of Novotny and also a close friend of his son, Anton Jr. — with whom he organized reputedly "wild parties" in a Prague apartment — Sejna was a thief. He squeezed supplies, gasoline, illegal exemptions from military service, anything and everything, from his military career. In fact, on the very eve of his escape, he carried off a job: he sold his personal automobile, a Mercedes, at the highest possible price and asked Skoda to bring him one of their latest models so that he could try it out before buying. It was in this Skoda that he crossed the frontier.

Two days before he left, Sejna made the rounds of all his friends to put the bite on them — he needed to pay a "debt of honor," he said. The unhappy General Janko, chief of general staff, who was to commit suicide after Sejna's escape, entrusted him with his modest savings, ten thousand crowns.

Sejna was a true son of the people, as he loved to say. From a family of farm laborers, he went into the army in 1950 with only nine years of elementary school. This lack of formal education did not stop him from receiving startling promotions. Made lieutenant in 1953, he rose without stopping; in 1967 he was promoted to general by Novotny himself.[9] In 1956 he had been elected deputy of Litomerice. His double functions were to permit him an extraordinary career as liar and adventurer.

But Sejna had taken with him more than stolen money (estimated at three hundred thousand crowns) and the regrets of some pretty women on that fateful March 10. The officers of the Pentagon who welcomed him so eagerly in Rome had not come for the story of his amatory prowess. The Czechoslovakian press, usually very discreet in spite of their "liberalization" on matters of this sort wrote on March 11:

> General Sejna has taken abroad with him military documents of the highest importance. . . . He was up-to-date on all the official reports between the high command of the army and the supreme organizations of the state and of the party. . . . He was equally well informed on economic affairs. These are solid gold for Western information services. Moreover, Sejna took part in the most secret conferences of the ministry of defense, and he has an excellent memory.[10]

Other organs of the press announcing the emergency arrival of the Soviet General Ivan Yakubovsky, commander-in-chief of the Warsaw Pact, recalled that Sejna was often the Czech delegate to the conferences at the combined headquarters of this important organization.

The Sejna affair sounded Novotny's death knell. The former secretary-general made Prague laugh until the tears came when he published a communiqué stripping his old friend General Sejna of his rank and removing all his decorations. The press and radio ran riot; meetings, held all over the country, demanded the resignation of the president and his principal supporters.

For ten days Novotny obstinately fought every step before sending in his resignation to the Presidium on March 22. The experiment of democratic socialism could make a second start.

Once again, however, in spite of the advantage this unprecedented military scandal gave him with the Russians, Dubcek would not twist the sword in the wound. Neither Anton Novotny, Jr., nor General Mamula, the "index card" man, was disturbed. The minister of defense, Lomski, kept his position, denying all participation in the January "upheavals"; of Sejna, he said in pitiful excuse, "I was mistaken in him."

On March 22, 1968, the future of Czechoslovakia was a question mark. In the midst of their widespread merrymaking, people paid more attention to appearances than to subterranean currents. The alliance, unexpected from the outset, of intellectuals, economists, and Slovaks had made possible the overthrow of a dictatorship which had seemed the most solidly established of any in the bloc of the U.S.S.R. satellites and by a process not only peaceful but also conforming to the internal logic of the system, to "socialist legality."

With only the weapons of the mind to end such a well-polished machine of oppression, a little worn, of course, but possessed of a powerful army, a formidable police force which had imprisoned, tortured, and assassinated more political opponents than that of any other "popular democracy" in twenty years (some 150,000 victims) to make so radical a revolution without firing a single shot established Dubcek and his friends on a sound strategic basis.

"Power was not in conquering; it was in seizing," an intimate of Dubcek's told me joyously on the dazzling morning of April 1, watching the happy crowd flow through the Narodni, the great Prague boulevard.

A socialist power, which was to begin with romantic zeal and to concern itself with dialogue and liberty. And I thought, like so many other foreigners who were living through those exalted days with me, that we were going to rediscover the loves and nostalgias of our twenties. "This star that rises in the East . . ." — we thought to see it twinkling over Prague.

Notes for Chapter 2

1. Though rallying to Dubcek, who harangued them from a balcony on the historic square of Prague in January, the veterans of the workers' militia did not become any the less a conservative element. Put to the proof, they did, however, remain loyal to Dubcek.
2. The Czechoslovakian army consisted of fourteen divisions, of which four were T55 tanks (3,200 tanks in all), an airborne brigade, 2,000 pieces of artillery plus missiles, an air force of 50,000 men with 600 modern fighter planes, 300 training planes, 100 combat helicopters, and 50 large troop transports, among other matériel.
3. During the opening inquiry into this affair several months later, on March 15, 1968, General Janko committed suicide.
4. "The Truth About a Letter: The Events at the Ministry of Defense of October 1967 to January 1968," C.T.K. (Ceteka) *Daily Press Survey* (April 8, 1968).
5. The Prague cinema studios.
6. Dubcek's election resulted from a laborious compromise and from an error of judgment. The progressives had put forward the names of Ota Sik, Smrkovsky, and Cernik, which were refused by the conservatives, who for their part also could not get enough votes for their candidates Lenart, Simunek, and Lastovicka. When Dubcek's name was mentioned, Novotny made no objection, being persuaded that the "Slovak" would not be accepted.
7. He had previously never received *any* bourgeois journalist, and one could count on the fingers of one hand the "journalists" from the U.S.S.R. and the people's democracies who had met him.
8. With friendly consideration for his future biographers, providence caused Alexander Dubcek to be born in the house of the greatest hero of his country, the nationalist writer Ludjovit Stur, the "awakener of the Slovak soul."
9. There was no sign in his past that he was predestined to such a brilliant military career. In a production on Czech television devoted to his story, filmed in his hometown, the childhood friends of "joyous Janot" said that he had inhaled ground cinnamon the day before his army medical examination so that spots would show up on his lungs when they were x-rayed. In spite of that he was found fit for service — to his great disappointment.
10. *Kulturni Noviny*, March 11, 1968.

3.

Five Months: A Lifetime
... March 22–August 22, 1968

Heatwave — Spring Cleaning (April) — The Party and Its
Policy — The Parade (May) — The Program — The Quarrel
— Delusion — The Spirit of Munich (June) — The Czechoslovakian Case — Appendix: Two Thousand Words — Letter
from the Five — Prague's Reply

[Heatwave]

Between March 22, the date of Novotny's resignation of his
duties as president of the Republic, and August 22, the "day of
the tanks," democratic socialism existed for five months: five
exalting months, trying months, when the two nations of the
Republic tried to build their future on new foundations, when
everything was open to question, when everything was happening at once, when the reactions within the country were com-
pounded by verbal terrorism of unprecedented violence, prelude to aggression, by the U.S.S.R. and the Warsaw Pact allies.

In the first days of April, a wave of unseasonable heat
prompted people to put away their jackets, to bring out light
dresses. Prague had never been so beautiful. Crowds of tourists
began to flood the city. On the old Charles Bridge, threatening
to collapse after four centuries of good and loyal service, a

78

footbridge of wood was thrown up; a placard indicated in several languages that the bridge was to be rebuilt. A mischievous hand had written under it "And also the Republic." The leaders of the new Czechoslovakia were smiling, exhausted, and eloquent. Hundreds of journalists came from all parts of the world to witness this fabulous marriage of socialism and liberty in a city made for a fairy tale.

The new masters of the party and the renovated state were talkative; only gradually would they learn to be silent — when *Pravda, Tribuna Ludu,* and *Neues Deutschland* began to scold. I was to cover nearly all the important events during these five months for a big Paris weekly. In the last days there were more than a thousand journalists in Prague; many were from as far away as Japan and South America. I *never* saw a journalist from the U.S.S.R. or the "hard" socialist countries; all the newsmen I interviewed found this to be the case. Where, then, were hidden those "special correspondents" from the Soviet press and the satellites who during the weeks and months, in a growing crescendo, emptied on that unhappy country oceans of filth called "reporting" or "eye-witness reports"?

In this period of optimism the tactic to be adopted by the Dubcek team was outlined. One evening at a reception, Miroslav Galuska, minister of culture and information, euphoric, a glass of champagne in his hand, confided in me. He was a young man, forty-six years old, slim, nervous, polyglot, and cultivated. He had been successively ambassador to Great Britain — this was immediately apparent from the cut of his clothes and the choice of his ties — joint editor-in-chief of *Rude Pravo,* and general commissar of the Montreal exposition. He was spoken of as a young man full of promise, which he fulfilled.

I told him of my astonishment at the mildness of the new

team toward men who had openly sworn its downfall. Public opinion held them in abhorrence. Little by little, as elections could be held, they would be effectively eliminated. But keeping them in office under the pretext of ultimately converting them, was it not like entertaining the enemy in one's house?

Galuska denied this: "Conservative forces here are definitively beaten. But we must play the game of democracy fairly with everyone. It is better if Dubcek's political and ethical generosity permits these people to stay, to continue to sit until the elections remove them. We do not wish to take the part of the progressive majority against the opposition, as was always the practice when the conservatives were in power. Perhaps this makes for difficulty today, but in the future I believe that this will be a great source of confidence. We do not wish to destroy the opposition but to convert it to our beliefs by strictly legal means. We do not wish to make use of means that are anything but strictly legal. We got rid of Novotny legally. We will give its true significance, its original meaning, to 'socialist legality.' "

[Spring Cleaning (April)]

Noble ideas. But the race against time between the socialist democracy aborning and the irreducible hostility of the Stalinists, supported by Moscow, had already begun. January was a surprise, a sort of legal coup d'etat, with its reversal of trends within the Presidium and Dubcek's nomination to the post of first secretary. Brezhnev, when called to the rescue by Novotny, had underestimated the scope of events. He realized too late that he had not been witnessing a simple struggle between clans but a revolution. He lost the first game. But the Central Committee and the National Assembly were still comfortably filled with Novotnyans, and so were the workers' militias and the party machine, that huge, octopus-like bureaucracy. Moscow would do everything in its power to keep Dubcek and his friends from getting control of the party. As little by little the conservatives were eliminated by the natural process of elections within the party, Moscow's tone grew more heated. Regional elections swept the Novotnyans out of the Central Committee. But according to the letter of party law, the newly elected members had to wait until the Extraordinary Congress of the party in September to take their places. To Moscow, this meant — in spite of press campaigns, prolonged maneuvers on Czechoslovakian soil, threats of economic sanction — the end of all its hopes of correcting the situation from within. To Brezhnev, it meant that the September congress must never meet. It would meet, but secretly, in a factory and in a Prague occupied by five hundred thousand soldiers brought in from Moscow, Warsaw, Budapest, Sofia, and East Berlin, brought to reestablish "the shining way of socialism," according to the terms of the first communiqué of the occupation forces.

The anticipated regional elections and the convocation thereafter of the Extraordinary Party Congress were the great issues which concerned the new leaders during those first April days. They had the wind behind them and knew themselves carried forward by an unprecedented wave of popular enthusiasm. For a long time the statesmen of communist Czechoslovakia, not knowing popularity, had contented themselves with the dreary ersatz of command demonstrations. To rediscover popularity was like finding the fountain of youth. But this popularity was not without some little impatience on the part of the public, and the press. The country was unrecognizable, wildly gay. In Bratislava, Mnacko told me: "We are still drunk on the liberty which we are advocating, and we don't yet know the limits of our responsibilities. I love this crazy period."

The Stalinists cleaned house and cried their guilt at all levels. Two hundred newspaper censors apologized publicly to the journalists and asked to be relieved of their function. Security agents went on television to express their repentance: they had acted badly; they would not do it again. Former torturers, members of the political police, committed suicide. The weekly *Mlady Svet* revealed that a great number of these Stalinists had recourse to plastic surgery; new faces would make them unrecognizable. Others were hiding in villages under assumed names. Though no one bothered them, the Stalinists felt the accusation of reproachful looks, which became unbearable to them, sharper than the instruments which they formerly used on their victims. Slogans bloomed on walls, but they did not speak of vengeance and demanded no price in blood. They only asked that those responsible for the mistakes of the past go, that they leave. The *Rude Pravo* itself, the most timid of the "liberated" papers, demanded a purge: "The option to retire quietly someplace should be offered to certain officials. Their retirement is one of the guarantees that the development of socialist democracy will be lasting and that there will be no retreat to the past to fear."

Dubcek and his friends had every reason to rejoice. Old General Svoboda, "hero of the Soviet Union," had been elected president of Czechoslovakia almost unanimously. He had also been elected by secret ballot, which was used for the first time by the National Assembly. The public viewed him with less unanimity than did the deputies. Many citizens still resented his passivity at the time of the 1948 crisis, when the army could have stopped the workers' militias. Everybody was worried about his age; he had been sick recently, and there was fear that his faculties might be impaired. But this was only a detail in this great spring housecleaning. The government was to be remodeled and the Central Committee of the C.P. was going to make every effort to institute new liberties. On every side these liberties were "anticipated." The press was free before its freedom was guaranteed. Political clubs were organized but barely tolerated. The members of Sokol (the nationalist Czech youth movement) took their old uniforms out of mothballs; country priests organized their first processions. Everyone took advantage of a climate rather than any legislation. During these five months the climate was that of a continually alternating hot and cold shower. No one knew exactly what was forbidden, what was tolerated, what was authorized. Nevertheless, for the first time, fear disappeared from the atmosphere of a communist regime (except for the fear of a Russian invasion, which lurked in everybody's subconscious from the very beginning), in spite of the legislation which remained Novotnyan and of government personnel which really was not replaced except in the highest echelons. Throughout this period I saw bitter, disappointed people reproaching Dubcek for his slowness, his indecision, but no one feared for his own security from the government at least.[1]

[The Party and Its Policy]

At the Central Committee's session on April 1, which inaugurated the question which would dominate the five months preceding Soviet aggression and would finally furnish its pretext, it was asked: was the monopoly of power by the Communist party compatible with democracy? In communist jargon this monopoly was called "the guiding role of the party."

After the election of the president of the Republic, the formation of the Cernik government, and the meeting of the first plenum of the Central Committee of the C.P. of the new era, Dubcek's team was at a crossroads. Did it want "revolution" — a change of regime — or would it make do with a simple tactical maneuver destined to overcome those pressing difficulties, economic and political, which had precipitated Novotny's downfall?

If the Czechs and the Slovaks had been alone, their response would not have been in any doubt. Josef Smrkovsky, whom I met the day of his election (by secret ballot) as president of the National Assembly, told me of his joy at *not* having been elected unanimously.[2] "The end of the rule of unanimity is the beginning of democracy," he said. He willingly admitted that for the moment there were no legal guarantees of democracy, and that such would require a good deal of time. One could not rebuild in a few months a complex of laws, rules, customs, and structures which it had taken twenty years to construct. The spirit of January must remain, through the press and dialogue with the citizens, the stimulant for forward movement. The party was preparing a program of action which would be "something which has never before been seen in the socialist world." The party and the government would each have its own limited sphere of action. The party's monopoly of power was to cease. The supreme bodies of the state were to be divided into legislative, executive, and judiciary functions, all under the vigilant control of parliament and the critical eye of the press.

As to what would constitute "guiding role of the party," Smrkovsky and most of the other leaders of the new direction remained vague. Later they were to make this guiding role all important, this decision was to be unanimous, as if they were obeying an imperious directive. It would prove difficult to decide whether the progressivism of Dubcek and his friends stopped at the taboo of the "monopoly" of power of the C.P. or whether they feared to approach the question while pressures were being exerted by conservative forces inside the party and by sister parties from Moscow to East Berlin. It is reasonable to assume that the second hypothesis is the correct one.

The first antiliberal offensive was not long in coming. Inside the factories, the Novotnyans, not daring to show themselves, passed out anonymous leaflets. By chance, on one of my trips, I saw several samples of their literature, mostly mimeographed sheets. At the Skoda factories in Pilsen, one of these warned the workers: "Dubcek and his crew will turn the factories over to the capitalists. A time of unemployment will return. Awake, Comrade, before it is too late." In Kosice, in the iron works, a tract accused Dubcek of having sold out Slovak interests to the Czechs. Elsewhere the Jews were denounced: "the Zionist hyenas" Goldstuecker, Ota Sik, and Kriegel. Cestmir Cisar, a pure Moravian Aryan who also passed, I never knew why, for an "anti-Semite" in orthodox Jewish circles in Prague, was himself judaized by certain of these leaflets.

Intimidating maneuvers were initiated outside Czechoslovakia. On March 23, Dubcek left for Dresden to reassure the orthodox of the block. All the arguments, all the tricks of blackmail and intimidation (including "military maneuvers"), which were to culminate in tragedy in the month of August were started in Dresden. Czechoslovakia, formerly the most docile of the satellites, was an irreplaceable part of the heart of the communist system. Strategically, the Bohemian plain is the pivot of the defense system of the Warsaw Pact. Economically, Czechoslovakia plays an essential role in Comecon, the common market of the East. It had also contributed the largest part of the communist aid to the Arabs, Cuba, and Vietnam. Finally, the defection of Prague threatened to precipitate the downfall of the most hated regime in Europe, to challenge the very existence of the German Democratic Republic.

Dubcek was ready to guarantee the active participation of his country in the Warsaw Pact, less for tactical reasons than because all Czechoslovakians, including the anticommunists who had been traumatized by Munich, deeply believed that the security of their country depended on its alliance with Moscow. However, Dubcek intended to dissociate the military aspect from both internal evolution and economic problems.

85

Not to shake off the yoke of Comecon was to make impossible the deep structural reforms demanded by the ruined economy and by the "Czechoslovakian way of socialist democracy." At the same time, to put a brake on political liberalization was to make impossible economic reforms which demanded new methods in a new psychological and social climate. His argument was both tight and tenuous, but still there was a discussion. Did Dubcek believe he was understood? He was optimistic when he returned from Dresden. He explained to the Presidium and to the Central Committee that even if one path was blocked — foreign policy — the two others were open.

At the beginning of April, the military authorities and the ministry of foreign affairs exhibited an "orthodox" zeal which was quite ridiculous. Barbed-wire fences along the Bavarian and Austrian borders, which had been removed the previous month, were put back into place "with interest." On television screens, the amused though concerned people of Prague watched frontier patrols accompanied by police dogs mount vigilant guard. For good measure, Dubcek sent a message of congratulation to the valiant soldiers who were stemming the tide of threatening troops from NATO. A tragicomedy.

At the Cernin palace, headquarters of the department of foreign affairs, the very men who had expressed to me such reasonable ideas on the subjects of Israel ("We should renew our ties as soon as possible with the Jewish state. The hasty rupture was a tragic error") and West Germany now held opposite views, more formally expressed than those of Moscow or Warsaw but the same. By throwing the country's foreign policy to the wolves, could they save the rest?

[The Parade (May)]

The first of May in Prague was an apotheosis. No one cared about the bitter press campaigns which appeared in the press of sister countries. An immense crowd swept over the Na Prikope, the great boulevard of Prague where Svoboda, Dubcek, Kriegel, and other stars of the new direction were to receive acclamations from 8 A.M. to late in the afternoon. The anarchistic parade, well-behaved and totally spontaneous, included not only the workers' militias and Pioneers but resistance fighters, deportees, former members of international brigades, sokols, and old legionnaires. Dubcek, radiant, smiled broadly, raised his arms, kissed children, signed autographs. The crowd applauded everybody. There were the very orthodox placards of party members who had not yet renovated their workers' slogans and those of unexpected demonstrators who were members of the new Club of Committed Nonparty Members.[3] These last carried slogans which were particularly new to Prague, even in those first months of democratization: "Are six million citizens without a party worth less than a million communists?" "No democracy without opposition"; "Who fears opposition fears for his position." And also: "Our hands are clean," "Free elections," "No more political police."

Dubcek's speech was both vague and generous, like all his statements during this period. He spoke of "the renewal of life, the vigorous development of socialist democracy." He asked all to unite for the realization of the party program adopted at the end of the Central Committee's plenary session on April 5, in order that each citizen "shall contribute in some modest measure to making socialism more attractive to the world."

[The Program]

This program was passed in Prague almost unnoticed by the masses; no one had taken the trouble to read the heavy forty-thousand-word document, which was quite ambiguous and yet presented the most liberal program ever adopted by a Communist party.

Compared to policy before January, the program was, no doubt, revolutionary. After the thaw, however, the laborious text fell a little flat: a significant part of the program had already been put into practice de facto if not de jure — the abolition of censorship, the right to a passport, the freedom of assembly and of speech, and so on. Many points were of a worrisome (or reassuring) obscurity. Others were more or less declarations of intention.

The intellectuals felt that this laborious text was probably the maximum that could be won from the present Central Committee with its substantial minority of conservatives but that it was "the minimum which should be expected from the next Central Committee." [4]

It is curious to observe that, though a barrage of "ideological" criticisms would burst forth from Moscow and the other "hard" capitals, this text was never considered by the dogmatists as a subversive "program of action." The letter of the law is not to be questioned in the U.S.S.R., an attitude dating from Stalin's era. The spirit which reigned in Prague and not the "tables of the law" worried the dogmatists.

Such as it was, with its omissions and willful ambiguities, the program was a way station to democratization and a preliminary to the solution to the "national problem." It presented several notable points:

- A federal system will progressively replace the centralized structure governing Bohemia-Moravia and Slovakia.

- The parliaments of these federated states will become true legislative assemblies.
- On the national level, the state and the party will limit their spheres by lessening their controls. The central parliament must realign itself through its legislative role. The electoral laws in force shall be revised and the slates presented to the voters shall permit a real choice, shall present more candidates than there are offices.
- The rights of businesses in economic matters shall be enlarged. They shall themselves decide on their programs and shall be assured autonomy in their financial management.
- At the head of enterprises shall be placed, at the regional level, economic councils where shall be seated an equal number of representatives of unions, banks, and consumers. These councils will appoint and remove managers, thus enlarging the concept of self-management, which also extends to universities.
- Suppression of censorship in the press, radio, and TV, full liberty of artistic and cultural creativity, freedom of assembly. . . . The program of action foresees police reform and the end of the endless *nomenklatura*, that species of permanent certificate of good conduct which up to now has prevented "No" parties from occupying responsible posts. This prohibition in any case has not been in effect for years.

The euphoria of liberation and the feverish work to stabilize the experiment were abruptly disturbed on May 4; the people of Prague learned of the impromptu and secret visit which Dubcek and Cernik had just paid to Moscow. The country entered its first period of serious tension which would culminate, on June 15, with the famous letter from Warsaw and Prague's reply several days later.

[The Quarrel]

The quarrel between Soviet dogmatism and Czechoslovakian reform is contained in its entirety in these two important documents, the letter and its reply.[5] The subsequent polemics — the laborious communiqués of Cierna, Bratislava, and finally Moscow, after the invasion — were only exhaustive variations on the same theme. All communiqués would mention the atmosphere of "frankness and comradeship," which in neo-Stalinist jargon means the deepest disharmony. Dubcek lost his gamble to keep two paths open by accepting a roadblock on the third. The Soviets wanted and would increasingly demand — to the point of rupture and aggression — total and unconditional alignment in all areas.

In four months — apparently fertile, filled with the sound of boots, packed with innumerable conferences and trips — nothing happened. This account can no longer be political analysis; it must become purely chronological. The Russians demanded, threatened; the Czechs wrangled, reasoned, tried to wear them out, without letting go of their point of view. Dubcek in the Kremlin, in Cierna, at Bratislava, was Daniel in the lions' den, Jan Hus at the stake in Constance, Galileo before his inquisitors. The atmosphere grew heavier every day. Too many people remembered Munich not to feel a sensation of oppressive fatalism. The journalist's task became more and more difficult: "sources" of information progressively dried up. Friends "in high places" fled or were obstinately silent. One of them, a member of the secretariat of the Central Committee, both overwhelmed and irritated, said to me one day: "What do you want me to say? I know nothing. And probably Dubcek doesn't know any more; we're waiting."

Nerves cracked. I saw a woman burst into tears in a government office where journalists were getting information. A Scandinavian colleague thoughtlessly patted her shoulder, saying: "I know. I was at Budapest. 'They' are capable of anything." The poor woman burst into tears again and the other stenographers caught her weeping; we stood in an office full of hysteria. Just a small scene in that long period of waiting. Rare, in fact. Both men and women in Czechoslovakia gritted their teeth: "Business as usual."

[Delusion]

By the end of May, some of the beautiful resolves of the thaw had disappeared. Meeting on May 21 and 22, the Presidium and the secretariat of the Central Committee put an end to hopes of creating a movement of political opposition in Czechoslovakia; the resurrection of the Social Democratic party was forbidden: "Such a demand is motivated by the desire to disrupt the unity which exists in the heart of the working class and thus to return to the situation existing before February 1948," said the communiqué dryly, and spoke, on the other hand, of the reactivation of the phantom National Front, which grouped around the C.P. the two embryo parties authorized since the Prague coup, the Populist (Christian) party, and the National Socialist party. The National Front was to be enlarged by including "social groups" — representing farmers, national minorities, youth, and so on — and was to be steered, as was proper, by the C.P., "guiding force," keeper of the Marxist-Leninist concept of the structure of socialism. The ministry of the interior, going even further the next day, forbade any attempt to organize a new political party.

This burst of orthodoxy came just in time to reassure Aleksei Kosygin, who was taking the waters at Karlovy Vary. But officially, the elderly Josef Pavel, minister of the interior, whose tormented clown's face reminded one a little of Kosygin, wanted to reassure the political clubs, which had never had any legal existence. They were always welcome, were tolerated, and their authorization would take place after the Extraordinary Congress in September, that "promised land." For many of the people of Prague, the expression "after the congress" took on something of the meaning of "after the flood."

May was the month of delusions and of the first bitterness. The precautions taken by government circles not to be compromised in the eyes of Moscow by showing too much intimacy and cordiality to noncommunists or Western visitors bordered on the ridiculous. Appointments were canceled without reason, but X or Y would subsequently send someone to excuse him, pretending a conflict. Important personalities from the Western political or economic worlds were received almost clandestinely. What was said one day was disavowed the next.

Censorship, which had really and truly disappeared, was succeeded by moral suppression enacted "with tears in eyes and hand on heart." As if not speaking a disagreeable truth to the sachems of the Kremlin was going to make these gentlemen more understanding. Have wolves ever been appeased by smiles?

May was the month of small intellectual dishonesties on the part of these new-style communists toward whom the whole nation had such a fraternal feeling. There began increasing insistence that in the prisons and camps the communist detainees were being molested by their companions in misfortune. The cases were extremely rare and, after all, the acts quite understandable.

The attempts by communist historians to reestablish the

truth about the events of the past twenty years, from the revolt of Prague and "victorious February," stopped. A thick veil of silence fell over the work of party economists who had begun to establish an honest diagnosis of the ills which the country was suffering after twenty years of colonization by the U.S.S.R. and its partners in the Comecon. To the journalists and diplomats posted in Prague who studied the press, it became evident that sentiment was replacing facts.

When the May session of the Central Committee opened on the 29th, democratization was in fact dying. What remained of it came from the achievements and momentum of the first months. No doubt the progressive elements were comforted to learn of the removal from the Central Committee of Novotny and six of his friends. A resolution was even adopted mentioning the right to strike.[6] But the insistent explanations that "socialist liberty" was not "bourgeois liberty," that "workers' democracy" was not "bourgeois democracy," were not motivated by the economic situation — the pretext used by the communists to monopolize "democracy" and "liberty" to their exclusive profit (as they monopolized the totality of power for two decades).

Paradoxically Cernik's government and Dubcek's party were simultaneously popular, upheld by the people unanimously, and yet very weak. Both lacked authority and in the long run were more loved than respected.

The conservatives held out, encouraged openly by Moscow and the satellites. The Soviet military units which had to participate in "maneuvers," according to the Warsaw Pact, arrived in the country on May 30. The exercises were not to begin until June 21; they would end on June 30. The economy was going from bad to worse; political preoccupations had prevented the initiation of even the most urgent reforms.

A secret rivalry existed between Oldrich Cernik, head of the government, and the ebullient economist Ota Sik, hailed as a miracle man but confined to an academic and honorific role. Moscow, while forbidding Prague to seek credit in the West, was in no hurry to negotiate the loan of $100 million in convertible currency promised since Dubcek's and Cernik's surprise trip on May 4. And the sum itself was ridiculous; the "raise" called for was estimated at $500 million.

In spite of words of appeasement from the most popular leaders of the new direction — Smrkovsky among others on the eve of an "explanatory" mission to the U.S.S.R. gave assurances that "we do not deviate from our chosen way, we shall not fall back one step, we shall not stop midway" — the atmosphere was one of pessimism and discouragement.

[The Spirit of Munich (June)]

The spirit of Munich, which alternated with the "spirit of Jan Hus," began to exert its depressing influence. A number of my friends were thinking of emigrating. Although freedom of movement was not really permitted, it was still easy enough to get a passport. Tomorrow might be too late.

For many intellectuals, this was not the time to become discouraged but the time to try to enlarge the openings, to profit as much as possible from the liberties permitted, and slowly, imperceptibly, "to bend the bars of the cage," by tricks and ruses à la Schweik. Dubcek would eventually try this tactic in his meeting with the Russians and their friends; but it was a great deal easier to trick Dubcek than Brezhnev.

The writer Jan Prochazka admirably expressed the feelings of all when he wrote (on June 25 in the monthly review *My 68*, "Us, in 68"):

If I were to sum up our actual situation, I would say that we have not ceased to march toward the abyss, but that happily we are marching a little more slowly. The improvement in our situation consists in the fact that we now are ruled not by a small royal court but by a larger royal court. Thanks to more clever methods, it even seems sometimes that we are ruling ourselves. Very little has changed, but everything has become more interesting.

It was in this context that the two-thousand-word bomb burst. Ludvik Vaculik once more lighted the fuse with a flamboyant text, signed by a hundred people from all walks of life, in which he recommended an active struggle against the conservatives in order to thrust democratization forward.[7]

Anton Liehm, who, along with Vaculik and several others, was an editor of *Literarni Listy*[8] in which this manifesto appeared on June 27, explained it further to me:

"We wanted to do something just before the summer holidays. We were afraid that during the holidays public opinion would relax its vigilance, which not only served as a goad but also was the only 'guarantee' of the continuation of the process. We wanted to take precautions. All those who helped Vaculik with the final edition of the text were, as was he, Communists of long standing, conscious of a liberal intelligentsia's dangerous tendency to become too avant-garde and thus to cut itself off from the working-class population. We were journalists and writers; it is possible we did not use the best form. We spoke what was in our hearts, ingenuously and without afterthought."

The outcry which this text provoked clearly demonstrated that the enemies, at home and abroad, of the Czechoslovakian experiment did have some afterthoughts.

I attended an official reception the day after the publication of "Two Thousand Words." I had occasion to converse with three active ministers, not the least important ones. In substance, they told me that none of them would have hesitated

95

to sign this text, "possibly correcting a word here and there." Nevertheless, "Two Thousand Words" prompted hostile reactions in both the party and the National Assembly, where one conservative deputy challenged the government to explain this "counterrevolutionary call to arms" and proposed martial law. Once more, the conservatives raised protest against freedom of the press, while *Literarni Listy* and the other papers which published the text were receiving tens of thousands of letters of approval.

In government circles no one attached great importance to the manifesto. Cernik entertained Vaculik and his friends at a very relaxed cocktail party in his home. Dubcek, appearing there briefly, expressed his basic accord with this text, which did honor to the courage of communist intellectuals. With the exception of the unshakable hard core, most of those who had at first condemned "Two Thousand Words" later adopted it and in fact used quotations from it to stud their speeches.

On the international level "Two Thousand Words" was to become the keystone of the evidence for the witch trial being prepared by the Moscow censors. In the first two weeks of July, the warnings to Czechoslovakia multiplied. On July 4, Brezhnev and Kadar reminded Moscow of "the vigorous reply made to the forces of counterrevolution (in Budapest) in 1956 for the benefit of the working class and the majority of the people." Not a day passed that harassed Czechoslovakian delegations in the capitals of the Soviet bloc did not receive "explanatory" visits, while Prague was crushed under an avalanche of messages, letters, motions, all touchingly spontaneous, in which the sister parties warned the new direction against the dangers of counterrevolution. This escalation of the verbal offensive was obviously intended to influence the militants of the nine extraordinary regional conferences meeting over the weekend of the first week in July to nominate candidates for the Extraordinary Congress in September.

The response to this democratic electoral campaign was not long in coming. *Pravda* fired its red bullets while meetings in factories in the U.S.S.R. affirmed the determination of the Soviet working class to defend socialism — in Czechoslovakia.

Soviet troops, whose maneuvers had ended on June 20, had not yet left the country. They left; then they came back: those quartered in East Germany discovered that they needed to return to the mother country and crossed eight hundred kilometers of Czech territory on the way with calculated delay.

Every day the Czechs grew more worried while awaiting the news. The troops would leave; they would not leave. General Dzur, the minister of national defense, contradicted himself in embarrassed explanations. In a news conference in Sweden, where he was on an official trip, Kosygin three times made a significant slip of the tongue, confusing Czechoslovakia and Hungary. And he was known as the moderate element in Moscow.

[The Czechoslovakian Case]

Sunday, July 14, the radio announced that the heads of five orthodox communist countries meeting at Warsaw were taking up the "Czechoslovakian case."

Forty-eight hours afterward, the teletypes released the terms of the famous "letter from the five," whose arguments would serve less than two months later as justification for aggression.[9] The judgment of Czechoslovakia in absentia rested on similar slogans which were repeated for months with monomaniacal insistence:

The evolution of developments in Czechoslovakia constitutes a danger for all the socialist countries; it is not an exclusively national problem but a common problem, affecting all the members of the Warsaw Pact.

Reactionary forces wish to do away with the guiding role of the party and have already taken possession of the press, radio, and television.

In Prague, once the first reaction was over, optimism returned. An Olympian calm prevailed in governmental circles which pretended to accept an exchange between the deaf in the hope that it would lead to an effective dialogue. Explain, explain again, a thousand times, if necessary. Over and over people repeated Thomas Masaryk's motto: *"Pravda vitezi"* (Truth will conquer). The answer of the Central Committee of the Czech Communist party was presented in a lengthy text, too lengthy, circumstantial, studied, irrefutably logical, entirely dignified.[10] It pretended that the adversary was acting in good faith.

Many were annoyed by this verbose document, believing that a brief polite reply was all that the sister parties' letter deserved.

Dusan Havlicek, the head of the press section of the Central Committee, an elegant man in his forties, prototype of the new-wave communist intellectuals, participated in the final draft of the text and tried to justify the length of the response to me: "You mustn't let the 'soft' parts of our reply keep you from seeing its 'hard' parts, the resolute and clear-cut affirmation of the principles of socialist democracy. Nothing essential in our program has been abandoned."

This pathetic justification continued to be offered until the very end, during all those tragic weeks when concession by concession, up to the point of aggression, the "essential" too would be abandoned. This letter had evolved from a compromise. The first draft was much "harder" and infuriated the centrists, who persuaded Dubcek to invite officially to Prague the ambassador from the U.S.S.R.; the latter spent a night with the Politburo moderating certain paragraphs.

Outside governmental circles, response was more emotional. *Literarni Listy* answered the ultimatum from Warsaw with a few harsh words: "A war of nerves cannot be waged against proud, determined, resolute men and peoples. With them, one can live only in friendship or in hatred. The Czechs and the Slovaks want to live in friendship with the Soviet Union. But they think little of those sacred cows of Marxism-Leninism which the Kremlin keeps in its ideological stables."

Oddly, the friends of Czechoslovakia seemed more worried than the interested parties themselves. The courage and the coolness of the Czechs, which were to stupefy the world after the aggression, were already revealing themselves.

"But then," sighed Jan Stern, the editorial writer of *Prace*, the union daily, "we are very much accustomed to crises. The situation is serious today, but it was serious in December, in January. It's been serious since the beginning of this new direction. We've had to get used to it. It's like the noise of trains for people who have the bad luck to live near a railroad station."

Notes for Chapter 3

1. In contrast, several liquidations of troublesome "witnesses" demonstrated the criminal activities of a group of hardcore Stalinists in the ranks of security. At the request of the government, the most absolute secrecy was maintained in these affairs.
2. Sixty-eight deputies voted against him.
3. The members pledged to the Club of Committed Nonparty Members (KAN in the Czech abbreviation) acclaimed President Svoboda but ostensibly ignored Dubcek.
4. The ways and means by which the system became democratic, by the play of free elections, are reflected in the party documents step by step. The statute proposals of the party made public at the beginning of August 1968, three weeks before the invasion, appeared distinctly more liberal than the content of the "program of action" published two months previously.
5. They are reprinted in the appendix to this chapter.
6. This congress would see the triumph of the Dubcek brain trusts, made up of brilliant young intellectuals of the party such as Cestmir Cisar, the jurist Zdenek Mlynar, and Ota Sik. Their resolutions burgeoned with new ideas on direct democracy, autarchy, ideology. Since the first years of Bolshevism, after the October revolution, no communist country had experienced such effervescence, such creative spirit. But once more, it applied only "inside the party." As in the republic of Athens, the overwhelming majority of noncommunist citizens of the Republic are out of the game. Before ending its session, the Central Committee planned a calendar which went well beyond the party congress in September. On October 28, the fiftieth anniversary of the founding of the Republic, the federation would be proclaimed. Before the end of the year mechanisms of autarchy would be installed and a new electoral law ratified. General elections were to be held in the spring of 1969, to replenish parliament and the regional councils. In less than a year, Dubcek claimed in his closing speech, "our country will have a new face."
7. This text is reproduced in the appendix to this chapter.
8. The name of *Literarni Noviny* after the thaw.
9. See the appendix to this chapter.
10. See the appendix to this chapter.

Appendix

Two Thousand Words . . . June 27, 1968 — Letter from the Five . . . July 19, 1968 — Prague's Reply . . . July 20, 1968

[Two Thousand Words . . . June 27, 1968]

The weekly Literarni Listy *published on June 27, 1968, under the title "Two Thousand Words," the following text signed by a hundred people from all walks of Czechoslovakian life. Its originator was, once more, the writer Ludvik Vaculik.*

This manifesto spoke out against the slowness of democratization.

The text by Vaculik and his friends at first aroused reservations among the Prague leaders, but after a period of reflection the party progressives adopted it and even made it their credo. Popular response was immediately enthusiastic.

For the Soviets and the orthodox communists, on the other hand, "Two Thousand Words" became the keystone of the case against the counterrevolutionaries. This text played a capital role in the unfolding of the Czech crisis.

The life of your nation, first threatened by the war, has subsequently known a dark period whose events have endangered its spiritual health and even its character.

It was with a sense of hope that the majority of the nation accepted the program of socialism. But the controls of command did not fall into good hands. The leaders' lack of experience as statesmen, practical knowledge, and philosophic culture would not have been important if they had at least been capable of listening to the opinions of others and if they had allowed themselves to be replaced, little by little, by persons more suitable.

The Communist party, which, after the war, enjoyed the confidence of the people, has gradually bartered that confidence for positions — to the point where it has all the positions and nothing else. We must say this, and those among us who are Communists know it. The party's self-deception about its achievements is as great as its deception of the people.

The policy of the leaders incorrectly transformed the party, which was a political party and an ideological group, into a power organization which has attracted avid egoists, clever cowards, and people with bad consciences. The rule of these has affected the party's nature and conduct.

Its internal organization does not permit honest men to acquire influence without enduring scandalous incidents or to modify the party to keep it in step with the modern world. Many Communists have fought this deterioration, but they have not succeeded in preventing what has happened.

The internal situation of the Communist party, serving as model, has provoked a similar situation in the state. The fact that the party is bound to the state has caused it to lose the advantages of distance from executive power. There are critiques neither of the activities of the state nor of economic organizations. Parliament has forgotten parliamentary procedure; the government has forgotten how to govern, and the leaders how to lead. The elections no longer have any meaning and laws have lost their validity.

We cannot depend on our representatives in any organization. If we did have confidence in them, we could ask nothing of them anyway, for they could do nothing. Worse still, we no longer have confidence in one another. Personal and collective honor has fallen.

Honesty leads nowhere and competence is no use. That is why most of the people are no longer interested in public affairs: they are interested only in themselves and in money. And the consequence of these deplorable conditions is that no one now can have confidence in money.

Relations between people are spoiled; there is no more joy in work. To sum up, the moment has arrived when the spiritual health and the character of the nation are threatened.

We are all — and above all those among us who are Communists — responsible for the actual state of things. The principal responsibility, however, belongs to those who were integral parts or instruments of that uncontrolled power. It was the power of one group's opinion instituted, from Prague to the least districts and communes, with the help of the party machine.

The machine decided what should or should not be done. It directed the cooperatives instead of the members of the cooperatives; it directed the factories and the national organizations instead of the workers and the citizens. No organization, not even a communist organization, really belonged to its members.

The principal fault and the greatest deceit of these leaders was that they justified their arbitrary acts by proclaiming that it was the will of the workers.

If we were to believe in this deceit, we would today have to blame the workers for the decline of our economy, for the crimes against innocent persons, for the imposition of censorship which interferes with everything written. It would be the workers who were responsible for the erroneous investments, the commercial losses, or the housing crisis.

Naturally, no sensible person believes in this culpability of the workers. Everyone knows that the working class, in practice, decides nothing; the worker functionaries are selected by someone else.

Many workers believe that they command, but the command is given in their name by a group of party and state machine functionaries especially trained for this job. In fact, these have replaced the ousted class and become the new authority.

It must be recognized that certain of these party functionaries had long realized that history was taking an unpleasant turn. One recognizes them today by the way they expose wrongs, rectify errors, and give the right of decision to members and to citizens in order to limit the power and effects of the machine's bureaucracy. They are united with us against the dated ideas underlying the system. But many other functionaries are opposed to change, and they still have weight. They still wield the instruments of power, particularly in the districts and communes where they can use these instruments in secret, without fear of hindrance.

Since the beginning of this year, we have been experiencing the rebirth of a process of democratization. This process began in the Communist party. We must say it, and those among us who are outside the party, and who up to recently looked for nothing good from us, know it too. We must add that this process could not have begun elsewhere. Only the Communists have been able to live a somewhat political life during the last twenty years.

Only Communist criticism was in a position to make itself known. Only the opposition within the Communist party had the privilege of being in contact with the enemy. The initiative and the efforts of the Communist Democrats were only the repayment of the debt contracted by the whole party against people outside the party which kept the latter in a position of inequality. That is why there is no gratitude due the Communist party, although it should be recognized that the party is honestly trying to use this last chance to save its honor and that of the nation.

The process of rebirth brings nothing very new. It is made up of ideas and suggestions many of which are older than the errors of our socialism, and others of which surface from below. They should have been expressed long ago, but they were stifled.

We do not nurse the illusion that these ideas triumph now by the force of truth. Their victory results rather from the weakness of the former leadership, worn out primarily by twenty years of unhindered power. Obviously all the undesirable elements hidden in the foundations and in the ideology of the system must have ripened before now manifesting themselves.

However, the significance of criticisms coming from circles of writers and students must not be underestimated. The social changes have their source in the economy. Words can have meaning only when they are pronounced in an environment suitably readied. "The suitably prepared conditions in our country" we must unfortunately understand to cover our general poverty and the total disintegration of the old system of government in which politicians of a certain type calmly compromise themselves at our expense. This truth is not triumphant: it is only the truth which remains when the rest goes down the drain. It is nothing to celebrate as a national victory. There is now only new hope.

We speak to you in this moment of hope, even though it is threatened. It has taken a few months to believe that we could speak, and certain among us still do not believe it. However, we have spoken and so many things have been revealed that we must express our intention of making this regime more humane. If not, the revenge of the old forces would be cruel! We speak to all those who have been waiting up to now. What actually happens next will be decisive for many years to come.

Now it is summer and the time for vacations, the time when traditionally one wants to let everything go. But we can be certain that our adversaries are not going to take any respite, that they are going to mobilize the people in their pay, and that actually already they are trying to prepare for a quiet Christmas vacation.

Let us be vigilant. Let us try to understand what is going to happen and respond to it. Let us renounce the impossible demand that one among us who is highly placed will always be able to give the exact interpretation of things and to draw the conclusion from it. Each of us must draw his own conclusions on his own responsibility. It is possible to come to a mutual agreement on the basis of conclusions only by discussion, which implies freedom of expression, which is in fact our only democratic accomplishment during this year.

In the coming days, we will have to prove our own initiative and our own determination. In the first place, we will oppose the opinion, if it manifests itself, that a democratic rebirth can come without the communists, or even against them; this would be not only unjust but also unreasonable.

The communists have well-established organizations; these organizations are necessary to sustain the tendencies of progress. They have experienced functionaries, and they also have in hand the controls of command. They have prepared a program of action which has been proposed to the public. It is a program aiming at reparation of the greatest injustices and they are the only ones in possession of such a concrete program. We should acclaim the establishment of a local program of action in each district and in each commune.

And now, suddenly, very ordinary and long-awaited measures are being taken. The Czechoslovakian Communist party is preparing for the congress which will elect a new Central Committee. We must demand that it be better than the Central Committee which is going out of office. If the Communist party actually declares that in the future it will found its supremacy not on force but on the trust of the citizens, let us believe it, as long as we can have faith in the persons which it has delegated to the districts and the regional conferences.

The people have feared for some time that the process of democratization would be stopped. This impression comes in part from the exhaustion caused by ferment of events and in part from the fact that the time of sensational revelations, dismissals of persons from high places, and speeches poisoned by an unprecedented verbal brutality has ended.

However, the explanation is simple: the struggle of the forces has become less visible. The battle is now given over to the substance and the application of laws, to the extent of the practical measures to be taken. More, we must allow the newcomers time — ministers, prosecutors, presidents, secretaries — the time to which they have a right to show that they can do something good or else that they are not attending to business. We cannot, for the moment, demand more of the central political bodies.

Practically, future democracy depends on what becomes of business and of what happens to the economy. In all our discussions, the economists have been important. It is necessary to seek out good managers and to assure them of good positions. It is true that we receive salaries poor in comparison with the salaries paid in more developed countries. We could demand more money, and it would be possible to print more bills, but their value would diminish. It is preferable to ask directors and presidents what they would like to manufacture, and at what price; to whom they would like to sell and at what price; what will be the profit, what part of this profit will be invested in modernization of production, and what part it will be possible to distribute.

The headlines of newspapers show that in the press there is a very severe battle going on the subject of democracy and leadership. Insofar as they are producers, the workers can intervene by the choice of persons whom they elect in the leadership of business and in the councils of business. Insofar as they are employees, they will act best for themselves if they choose as representatives capable and honest elements in the union organizations without consideration of political affiliation.

While it is understood that it is impossible to demand more at this moment from the central bodies, it is necessary to ask much more at the district level, especially from the communists.

We demand the removal of those who have abused their power, who have wasted the collective patrimony, and who have behaved in a dishonest or brutal manner; it is indispensable to find ways of making them leave. For example: public criticisms, adoption of resolutions, organization of demonstrations, forced retirements, strikes, collections for gifts to those who are leaving.

At all times, we must reject illegal, brutal, and incorrect methods, because they will serve to reflect on Alexander Dubcek. We must speak out against the sending of insulting letters so that if our adversaries receive any, they will be well aware that they have sent them to themselves.

Let us bring the National Front back to life. Let us demand public meetings and national committees. Let us establish special committees and commissions of citizens to take up questions which are unanswered by functionaries. It is simple: it is enough that several people meet, elect a president, write an official report, publish their conclusions calling for a solution, and refuse to allow themselves to be intimidated. Let us transform the regional and local press which blows the trumpet sounding official views and makes of it a forum of all political elements. Let us demand the formation of editorial committees composed of representatives of the National Front or even create new newspapers.

Let us establish committees for defense of the freedom of expression. Let us organize our own rules of order for our meetings. If we have wind of strange news, let us verify it. Let us send delegations to people who are involved, and let their responses be published and if possible posted.

Let us give our support to the security agencies when they pursue criminals and common-law delinquents. We have no intention of provoking anarchy or a general state of insecurity. Let us avoid discord between neighbors; let us renounce political ill will. Let us unmask informers.

Vacation trips to the country have awakened interest in constitutional adjustments between Czechs and Slovaks. We consider that federation is a way of resolving the question of nationalities. Besides that, it is one of the important measures which will permit the institution of democratic conditions. But this measure will not by itself assure a better life to Slovaks and it will not resolve the problem of rule, whether it is in the region of the Czechs or in Slovakia. Party bureaucracy and that of the state will continue to rule more than ever, even in Slovakia, under the pretext that it has been given a greater liberty.

The possibility of witnessing the intervention of foreign forces in our internal evolution has lately been a great source of apprehension. In the face of superior forces, all we can do is hold our own and not take the initiative. We give the assurance to the government that we shall support it, even with arms, so long as it does what it has been mandated to do. And we give to our allies the assurance that we shall respect our treaties of friendship, alliance, and trade. Vehement reproaches and latent suspicions will not be able to do anything but make the position of the government more difficult.

In any case, we shall only have equal relations with other countries if we improve our internal situation and if we push our rebirth to a point making it possible one day to elect statesmen endowed with enough courage, honor, and political wisdom to establish and maintain such relations. Herein lies, let us note in passing, the problem of governments of all the little states in the world. This spring, as after the war, a great opportunity was given us; once more we have the possibility of taking up our common cause, which to all intents and purposes we call socialism, and the possibility of giving it a form corresponding better to the good reputation we used to have and to the relatively good opinion which we used to have of ourselves. This spring has just ended. It will never come back. This winter we shall know all.

On this note we conclude our statement to workers, peasants, functionaries, artists, scholars, technicians — to everybody. This statement has been made at the suggestion of scholars.

[Letter from the Five . . . July 19, 1968]

This is the entire text of the letter addressed to the Czechoslovakian Communist party by the five powers that met at Warsaw on July 14 and 15.

Dear Comrades, In the name of the central committees of the workers and communist parties of Bulgaria, Poland, the Democratic Republic of Germany, Hungary, and the U.S.S.R., we address this letter to you, inspired by sincere friendship based on the principles of Marxism-Leninism and proletarian internationalism, with a view to strengthening the position of our common cause — socialism — as well as the security of the socialist community.

We are profoundly concerned by the development of the situation in your country. It is our deepest conviction that the attacks from the forces of reaction, supported by those of imperialism, against your party and against the foundations of the socialist system in Czechoslovakia threaten to divert your country from the socialist way. Thus it is a danger to the interests of the socialist system as a whole.

This concern was expressed at the meeting at Dresden, during bilateral meetings, and in letters which have recently been addressed by our parties to the Central Committee of the Czechoslovakian Communist party.

Recently we proposed to the Presidium of the Central Committee of the Czechoslovakian Communist party that it hold a new meeting on July 14 to promote an exchange of views and information on the situation in our countries and on the development of events in Czechoslovakia. Unfortunately, the Presidium of the Czechoslovakian Communist party did not take part in the meeting and did not take advantage of the occasion to discuss the situation collectively with its comrades.

We should like you to understand us and to interpret our objective correctly. We have not had and we do not have the intention of intervening in affairs which are of exclusive interest to your party and your state or of violating the principle of independence and equality of socialist countries.

We do not come as representatives of the past wishing to importune you by demanding that you correct errors and deficiencies, including the violation of socialist legality.

We are not interfering in methods of planning and management in the Czechoslovakian economy, in your activities designed to ameliorate the structures of the economy and develop socialist democracy.

We salute the regularization of relations between Czechs

and Slovaks on the basis of principles of fraternal cooperation in the framework of the Socialist Republic of Czechoslovakia.

But at the same time, we cannot accept that foreign forces should lead your country from the way of socialism and expose Czechoslovakia to the danger of being divided from the socialist community. This is not solely your problem. This is the problem of all the communist and workers' parties of all the countries which are joined by bonds of cooperation and friendship. It is the common problem of our countries, which are united by the treaty of Warsaw to assure their independence, peace, and security in Europe and to raise an indestructible barrier against the aggressive and retaliatory maneuvers of imperialism.

The peoples of our countries achieved victory over the fascism of Hitler at the price of enormous sacrifices and obtained liberty, independence, and the possibility of following the way of progress and socialism.

We shall never consent to seeing endangered the historical achievements of socialism, independence, and the liberty of our people; we shall never agree that imperialism, whether peacefully or not, whether from within or from without, should create a rift in the socialist system and change the balance of power in Europe in its favor.

The strength and the firmness of our alliance depends on the internal strength of the socialist system of each one of our countries and the leading role of the party in the social and political life of our peoples and our countries.

Any undermining of the role of the Communist party leads to the liquidation of the socialist system and socialist democracy. Thus the basis of our alliance, even the security of our countries, is threatened.

As you know, our parties welcomed with understanding the resolutions which were adopted at the plenary session of the Central Committee of the Czechoslovakian Communist party of last January. We began with the premise that your party, having the reins of power firmly in hand, would guide the whole process according to the interests of socialism and would not allow reactionary anticommunist forces to use it for their own designs. We were convinced that you would safeguard the Leninist principle of democratic centralism.

We spoke several times of these problems in the course of our meetings and you assured us that you saw clearly the danger which you were resolved to oppose. Unfortunately, it did not happen thus. The forces of reaction, making use of the weakening of the leadership of the party and using demagogically the principle of "democratization," launched an attack against the Czechoslovakian Communist party and against its legitimate functionaries, with the well-defined purpose of eliminating the leading role of the party and bringing about the confrontation of Czechoslovakia with the other socialist countries.

In recent times, political organizations and clubs formed outside the framework of the National Front have become essentially the headquarters of reactionary forces. The Social Democrats tried obstinately to form their party. They organized clandestine committees and wished to take over the leadership of the country in order to restore the bourgeois system. Forces opposed to socialism, together with revisionist forces, took over the press, radio, and television of your country. They used them to undermine friendly relations between Czechoslovakia and the other socialist countries.

In spite of the resolution adopted in May by the plenum of the Central Committee of the Czechoslovakian Communist party, reactionary attacks were not repulsed. The forces of reaction were thus able to publish their political platform in the document entitled "Two Thousand Words," which constitutes an open opposition to the Communist party, an appeal to the struggle against constitutional power. This statement constitutes a serious threat to the party, to the National Front, and to the socialist state. This statement is essentially a political program of counterrevolution. No one should allow himself to be deceived by the allegations of the authors of this document that they do not intend to overturn the socialist system nor act without the communists nor break the alliance with the socialist countries. These are only empty phrases which try to legalize this platform of counterrevolution and weaken the vigilance of the party and the working class.

Antisocialist and revisionist forces abuse the activity of the Communist party, press attacks against functionaries of the party, and soil the names of honest Communists who are devoted to the party.

Thus there has been created a situation absolutely unacceptable in a socialist country. In this atmosphere, attacks are launched against both Czechoslovakia's foreign policy and, especially, its alliance with the socialist countries.

Voices are also raised for the revision of our common coordinated policy toward the Federal Republic of Germany in spite of the fact that the West German government continues its policy, which is hostile to the interests of our security.

In your country, the course which events have taken in these last months indicates that the forces supported by imperialist counterrevolutionary centers have launched massive frontal attacks against the socialist system. It is evident that the reactionary centers of imperialism were united before the events in Czechoslovakia and are now doing everything to make the situation even more tense and complex. The bourgeois press, hailing "democratization" and "liberalization" in Czechoslovakia, pursues its campaign of calumnies against the socialist sister countries. The leading circles of the Federal Republic of Germany are particularly active and try to use the events in Czechoslovakia to create conflicts among the socialist countries in order to isolate the Democratic German Republic and to achieve their vengeful intentions.

Do you not see the danger? Is it possible in such a situation to remain immobile and limit oneself to declarations of fidelity to the cause of socialism and the obligations which alliance entails? Do you not see that counterrevolution is in the process of conquering position after position? Do you not see that the party is losing control over events and that it is more and more in retreat before the pressure of anticommunist forces?

Your press, your radio, and your television together have begun a campaign against the military exercises of the forces of the Warsaw Pact. Does this not waken distrust and hostile sentiments toward the Soviet Union and the other socialist countries? Events have developed to such a point that the maneuvers which have been organized with the participation of Soviet units are now used to prefer accusations of violation of the sovereignty of Czechoslovakia.

The hidden motive of this campaign is to deceive the Czechoslovakian workers and to place in doubt the truth that Czechoslovakia cannot safeguard its independence and its sovereignty except by being a socialist country.

According to our conviction, the situation which has arisen in Czechoslovakia endangers the socialist foundation of the country and threatens the essential common interests of the other socialist countries. The peoples of our countries will never pardon us for indifference and negligence before such a danger.

Our countries are linked by treaties and agreements. The important common obligation of our countries and our peoples is founded on the common effort to defend socialism and to guarantee collective security of the socialist countries.

Our parties are responsible not solely to their own working classes but equally so to the international working class, to the international communist movement, for their acts. They cannot withdraw from these obligations. Thus we should unite for solidarity in the defense of socialist achievements, our security, and our international position.

Thus we are of the opinion that resolute opposition to attacks from anticommunist forces, a committed struggle to maintain the socialist system in Czechoslovakia, is not only your task, but equally ours.

The cause of the power of the working class, of the defense of the achievements of socialism in Czechoslovakia demands:

- A resolute and courageous offensive against antisocialist forces of the right, in order to mobilize all means of defense which are at the disposition of the socialist state
- The cessation of activities of all political organizations which take a position against socialism
- Utilization of all means of information — press, radio, and television — in the interests of the working class, the workers, and, in that, socialism
- The closing of party ranks around the principles of maintenance of democratic centralism and the struggle against those who use the forces of the enemy.

We know that in Czechoslovakia there are forces capable of defending the socialist system and fighting antisocialist elements. The working class, the progressive intellectuals, the majority of workers in Czechoslovakia, are ready to do everything necessary for the development of socialist society. The actual task is to mobilize these forces in the struggle against the counterrevolutionary forces and to consolidate socialism in Czechoslovakia. We are convinced that the Czechoslovakian Communist party will entirely assume its responsibilities and will take the measures necessary to combat reaction. In this struggle, it can count on the solidarity and the support of the socialist sister countries.

[Prague's Reply . . . July 20, 1968]

This is the entire text of the reply by the Czechoslovakian Communist party to the July 19, 1968, letter.

The Presidium of the Czechoslovakian party has examined from all points of view the letter which was addressed to the Central Committee of our party by the representatives of the parties of the five socialist countries at the time of their meeting in Warsaw.

It is emphasized in this letter that it is motivated by concern about the subject of our common cause of reinforcing the position of socialism. That is why, with the same intention, we wish to express as openly our attitude concerning the questions which are raised in the letter.

But at the same time we are fully conscious that it is scarcely possible by an exchange of letters to illuminate entirely a problem as complicated as the one which is the object of general attention. This is why our reply does not propose such goals. Quite the contrary, we envisage direct mutual meetings of the parties.

Many of the fears exposed in the letter have already been expressed in the resolution of the Central Committee of the Czechoslovakian Communist party, meeting in the month of May. However, we believe to be of chief importance the accumulation of contradictions, during the years preceding the plenary session of the Central Committee of the Czechoslovakian Communist party of January, which caused the actual political situation. It is scarcely possible to resolve these contradictions in a satisfactory manner at one stroke in a short space of time. This is why it is inevitable that, in the political line of the program of action of our party, the main current of healthy social activity should be accompanied by extreme tendencies,

117

that the remains of the antisocialist forces in our society seek now to exploit the situation, and that at the same time dogmatic and sectarian forces linked to the erroneous policy before the January plenum should continue their activity.

In this complicated situation the party itself could not be spared the internal contradictions accompanying the process of unification on the line of the program of action. Among the negative phenomena of this process also figure the violations of the principles of democratic centralism in the conduct of certain communists, which are due first of all to the fact that during long years the former leadership of the party applied bureaucratic centralism and repressed the internal democracy of the party.

All this prevents the achievement of only those results which we most wish to obtain in party policy. We do not wish to hide these facts; we hide them neither from the party nor from the people. That is why the May plenum of the Central Committee openly declared that it is indispensable to mobilize all forces against possible civil conflict and against threats to socialist power in Czechoslovakia.

Our party has also unanimously declared that, if such a threat should arise, the party would use all means to defend the socialist system. Thus we ourselves see the possibility of such a danger. We understand that this cannot leave the parties of the socialist countries indifferent.

However, we do not see real reasons for qualifying the actual situation of our country as counterrevolutionary, for declaring that the foundations of the socialist regime are menaced, that a change in our foreign policy is being prepared, or that there is a concrete threat that our party will dissociate itself from the socialist community.

Our alliance and our friendship with the U.S.S.R. and the other socialist countries are deeply rooted in the social regime, in the traditions and the historical experiences of our nations, in their interests, their sentiments, and their thoughts. The liberation from Nazi occupation and the embarkation on the way of a new life are constantly linked in the consciousness of our people to the historic victory of the U.S.S.R. in the second world war and to respect for the heroes who gave their lives in this conflict.

It is also there that the program of action of our party begins, there that we reclaim this tradition for ourselves as a point of departure.

The fundamental direction of the foreign policy of Czecho-slovakia arose and was established at the time of the struggle for national liberation and in the process of socialist recon-struction of our country; it moves toward alliance and coopera-tion with the Soviet Union and with the other socialist coun-tries. We behave in such a way that friendly relationships with our allies, the countries of the world socialist community, will deepen on a basis of mutual respect, sovereignty and equality of rights, and international solidarity. In this sense, we con-tribute more actively to the common activity of the economic council of mutual aid and the Warsaw treaty.

Mention is made in the letter of attacks against our socialist foreign policy, of plots against our alliance and friendship with the socialist countries, of voices demanding the revision of our common and coordinated policy as to the Federal Republic of Germany; it is even stated that seductive moves on the part of the authorities of the Federal Republic of Germany find a re-sponse in the circle of leadership in our country.

Such statements astonish us, for it is a well-known fact that the Czechoslovakian government practices a consistent social-ist foreign policy whose principles have been formulated in the program of action of the Czechoslovakian Communist party and in that of the government. These documents, the speeches of the responsible Czechoslovakian leaders, as well as our other acts, arise from the principles of socialist internationalism, from the alliance and the development of friendly relations with the Soviet Union and the other socialist countries. We believe that it is these facts which are decisive rather than the irresponsible voices of certain individuals which are raised among us.

Given the bitter historical experiences of our nations with imperialism and German militarism, it is unimaginable that a Czechoslovakian government, whatever it was, could ignore these facts or lightly risk our country's destiny. So much the less could a socialist government do so, and we must deny any suspicion in this direction.

In that which concerns our relationships with the Federal Republic of Germany it is a well-known fact that Czechoslovakia, although that country's neighbor, was the last to take certain steps toward a partial adaptation of mutual relations, economic in particular; the other socialist countries had modified their relationships with the Federal Republic of Germany in one way or another, much earlier, without awakening any fears whatsoever.

At the same time we respect and responsibly defend the interests of the German Democratic Republic, our socialist ally, and we do all that is necessary to strengthen its international position and authority. All the speeches of the leaders of our party and the state have expressly confirmed this during the whole period following January 1968.

The agreements and treaties uniting the socialist countries represent an important element of mutual cooperation, peace, and collective security. Czechoslovakia entirely respects its conventional engagements and it still is developing the system of agreements with the socialist countries, which is demonstrated by the new treaties of alliance recently concluded with the People's Republic of Bulgaria and the People's Republic of Hungary, as well as by the treaty in preparation on friendship and cooperation with the Socialist Republic of Rumania.

Like the authors of the letter, we will never accept that the historic achievements of socialism and the security of the nations of our country should be threatened or that imperialism, in a peaceful manner or by violence, should shatter the socialist system and modify the balance of power in Europe in its favor. The principal content of our evolution after January is just this tendency to increase the internal strength and the stability of the socialist regime and thus that of our relationships of alliance. The maneuvers of the armed forces of the Warsaw treaty on Czechoslovakian territory constitute a concrete proof of our faithful fulfillment of commitments of alliance. In order to assure the success of these maneuvers, we have, on our side, taken all necessary steps. Our people as well as the members of our army have welcomed the Soviet army and the allied armies to our territory in a friendly way. The supreme leaders of the party and the government, by their presence, have testified to the importance we attach to these maneuvers and the interest we take in them. The confusion and certain doubts expressed in our public opinion appeared only after the reiterated changes in the date of departure of the allied armies from Czechoslovakia at the end of the maneuvers.

The letter from the five parties treats also with certain problems of internal policy of the present time. We accept the assurance that this interest is not intended as interference "in methods of planning and management in the Czechoslovakian economy" or in our "activities designed to ameliorate the structures of the economy and develop socialist democracy" and that our efforts to balance "the relations between Czechs and Slovaks on the basis of principles of fraternal cooperation in the framework of the socialist republic of Czechoslovakia" are hailed.

We approve the opinion according to which the strength and the stability of our relations — which are indisputably in the vital common interest of all of us — depend on the internal strength of the socialist regime of each of our countries.

We do not doubt that to undermine the leading role of the communist parties would represent a threat of extinction to the socialist regime. This is why it is absolutely indispensable that we understand one another in order to determine correctly on what the strength of the socialist regime in Czechoslovakia actually depends, as well as to strengthen the leading task of the Communist party.

Taking past experiences into account, the program for action of our party stipulates that:

Today it is particularly important that the party practice a policy permitting it to deserve fully the leading role in our society. We are persuaded that in the actual situation, it is here that the key to the socialist evolution of the country lies.

The Communist party depends on the voluntary support of the people. It does not derive its leading role from the fact that it reigns over the society, but from the fact that it serves with greatest devotion its free and progressive socialist evolution. It cannot acquire its authority by force, but it must do so constantly by its laws. It cannot impose its line by commands, but only by the work of its members, by the truth of its ideals.

We do not conceal — and we said as much at the time of the May plenum of the Central Committee — that there actually exists a tendency to discredit the party, to contest its moral and political right to lead the society. However, if we ask ourselves whether it is correct to assume that these phenomena represent a threat against the socialist regime, that they signify the end of the leading political role of the Czechoslovakian Communist party under the pressure of reactionary, counterrevolutionary forces, we arrive at the conclusion: in no way whatever.

The guiding role of our party has suffered gravely in the past from the distortions of the 1950's and from the irresponsible eliminations by the leadership with Anton Novotny at its head. By his mistakes, moreover, numerous social conflicts were deepened between Czechs and Slovaks, between intellectuals and the working class, between the younger generation and older people. The irresponsible solution of economic questions has left us in a state which does not permit us to resolve numerous legitimate economic claims of the workers and, because of this, the efficiency of the whole national economy is seriously disturbed. Under this leadership, the masses' confidence in the party diminished, and voices of criticism and opposition made themselves heard. However, all that was "regulated" by the replies of the powers to legitimate discontents, to criticism, and to the irresponsible attempts to resolve social problems in the interest of the party and its leading position.

Instead of eliminating errors little by little and in a considered way, new errors accumulated and consequently contradictions to the subjectivism. During the years when objectivism could little by little have developed socialist democracy and applied scientific management, contradictions and social difficulties were sharpened by subjective inefficiency. Nevertheless, it seemed that all was well in Czechoslovakia. The first stage of the evolution was set in motion without conflict: the real drop in confidence in the party was masked by external forms of management by party directive.

Although this regime represented itself as a firm guarantee to the interests of the whole socialist bloc, internally problems grew whose true solution was blocked by the interference with the new creative attitudes by those in power.

Any sign, whatever it was, of return to these methods would rouse a crushing resistance from the majority of party members, opposition from the workers, the laborers, the peasants of the cooperatives, and the intellectuals. By effectuating such a thing, the party would in fact threaten its political role of leadership and create a situation which would really produce a struggle for power. Then socialist achievements of the people would indeed be threatened, as would the socialist community's common interests in the anti-imperialist front.

We agree that one of the first tasks of the party is to stop the powers of the right and the antisocial forces. To this end our party set in motion a political tactic in the May plenum of the Central Committee and it is resolving these questions according to this approach. This tactic consists of a series of steps which will be crowned with success only if we unite the necessary conditions with their progressive realization over a period of several months.

The condition for success, according to us, is that the realization of the program of action and the preparations for the party congress must not be threatened by any incorrect act which would provoke political conflict in our country. The May plenum of the Central Committee has clearly expressed this in its resolution.

Actually, the party believes that the fundamental task is to avoid threats to the socialist character of power and to the social regime from anticommunist tendencies or conservative forces which would like a return to the situation before January 1968 and which have not assured the development of socialism.

Our party has defined the principal goals and the following steps of the political task:

1. Dissociate the whole party from the distortions of the past, responsibility for which devolves on certain members of the former party leadership; these persons must accept in full this responsibility.

2. Prepare the Fourteenth Congress Extraordinary of the party, which will forward the development of the political situation following the January plenum and according to the principles of democratic centralism in the party; determine the obligatory line for the whole party; take a political position in that which concerns the federative organization of Czechoslo-

vakia; and adopt new statutes and elect a new Central Committee, to the benefit of the full authority and with entire confidence in the party and in all the society.

3. After the Fourteenth Congress, attack offensively the solution of all fundamental questions of internal policy: improvement of the political system based on the socialist platform of the National Front and social self-management, the juridicial solution of the federal state, elections of representative bodies of the state (federal, national, local), and the composition of a new constitution.

We find ourselves now at the stage of political struggle for the actualization of the line of the May plenum of the Central Committee of the Czechoslovakian Communist party. It is a true struggle in which we recognize not only victory but also failures; but the results of isolated battles do not permit a correct estimate of the result of the whole struggle. Nevertheless, we believe that since the May plenum we have succeeded in consolidating the political situation.

These last days, the extraordinary district and regional conferences have shown clearly that the party is uniting on the line of the program of action. Delegates to the congress have been elected whose choice guarantees that the progressive core of our party, not extremist views, democratically consulted, will decide the future line of the party. The representatives of the new leadership of the Czechoslovakian Communist party attached to the line of the program of action and the May plenum of the Central Committee have all been proposed by regional conferences for the new Central Committee. The party is thus progressively gaining a certain stabilization, and the essential preparations for the congress are proceeding successfully.

In accordance with the resolution of the May plenum and on the initiative of the Communists, the National Front is working out a socialist platform of political importance. All the political formations of the National Front on June 15, 1968, adopted a program which recognizes the guiding role of the Czechoslovakian Communist party, a role acquired historically; this statement expresses the socialist principles of internal and foreign policy. At this very moment the National Front is examining a statute constituting an obligatory organizational norm assuring socialist political orientation of all parties and all organizations.

According to the law concerning judiciary rehabilitations, we are in principle correcting the painful problem of illegal confinement of innocent people committed in recent years. This measure has obviously attracted the attention of public opinion and the information media.

In September, immediately after the party congress, certain new and important laws will be discussed: the constitutional law on the National Front should confirm the enduring existence of a system of political parties on the basis of the National Front; a law on the right of assembly and association should define the legal rules of existence and of activity of different voluntary organizations, associations, clubs, and so on. This will permit us effectively to face attempts of anticommunist forces and to establish the bases of the organization of public activity.

The Communists also are regulating in the spirit of the resolution of the May plenum important questions as to the work of the unions and the business councils of the workers. To sum up, the party has successfully opposed a political demagogy seeking to make use of justified claims of the workers to disorganize our regime and to release a spontaneous movement in the name of "workers demands" for the purpose of aggravating the economic and political situation in the country. We are also regulating, as much as possible, certain burning social and political questions, including among others the increase of pensions and adjustments of the lower salaries. The government first and foremost is concerned with the fundamental economic problems of the country in order to give new drive to the development of production and to be able to proceed to the betterment of the standard of living of the people.

We have taken the necessary measures to assure the security of our frontiers. The party is bringing its full weight to bear on the consolidation of the army, security, public ministry, and the courts. The party has taken a clear position on the question of popular militia, which has expressed its full support of the new leadership of the Czechoslovakian Communist party and its program of action. This important measure has been favorably received, it is known, by the workers in Czechoslovakia but also in the U.S.S.R.

We consider these measures as the important results of the application of the line of the May plenum of the Central Committee of the Czechoslovakian Communist party, as significant indications of the consolidation of the political situation, and as confirmation, not only stated but authentic as well, of the leading position of the party in our country.

Nevertheless, we see, and we do not wish to hide, that the application of all the conclusions of the May plenum is not satisfying. It also appears that in the course of public meetings and in the information media voices and tendencies make themselves heard against the positive efforts of the party, the organizations of the state, and the National Front. We consider the solution to this question a long-term task and we are applying the resolution of the May plenum of the Central Committee according to which "political leadership cannot be applied by the old administrative methods of power."

The Presidium of the Central Committtee of the Czechoslovakian Communist party, the government, and the National Front have unanimously rejected the two-thousand-word appeal, which calls for anarchic actions and the violation of the institutional character of our political reform. It must be clear that after this rejection such actions have no longer occurred in our country and the results of the appeal of "Two Thousand Words" did not, in fact, threaten the party, the National Front, or the socialist state.

A persisting negative characteristic of our reality is the campaign of unfounded lies against different militants and public personalities, including members of the new leadership of the Communist party, campaigns carried out from extremist positions on the right and left. The secretariat of the Central Committee of the Communist party and the leaders of the party have unequivocally and concretely condemned such methods.

We know that this situation was made possible by the abolition of censorship and by the establishment of freedom of expression and the press. By this fact, what was formerly passed on secretly can now be said openly.

However, if we ask the question "Is it correct to equate such phenomena with a disappearance of the leading role of the Czechoslovakian Communist party under pressure from reactionary, counterrevolutionary forces?" we arrive at the conclusion that this is not the case. All this is only a part of our political reality today. There is, in fact, a second part, in our opinion, determining that same reality: the increasing influence of the new democratic policy of the party in the eyes of large masses of workers, of the absolute majority of the population. The immense majority of citizens of all classes and levels of our society has declared for the suppression of censorship, for the freedom of speech. The Czechoslovakian Communist party is trying to prove that it is capable of exerting political leadership otherwise than by bureaucratic and police methods, above all by the strength of Marxist-Leninist ideas, by its program, by its just policy supported by the whole population.

Our party cannot bring victory to the difficult political struggle unless it can actualize the tactical line of the May plenum of the Central Committee and regulate fundamental political questions in the Fourteenth Congress Extraordinary in the spirit of its program of action.

This is why we consider all pressure exercised to oblige the party to engage in another way — that is to say, to resolve the fundamental questions of policy otherwise and at another time than in the Fourteenth Congress — as the principal threat against the fruitful establishment of the leading role of the party in Czechoslovakia. Such pressures are deployed by internal extremist forces of the right as by the dogmatic conservative and sectarian forces hoping for a return of the situation of before January 1968.

The development of the situation described in the letter of the five parties and the certainly sincere advice which it formulates do not take into account all the complexity of the dynamic social movement as it was analyzed by the plenum of the Central Committee of the Communist party of Czechoslovakia and the complex conclusions adopted by this plenum.

Our Marxist-Leninist policy cannot be based only on superficial phenomena which do not always accurately reflect the deep causes of social evolution, but it must seize the essence of that evolution and direct itself accordingly.

At this actual moment, the parties can serve the interests of socialism in our country in the first place by expressing their confidence in the leadership of the Communist party of Czechoslovakia and their full support of its policy. This is why we have proposed bilateral meetings of representatives of our parties as a preliminary condition to the fruitful common negotiations, in order that common discussions may be founded on deeper mutual consultations based on objective information.

We sincerely regret that these proposals have had no results. It is not our fault that the Warsaw meeting took place without our participation. Twice we have examined the proposals of the five parties for the convocation of this meeting at the Presidium of the Central Committee of the Czechoslovakian Communist party (July 8 and 12) and we have immediately communicated our opinion on the manner of preparation of this meeting as we thought most correct. Unfortunately, our proposals of July 12 were useless for, without waiting, a meeting had already been called for July 14. This was learned by us on July 13, in the afternoon, through the intermediary of the Czechoslovakian press agency [C.T.K., Ceteka] when the representatives of the five parties were already arriving in Warsaw.

In none of the points of view which we have submitted to the five parties have we ever refused the principle of participation in a common meeting. We have only expressed our own opinion as to the actual time and as to its way of preparation, in order that it might be organized with objectivity and founded on more complete information as to our complex problems. From the content of the letters of the five parties which were addressed to us between July 4 and July 6, 1968, we have in fact deduced that such information is absolutely indispensable if we do not want to end with negotiations whose success is compromised in advance by unilateral and incomplete information of the great majority of participants in consultation on the real situation in Czechoslovakia.

This is the meaning of our proposals for preliminary bilateral discussions. We were in no way motivated by the intention of isolating ourselves from the community of our parties and our countries but, on the contrary, by the desire to contribute to its development and its consolidation.

We believe that the convocation of a meeting in which the policy and activity of a party were to be evaluated without the participation of its representatives does not serve the common cause of socialism. We consider valid as always the principle expressed in the declaration of the Soviet government of October 30, 1956, saying: "The countries of the larger community of the socialist nations, united by common ideals for the improvement of socialist society and the principles of proletarian internationalism, can establish mutual relations only on the basis of full equality of rights, respect for territorial integrity, independence, national sovereignty, mutual noninterference in internal affairs." These principles, as we know, were confirmed and adopted by the conference of representatives of communist parties in Moscow in November 1957.

In all our activity we wish to continue to strengthen and to develop the great international traditions which, in our opinion, must also comprise the understanding of the common interests and goals of the progressive forces of the world as well as understanding of specific national needs. We are anxious that our relationships should deteriorate no further and we are desirous of contributing on our behalf to the appeasement of the situation for the benefit of socialism and the unity of the socialist countries. On our side, we will do nothing which could be in conflict with these goals. But we expect of the other parties that they help us in our efforts and show understanding of our situation.

The next session of bilateral negotiations proposed by us — in the course of which would be examined, among other things, the possibility of a common meeting of the parties of the socialist countries, a meeting whose program, whose composition, whose place and date, would be fixed in these bilateral discussions — appears to us to be an important task.

We shall consider it decisive that we hear, as soon as possible, about positive measures which will assure the continuation of our friendly collaboration and which will give evidence, in a convincing manner, of our common will to develop and consolidate mutual friendly relations, this in the interest of our common struggle against imperialism, for peace and security of nations, for democracy and socialism.

4.

Toward the End
... July 18–August 22, 1968

Voices of Unanimity (July) — A War of Nerves — The Last Chance — The Appeal — One Moment in Time — The Last Days (August) — Appendix: The Citizens' Appeal — Bratislava Communiqué — Tass Communiqué

[Voices of Unanimity (July)]

On the evening of July 18, Dubcek in the best of form gave before television cameras the firm and dignified speech for which the world was waiting:

> We are determined — and in this matter we count on the support of public opinion — to continue the policy which we adopted at the January plenary session of the Central Committee, the policy desired and supported by the Czech and Slovak nations. We wish to create a socialism which has not lost its human character. We have paid dearly for the previous practice of making decisions without taking into account the will of the people. The masses were not content with the former leadership. The Communist party cannot change the masses, but it can change

132

the leadership. After long years of silence, each of us can express his opinion with dignity; socialism begins to become the business of the whole people.

Dubcek objected categorically to the Warsaw ultimatum; his response was even more negative than the official reply of the Central Committee: "Public opinion was thunderstruck by the pronouncement of the Warsaw conference and by our nonparticipation in that meeting." It was equally disturbed

by the attitude taken by the five sister parties regarding the situation in Czechoslovakia. I want to believe that we will be able to refute the same evidence not only before our own nation but before the whole communist movement. We are grateful for any support given us by our sister parties. We certainly do not wish to impose our methods on them, for we would thus negate our own belief that each party should model its policy according to its own specific conditions. But we desire that socialism may be firmly rooted in our country, that it may be a socialism in harmony with the socialist conscience of our people.

Millions of hands applauded the relaxed and smiling face which appeared on little screens across the nation. Dubcek had every reason to be satisfied with the trumps he held in readiness for the imminent confrontation with the base censors of Warsaw.

Dubcek had obtained from the Central Committee unanimous support for his policy. Rumor had it in Prague that the news of this support had upset Brezhnev: "Even Kolder?" the master of the Kremlin had asked anxiously in one of his almost daily telephone conversations with Dubcek.[1]

The unanimity of the Central Committee was only a reflection of the extraordinary unanimity of the whole Czech people. In his archbishop's palace in Hradschin, Monsignor Frantisek Tomasek, head of Czechoslovakian Christianity, spoke to me of the problems of his church, the seminaries, religious education. He stopped suddenly, sighed, and spoke these startling words to me: "I believe that for the first time in my life I am going to have to pray for the head of a Marxist state. A Christian can only pray. With men like these in power here today, the church can envision peaceful coexistence. But if they leave, everything will again be uncertain, and not only for us."

A fine rain fell on Prague and its green cupolas. Through the window of the episcopal palace, I watched a troop of Pioneers cross Hradschin Square on the run. Some of them carried red flags and wore armbands.

"We have no other choice than resistance or capitulation. It will be resistance à la Schweik, or perhaps à la Jan Hus, though I don't think we'll go that far, but we will not give in. Our patience and composure must not be mistaken for weakness. The Czech people are tenacious and the communists in this country are not going to take lessons in socialism from anyone." These are the words of my friend Pelikan. Jiri Pelikan, head of television, member of the Central Committee, and deputy and president of the foreign policy group in the National Assembly, looks like a wrestler. His proposals reflected what Czechs and Slovaks were saying and thinking during that uncertain summer of heat waves and rainstorms.

"And if the Russians?" Pelikan shrugged his shoulders. He did not believe in this eventuality and enumerated to me all the reasons why Prague could never be Budapest. "But if one were to consider the improbable . . . as a working hypothesis?"

His reply was, "We would find new forms of passive resistance, but we would not surrender." [2]

In July television played the decisive role that it had in January. Every evening television viewers saw for themselves the piles of letters and petitions which arrived from every part of the country, urging the Communist party and the government to be firm. The behavior of the masses themselves was expressed in a style hitherto unknown to the communist world. There were no prefabricated or manipulated meetings in the factories or on the collective farms, no slogans recited in chorus by a well-rehearsed crowd, no forms typical of the Soviet pattern. The man in the street sent his letters to the radio stations and newspapers like a reader of *The Times* or *Le Monde*.

The letter from Warsaw had ironically strengthened Dubcek's position. The most reserved intellectuals no longer accused him of centrism or half-heartedness; the Slovaks, whose egalitarian demands at one time had driven the central government to distraction, found themselves shoulder to shoulder with the Czechs.

Dubcek, basically an extremely modest, even timid man, had previously refused any publicity. During these tense days a picture story appeared in the weeklies revealing the private life of the secretary. In the incongruous holiday atmosphere of a Prague where crowds of Soviet tourists met troops of American ladies in flowered hats, the Western journalists were ironically the most pessimistic. And finally even they allowed themselves to be persuaded that another Budapest was impossible.

In the secretariat of the Central Committee — where there were some complaints about the alarmist tendencies of the Western press — I was assured that the Soviets would never be so foolish, that the European communist movement would never recover from such a blow, that the entire European left viewed the letter from Warsaw as the last threat brandished by an outdated system of government and believed Prague's resistance to be the dawn of a new era.

Dubcek knew all that. He knew that he was not alone. Mar-

shal Tito and Ceausescu, speaking for Yugoslavia and Rumania, had made very clear their disapproval of the restraints
which the Warsaw five intended to impose upon Prague. The
spirit of the prewar "little entente" seemed to be coming to
life again under the folds of the red flag. And there were
others; the French and Italian communists especially wanted
to protect their futures.

Waldeck Rochet, general secretary of the French Communist party, and Giancarlo Pajetta, number two in the Italian
Communist party, were in the office of Mikhail A. Souslov,
secretary of the Soviet Communist party in charge of relations
with foreign Communist parties, when they first scanned the
text of the letter from the five on July 15. They needed to read
very little — "We will not consent," "We will not admit" —
to understand that things had taken a turn for the worse.

They pleaded their case, their concern for their futures, passionately, considering problems of the Moscow-Prague crisis
from two viewpoints. They first represented the interests of
international communism. It had been admitted, they demonstrated, that each country could and should alone determine its
approach to socialism, which admission presupposed Moscow's
noninterference in Czechoslovakian affairs. In this sense the
Warsaw conference was in itself an error. Condemnation of
Dubcek's policy would be a more serious mistake. Intervention
would be the fatal error.

The second part of the argument presented by the French
and the Italians, who in effect acted as spokesmen for the communist parties of the world, represented the interests of these
parties in the capitalist world. Another Budapest would ring
the knell not only for the French communists, already weakened by their recent defeat at the polls, but also for the Italians, who had just won some votes thanks to their relative autonomy and freedom of speech.

Souslov appeared shaken, but the other Soviet spokesmen

were unmoved. They were persuaded that Dubcek represented no more than a minority and that the Warsaw letter would galvanize the "good" communists.

In Prague, Stepan Chervonenko, the Soviet ambassador, paid longer and longer visits to Novotny's villa, although the conservatives no longer dared show themselves by day for fear of being lynched. People were aware that these renegades were "organizing" and spreading poison in the Kremlin. ("Intelligence" would receive formal proof that entire passages from the letter from the five had been written by Czechoslovakian hands.) But Dubcek believed that the Soviets were deceived and would eventually return to better sentiments. He was relatively optimistic after the short visit from Waldeck Rochet on July 19. The French politician was himself blackly pessimistic. He proposed that a meeting of the European communist parties examine the "Czechoslovakian case." Dubcek refused, firmly but politely. He still thought that bilateral encounters were more fruitful than forums. (Besides, he had in his pocket the U.S.S.R.'s proposal for a meeting between the presidiums of the two countries' communist parties, a proposal to which Radio Prague alluded on the evening of July 19 without indicating either the place of the meeting or the composition of the delegations.) Beyond this, Dubcek, like all his compatriots, assumed that the "case" to be examined was that of the neo-Stalinist dogmatism of the Soviets and their friends rather than his own. An echo of that state of mind is evident in the witticism told me by a member of the Central Committee: "We have no problems here, but clearly Brezhnev has some. We should examine them with goodwill."

The Czechs did favor an international meeting of the communist parties to examine the general situation of international communism, but they thought that the Soviets would prevent such a meeting from taking place.

[A War of Nerves]

The carrot, a meeting of the presidiums, did not preclude the stick, a war of nerves. Friday, July 19, anti-Czechoslovakian propaganda reached new heights. *Pravda* announced a plot by NATO to detach Czechoslovakia from the Warsaw Pact and disclosed the discovery of an arms depot. This last affair is worth a pause. On July 12, the police of Karlovy Vary, alerted by an anonymous telephone call, discovered under a bridge in Sokolov in western Bohemia twenty Thomson machine guns, thirty revolvers, and ammunition in new plastic bags. Supposedly the matter was kept absolutely secret, yet it was revealed to Moscow and Sofia before it was heard in Prague. This incident, unquestionably a provocation, was the first of a whole series of similar incidents in which the hand of the East German special services was soon evident. Still more disturbing was the announcement of the catastrophic returns to Moscow of Marshal Andrei Grechko, Soviet minister of defense, from Algiers, and of Marshal Ivan Yakubovsky, commander-in-chief of the armies of the Warsaw Pact, from Prague. The Red Army paper *Krasnaya Zvezda* commented on the Czechoslovakian situation from the "military" point of view. The conflict, up to this time "ideological," took on more and more alarming character with the military's full-fledged entry into the debate.

In the days to come, bitter controversy developed between Prague and Moscow over the place and manner of the meeting. The Soviets insisted that it be in the U.S.S.R. (they proposed Kiev or L'vov); the Czechs wished to have it in their country. A wind of dissension blew over Czechoslovakia. Those in the confidence of the party assured me that the encounter, if it took place, would be brief: "Dubcek will be satisfied to sum up the reply of the Central Committee to the letter of the five."

With the full and entire agreement of the Presidium — which was to disavow this later — General Prchlik asked for a reform of the Warsaw Pact and gave assurances that he had not found any secret agreement signed by Novotny outlining clauses other than those already known and found in the archives of the ministry of defense. Moreover, he announced the final departure of the last Soviet troops — who were on maneuvers which had been dragged out on various "technical" pretexts — and gave figures, an itinerary, and an evacuation calendar. It was a masterly bluff. (The press began each day by announcing the presence of Russians in such and such a place in the country, which would bring a rush of newsmen and cameramen in search of pictures.) There was no confirmation of Prchlik's release; the Russians gave evasive and dilatory answers. Moscow would not forget Prchlik's audacious stroke, and henceforth he took the Number 1 position in the already long list of "men to be eliminated" in Prague. Nevertheless, Dubcek clearly indicated through Prchlik's bluff that the Czech leadership considered complete evacuation by Soviet forces a preliminary condition to the coming discussions.

On July 22, a communiqué from Tass Agency announced that the meeting would be held in Czech territory on July 31. But a new offensive, more threatening than previously, was being launched. Moscow had just discovered that the West German frontier of Czechoslovakia was vulnerable; the "proof" — the arms depots recently discovered and the maneuvers of the Black Lion Bundeswehr in Bavaria. These maneuvers had been canceled for several days, but Moscow pretended not to know this and expressed with sinister humor concern about the arms which their own agents provocateurs hid "so amateurishly that a schoolboy would have blushed for it" (as the Prague daily *Mlada Fronta* wrote). A spoken note warned the Czech government that "threatening concentrations" of "German retaliatory forces" were gathering on the frontiers. Pankow, fanning the flame, announced a probable "Sudeten" uprising.

The hallucinatory style of the scenario recalled the one which had served as fuse for the six-day war in the Middle East. Then the Soviets had denounced imaginary concentrations of Israeli soldiers on the borders of Syria. Nothing could dissuade them; the Soviet ambassador to Tel Aviv refused to go to see for himself. Chervonenko now refused to go to the Bohemian "front." What he "knew" sufficed. Feverishly, the military authorities summoned journalists and gave them binoculars. There was not even a shadow of a German helmet in Bavaria. Television once more showed the frontier zone guarded by troops armed to the teeth; for good measure, Dzur had concentrated his armored divisions there. All this made no difference. Moscow would have this frontier "poorly protected," whether or not the Czechs protected it with a million men. Rarely since Hitler has the political cynicism of a great power attained this degree of ignominy.

As for the "Sudetens" whose insurrectionist tendencies had been detected by the "good" Germans of Pankow, some 70,000 remained of the 3.5 million before the war; their average age was sixty. East Berlin corrected its fire: "They will be joined by Sudeten refugees from West Germany." A radio commentator answered with a "droll tale" which went the rounds of Prague. He told about seeing one of the Sudeten refugees who had returned to the village of his birth in his luxury-model Mercedes burst into tears: "Are you weeping for the loss of your fatherland, the house from which you were driven, your wicked actions during the war?" "No," said the German, sobbing even harder, "I'm crying for joy to see how miserable you are and for having escaped the fate of these unhappy people. Thank you for driving me out."

Warsaw and East Berlin once more announced that Czechoslovakia was a veritable sieve and that numbers of "counterrevolutionaries" from all the socialist countries were using Czechoslovakian territory as an avenue of escape to the West. These were people from the jurisdictions of Poland and the Democratic Republic of Germany.[3]

On July 23, *Izvestia* announced with much ado that important maneuvers of the Red Army, necessitating the recall of many reservists, would go on until August 10 along the western frontiers of the U.S.S.R. from the Baltic countries to the Ukraine.

The press of the five "sister" countries redoubled its insults, which went from accusations of espionage directed at well-known Czechs to the denunciation of miniskirted workers in the streets of Bratislava. In East Germany, Ulbricht had a barbed-wire fence erected on the frontier separating his country from Czechoslovakia.

[The Last Chance]

At Prague the composure was impressive: the belief that Moscow and its friends were "misinformed" was still maintained. The unions, the sporting groups, and various associations had sent out delegations and innumerable messages of explanation and had urged their opposite numbers to come and see for themselves; the Writers' Union invited Louis Aragon, Arthur Miller, Jean Paul Sartre, Bertrand Russell, and others to come. The newspaper *Prace* thought that these contacts had some value because errors would come to light. Under the by-line of its Moscow correspondent, it said:

In talking with certain people these days, one becomes aware that they are disturbed by the different points of view adopted by the communist parties of Western Europe and by those of certain socialist countries; [one realizes] that they are beginning to ask themselves if the Warsaw recommendations really correspond to the truth. People are beginning to wonder if this letter from Warsaw has not divided the communist movement instead of unifying it.[4]

In political and intellectual circles in Prague, one often heard this slogan, resolute and desperate at the same time: "We must succeed. Not only is it our country's last chance; it may be socialism's last chance in Europe."

And Mnacko, whose mood since his return from Israel had never been more pugnacious, said to me: "What is going on now didn't begin in January. For years and years we have been traveling in darkness, we communists who are not resigned to the caricature which has been made of our ideal. We have been asking ourselves for years: But what is this? Is this what is called socialism? Where is human nobility? Where is the socialist dignity of man? How can we change the system? How can we transform a socialism opposed to the individual into a socialism for the individual? Now, and only now, we have a chance to build a socialist democracy and establish its laws. It has never been tried before. Sometimes it makes me feel dizzy, but it is also the most stunning opportunity which has been offered to my generation. I believed our generation lost. For it is through our naiveté, our romanticism, our lack of political clarity, that we permitted this perverse regime to establish itself for twenty years. It isn't just Stalin, Gottwald, and Novotny who are to blame. We are too, all of us, from the beginning. We all have profited by the system and afterward we have drunk the cup to the dregs. That is why I do not believe we can be deceived a second time. We know all the tricks and all the masks. They won't teach Stalinist grimaces to old monkeys like us. If the irreparable does not happen, and I do not believe that it will happen, this process will go on to its conclusion."

It was during these days of waiting that I met that rare bird in Prague, a Soviet colleague. He was a journalist from the Novosti Agency, agreeable, intelligent, but expressing a chauvinism which froze my bones. Quite ingenuously, he said to me: "Do you know that passage in the second volume of Hasek's *Good Soldier Schweik* where Schweik literally drives an Austrian railwayman crazy by explaining to him for hours on end how the railways of the Hapsburg monarchy ought to run? The pretentiousness of the Czechs in teaching us what socialism is, is unbearable. They may still be Schweiks, but we aren't Hapsburgs. They'll find it out soon enough."

In Prague, nerves began to fray. Passing from optimism to pessimism and vice versa, people began to play little social games. The first subject was the concessions which the Russians would demand at the coming meeting of the presidiums. Some thought that the Soviets would present Dubcek with a real ultimatum in the form of the following alternatives: "We will let your experiment in democratization continue if we can group troops on the western frontier of Czechoslovakia, or else, no troops, but you must reestablish censorship." To those who refused any compromise, invoking Munich — "any concession exacted by threats will be followed by new demands" — the realists answered with formulas of conciliation.

The revelation of the plan, attributed to the conservatives, for a six-month cooling-off period for liberalization unleashed fury. Those in power were silent. Finally, to placate a thousand bad-tempered Western journalists, the Central Committee granted a press conference. It was held on July 24 by an obscure little functionary, Mr. Tichy, who offered assurances that the Czechs intended to remain firm on two points: the defense of the frontier and the policy of a free press.

It became evident that Dubcek had nothing to sell to the Soviets except minor concessions: nonrecognition of Israel, a refusal to entertain diplomatic and economic advances from West Germany, at the most only "mixed" military commissions on the frontiers. He was caught in a trap of his own making; he had accepted from the beginning the intermingling of problems rising solely from the sovereignty of the state with those concerning ideological affairs of the party.

The second social game in Prague was guessing who was a "traitor." Was it some member or other of the Slovak group of the Presidium — Bilak, Frantisek Barbirek, Alois Indra, the ebullient Kolder, Svestka, the sallow and fanatical editor-in-chief of *Rude Pravo?*

On July 25, when they bought their morning papers, the people of Prague were dumbfounded. The press announced the dismissal of General Prchlik, head of the eighth section of the Central Committee. It was true that dissolution of this office, which had played a sad role in the period of "the deformities of sociality legality," was in line with the renewal. But the dismissal came at a moment when there could be no doubt: it was a major concession to Moscow, which had not appreciated Prchlik.[5] The public was bitterly indignant. It was felt instinctively that in eliminating Prchlik, who had already saved the team of the thaw from Sejna's putsch, Dubcek not only tarnished his halo by betraying his friend but revealed himself to be considerably weakened. In official circles, foreign journalists were taken aside and told, under the seal of secrecy, that this was only one more "Schweikade," that Prchlik would keep his functions on the Army staff, and so on.

The atmosphere became more and more oppressive. The press revealed that at the Soviet demand absolute secrecy about the coming meeting was to be maintained. The rumor circulated among foreign journalists that it would be held in the last days of July in Slovakia. There was talk of either

Banska Bystrica or Kosice, of a castle in Bohemia, and even of a train. With much courtesy the government press services "apologized" to us for the silence that they were obliged to observe "for reasons beyond control."

On Wenceslas Square people snatched up newspapers. The headline of *Literarni Listy* proclaimed: "No Government Can Survive a Second Munich." One of the newspaper sellers was a "beatnik," sporting long hair and dirty blue jeans. He created a huge success by announcing "all the details on the upcoming kiss of peace between Brezhnev and Dubcek."

[The Appeal]

On Friday, July 26, tension was at its height. A persistent rain fell on Prague. The editorial offices of *Literarni Listy,* where I went to see my friends, buzzed like a beehive. This literary weekly, always in the front line of battle, put out a special four-page edition in the form of an appeal from citizens — a brief and incisive editorial, three symbolic photographs (the burial of a partisan in 1945, a mother and child, a ham radio operator with a group), three cruel caricatures by Jiranek and Steiger, and signatures, three pages of them in tiny print.[6]

From this Friday evening — when the supplement of *Literarni Listy* was exhausted after only a few hours on the streets — until the Monday of the official meeting, Prague lived through unforgettable hours of confusion and friendship, emotion and humor. In the editorial room of the journal which opened onto the quays of the Vltava, Pavel Kohout told me the story of this manifesto, conceived and written in a few hours:

"We began at four o'clock Thursday afternoon to discuss the text. On Friday it was printed in two hours. We had not foreseen that the next day thousands of young people, as if sprung from the sidewalks, would collect pages of signatures, and that on Sunday evening I would carry home in a big bag 85,507 signatures from a single street in Prague to be sent to the Central Committee."

For three days I saw groups forming in Wenceslas Square, in front of the central railroad station, in the old city, and in its adjacent quarters. Teams of volunteers brought tables into the street. A table was installed in the lobby of my hotel. As the employees signed, each one wrote beside his name his title: cook, chambermaid, elevator operator, down to the last scullery boy who put his greasy fingerprint on the paper. In the streets, in the midst of this civic mobilization, laughter mixed with tears, humor accompanied anguish. Before a large store in the center of town, as the students carefully compiled pages of signatures, often accompanied by addresses, someone said aloud: "Cross those addresses out; it will make it too easy for the police *afterward* . . ." Everyone laughed, however weakly. Farther on, one good woman, seeing a line, asked eagerly "What merchandise are they queued up for?" "For freedom," the crowd answered her. In the evening at a number of theaters the actors appeared in costume to read "The Citizens' Appeal" from the stage.

Signatures arrived by the cartload at television stations, newspaper offices, and the Central Committee. The fear that the Soviet Presidium would split the Czechoslovakian Politburo was dissipated by the strength of popular unanimity. It was given out that, although the six "soft" members of the Presidium — the three Slovaks plus Kolder, Jan Piller, and Svestka — certainly had differing opinions, they could not but be impressed by the tidal wave of swelling public opinion. Smrkovsky, faithful to his tactics, committed another calculated "indiscretion," announcing that any deviation from the agreed line of negotiation by a member of the Presidium would constitute a crime not only against the party but against the people.[7] He added as clearly as possible: "Such a traitor will not be pardoned by the people. We shall draw up our accounts when we return to Prague, both as a collective body and as individuals."

On Saturday, July 27, at 7:30 in the evening, Dubcek, his face drawn with fatigue but his voice strong and determined, announced to a television audience of millions of relieved Czechs and Slovaks his decision to "take not one single step aside from the path on which we have begun."

The weekend, sacrosanct in Czechoslovakia, had begun with Dubcek's hopeful words. On Sunday, the sun came out; as Soviet tourist buses stopped for a moment at the border of the Ukraine, promenaders went to Fucik Park (Prague's Luna Park) or wandered along the boulevards. And people continued to sign. Innumerable petitions were set out on little tables placed all over the city. In this conflict which matched the Soviet colossus against their little country, the Czechs did battle with no more than their good nature and their fountain pens.

[One Moment in Time]

At Cierna nad Tisou, a little frontier station on the far eastern border of the country, and a very short distance, three or four kilometers, from the U.S.S.R., the two presidiums confronted each other on Monday, July 29. Later it would be known through indiscretions that Dubcek and the progressives of his team, including Spacek, who had not yet recovered from an automobile accident, left for Slovakia simultaneously determined and despairing. They warned their families that the worst could happen and then left, little suitcases in hand, "like Jews under Gestapo occupation," to quote one of Dubeck's assistants.

147

To Dubcek was attributed this dreadful remark: "Where we are going, we must wear the faces of angels over the jaws of wolves." [8]

For four days, I watched a people hold its breath and wait with such a pathetic confidence in the rightness of its cause that few international postwar incidents seemed to me to be so representative of absolute crime, of sin against the spirit. The strangling of the Czechoslovakian revolution was not as spectacular as genocide. But is not destroying the hope of a people perhaps as tragic as destroying their lives?

On the eve of Cierna, I had met old Josef Boruvka, minister of agriculture and food production. A vigorous sexagenarian, this former farmer from eastern Bohemia reminded me of the Israeli "kibbutznik-ministers," [9] whom he resembled both in looks and in language. He could have been the twin brother of his friend Smrkovsky, whom he resembled in stature, in husky physique — enormous eyebrows under a cap of white hair, a face carved with the blows of a chisel. Like Smrkovsky he was one of the most ardent progressives in the government.

"I have never been so optimistic as to the outcome of this crisis . . ." he said. On the evening of the previous day he had dined with the president of the U.S.S.R. agricultural groups — fifteen million members — and afterward had shown him around his collective farm. The Russian was moved to tears by his conversation with the farmworkers and told him: "I have seen no counterrevolutionists here, nothing but good comrades, nothing but the kind of socialists we would like to have at home, Tovarich Minister."

"You see," Boruvka told me, "there is nothing to worry about this coming confrontation of presidiums. We welcome any confrontation with our Soviet friends. We will explain to them as many times as need be. And our friends will understand that we cannot take any other way, cannot depart from our national traditions."

The people would later know that during the four days of meetings at Cierna, during the thirty-nine hours of debate against the noisy background of the Soviet military "maneuvers," Dubcek and his friends kept their promises to the people, ceding nothing, retracting nothing.

The Cierna meeting can be reconstructed. For the Soviets the sole objective of the bilateral conference was to obtain an admission of defeat from their satellite. Since mid-July they had hoped that with the help of "maneuvers" their conservative friends would again master the situation in Prague so that there would need be no further foreign intervention. The unanimity of the Central Committee — where Novotnyans, isolated and discredited, no longer carried any weight — the cohesion of the Presidium, and the campaign of "signatures" reduced this hope to nothing. At the conference table at Cierna the Soviets had a single remaining trump, direct intimidation, which in their minds was synonymous with Canossa; it was Hitler's directive to Hacha, Montoire's interview with Petain, that ultimate step before military aggresssion. But at Cierna the betting was still open.

The first interview was icy. The Soviets called no one comrade except old Svoboda. Opening fire, they declared that counterrevolutionary forces were endangering Czechoslovakian socialism; proof — the letter from the workers of the Auto-Praga factory[10] and a press which "dishonored honest workers and socialism." The Czechoslovakian situation endangered all the countries of the bloc; the party had abandoned its leadership to uncontrolled elements who had conquered the press before taking power. The party's softness necessitated external intervention by the parties of the sister countries.

Dubcek answered vigorously. He said in effect: the letter

from the Praga workers, a solitary example, means nothing. Moreover, it should have been discussed a week ago when it was first received. There can be no question of reestablishing censorship; the press has been the architect of the nation's political awakening. It is managed by good Communists and honest citizens. Its contents are inspired solely by ideas contained in the party's program of action of April 5, which remains the keystone of our policy. At that time there was no criticism of this program. Why now? We have not in the least distorted the fundamentals of socialist propriety. Even in our economic reforms, what we envisage for small private property is well within what the Hungarians, the Poles, and especially the East Germans are doing. As for the leadership of the party, it has been not weakened but reformulated. Henceforth, the party wishes not to impose but to convince, "to merit its leadership by its devotion and the quality of its members. The principal embodiment of Czechoslovakian political life remains the National Front and we cannot a priori forbid any political party, any expression of opinion, which subscribes to the program of the Front." [11]

During the second day, the Soviets loosed a fierce attack against certain individuals: General Prchlik; Cestmir Cisar, the political secretary of the Presidium and the "pope of revisionism"; Josef Pavel, the minister of the interior "who caused the workers' blood to flow"; Ota Sik, the economist accused of returning Czechoslovakia to capitalism. The company present was not spared; Frantisek Kriegel did not escape some wounding references to his Jewish origins.[12]

The Soviets had endless lists in their dossiers. Nothing had escaped them; even insignificant interviews in the "bourgeois" press had been examined microscopically.

The Czechoslovakians held firm. They would cease their attacks against and caricatures of the sister parties only when the orthodox press did as much for Czechoslovakia.

And Cernik counterattacked with the Soviet violations of the Warsaw Pact which guaranteed his country's sovereignty. Intractable on the subject of their domestic policy, Dubcek and his friends tossed out ballast in the form of a modified foreign policy: Czechoslovakia would not recognize Israel, would make no new efforts to normalize relations with West Germany without Moscow's preliminary agreement, would continue to contribute their share of aid to "anti-imperialist forces."

The Soviets promised to make a definite decision on the long-deferred loan of four hundred million convertible rubles.

On Wednesday, July 31, although the atmosphere was glacial, the Czechs relaxed. Dubcek had his secretary shop for white shirts; he had not thought the meeting would last so long. He also put an end to the permanent alarm system which linked the Presidium and a secret wire-service center on the outskirts of Prague. If anything happened, instructions were to "tell the world the truth" by a network of transmitters. Part of this network would later form the astonishing epic of free radio after the invasion. In short, at no time did Dubcek foresee armed resistance, even if the irreparable were to happen. Late that Wednesday afternoon, General Svoboda gave a moving speech in which he praised humanist socialism to the skies and begged the Soviet comrades not to kill a great hope. Kosygin, Souslov, and even Brezhnev seemed moved and gave the old soldier an accolade. On the other hand, notable was the coldness of Alexander Chelepin and Pierre Chelest, members of the Soviet Politburo, whose ties to the military were well known.

On the morning of Thursday, August 1, the Russians conferred among themselves. At 1 P.M., when they returned to their places at the conference table, Dubcek knew that he had won the match. He did not know that this was to be only a brief respite. Within the shadow of the Soviet personages at the meeting — Kosygin, Brezhnev, Souslov — other members of the Politburo whose names no one knew outside the Soviet borders were already preparing for aggression.

The joint communiqué announced scarcely anything but the Bratislava meeting at which forty-eight hours later the satellites would endorse the laborious compromise of Cierna — a "compromise" which, for the moment, made it seem that the Czechoslovaks had not ceded anything at all.

In Prague, on the evening of Friday, August 2, an exhausted but triumphant Dubcek announced over the radio:

> We can be satisfied with the results of the spirit of the negotiations held at Cierna. We have kept the promises which we made. For the Czechoslovakian people, there is no other way but the one embarked upon in January 1968. Our Soviet comrades are convinced that we are ready to prove by deeds that we will not leave the socialist path.
>
> The two parties have shown each other that they are ready to take concrete measures to strengthen their cooperation in the frame of Comecon and in the Warsaw Pact.

He cut short all rumors which were circulating on the eventual "secret" agreements limiting Czechoslovakian sovereignty by the maintenance of foreign troops on the western borders of the country: "I wish to emphasize that the Czechoslovakian army is a firm link in the Warsaw Pact and a sufficient guarantee for the protection of our frontiers."

Relieved but still anxious, the public did not seem to share the optimism of its leaders. At Bratislava, where the meeting of the six opened on August 3, a brilliantly sunny Monday, Dubcek and his friends were wildly cheered; boos welcomed Ulbricht. The document[18] signed so flamboyantly in the court of Bratislava's city hall — opposite the "hall of mirrors" where

Napoleonic France, at the peak of its power, had sealed its victory with Austria — was the Austerlitz of democratic socialism. Omens were gloomy: at the moment of the signing, a violent, unexpected storm broke, pouring floods of water on the Slovakian capital.

The Bratislava communiqué was too ambiguous, in the opinion of both the international press and the Czechoslovakian people, to support either optimists or pessimists. A hypothesis suggested itself to the former: the Soviets had placed a limit on the Czechoslovakian experiment, particularly in the area of foreign policy, but otherwise the process could continue without hindrance. Lyrical passages all over the world praised the wisdom and political maturity of a Soviet Union which was finally de-Stalinized. The pessimists believed Dubcek had won only a respite: everything would depend on Prague's and Moscow's interpretation of the agreements of Cierna and Bratislava. And then, were there "secret clauses"?

The people of Prague argued endlessly. Sporadic palavers and free-for-alls, rather than demonstrations, remained the style of this still quiet revolution. This conflict evoked both Athenian democracy and Hyde Park soapboxes; members of the government and the Politburo, when questioned in the streets, explained themselves "family style" at the risk of getting pushed around. I never saw any of them with bodyguards. I never in those feverish days saw the police manhandle demonstrators. There was no trace of anarchy in this socialist republic whose features had been blurred but not obliterated by twenty years of Stalinism and whose national virtues survived: simplicity, faith in another man's word, and respect, a little formal, for intelligence. People greeted each other pompously as "Pan Ingenyr," "Pan Doktor," "Pan Professor" . . . In taverns people quietly enjoying their pleasures gorged themselves on beer. Even drunk, the Czechs had the placid and verbose dignity of peaceful souls. Most of the young people were on holiday. "Make your putsches in summer," advised Malaparte in his *Technique of a Coup d'Etat.*

After Bratislava, the Czechs and the Slovaks awaited the arrival of their friends, Tito the Yugoslav — the only one who had announced, during these cruel hours, "to move against Czechoslovakia is to rouse us" — and Ceausescu, the Rumanian. Their arrival, continually announced, was delayed; Dubcek was clearly afraid that the crowd's enthusiasm for the marshal would be accompanied by anti-Soviet cheers. In spite of the journalists' promise to use the soft pedal, *Literarni Listy* could not refrain from publishing a fierce "philological" analysis of the declaration of Bratislava and a biting "Letter from a Captain to a General" signed by Pavel Kohout, playwright and one of the authors of the "Appeal to the Citizens." The "Letter" was in homage to General Prchlik who, in spite of his disgrace, still bore the affection and esteem of the people.

The uneasiness born with the declaration of Bratislava did not die. How could both Dubcek and Ulbricht be "satisfied"? How could words mean the same thing in Prague and Moscow when Czechoslovakian ears no longer understood pseudosocialist jargon? Conscious of these doubts, the Czech leaders multiplied their explanations, trying to overcome the distrust which was bitter fruit from the past.

In newspaper editorials, particularly in the party paper *Rude Pravo*, it was a matter of demonstrating that the Czechoslovakian way and the unity of the socialist bloc, one day incompatible, were, the next, as complementary as thumb and forefinger: "We found a common language with our Soviet brothers. They understood us." And Professor Antonin Schneidarek, director of the party Institute of Political and Economic Research, explained how the crisis demonstrated positively the interdependence of the Czechoslovakian evolutionary process and the unity of the bloc: "First, unity of the communist parties is necessary to a country's free internal development. Second, the specific character of each socialist country increasingly influences the development of the others."

The formula seemed clear, although it recalled those optical figures in kaleidoscopes in which the eye can perceive either circles (Soviet influence) or squares (Czechoslovakian influence). But who was turning the kaleidoscope?

Schneidarek continued:

In the eyes of certain people, external political problems played a large part. They went so far as to consider the solution of these problems the basis for future development of democratic socialism in Czechoslovakia. This development seemed to be linked to foreign economic aid, to economic relations with the West and the Common Market, to our relations with West Germany and Israel. I believe that the importance of the liaisons has been much exaggerated. The drama of the democratic process will be played out in Czechoslovakia, not elsewhere. Of course it will not be played in a political void, nor outside the influence of the powers in that part of Europe. It is for this reason that the settlement of relations with the socialist states is the necessary preliminary to any future democratization.

And Schneidarek concluded pathetically: "How can those who see liberalization differently understand either the true situation or the crux of the problems still to be resolved?"

It could not have been more clear: Czechoslovakia had sacrificed all semblance of independence in matters of foreign policy. For the rest, it only asked to be let alone. Was Czechoslovakia in a sense to be a "Rumania in reverse" — Moscow-tolerated independent external politics (from Bucharest) at the price of rigorous orthodoxy within the borders? Observers could not but be skeptical. If Czechoslovakia could neither free itself from the yoke of Comecon nor ease it, if it was not permitted to solicit loans in the West and at the same time did not receive the amounts promised by the East, how could it begin the economic reform demanded by Ota Sik and his "economic council"? This economic reform had already been delayed for five months and all Prague was talking about Sik's bad humor and his threats to resign.

[The Last Days (August)]

However it was thought that the Bratislava compromise would authorize the completion of the legislative work and the democratic reform of the party, whose bylaws' projected revision was published in *Rude Pravo* on August 9, the day of Tito's visit incontestably opened a new breach in the traditional structures of dogmatism. This revision included the right of opposing minorities to exist within the party and extended the secret ballot to all ranks within the party. Other points of the plan extended democratic procedure to the executive apparatus and to the problem of nationalities.

But Dubcek gambled without luck. The same day in Moscow the Soviet Communist party published a seven-thousand-word document — its pretext being the preparation for Lenin's centenary in 1970 — whose spirit and letter were antithetical to the new bylaws of Czech communism.

Tito had barely left when an unforeseen visitor was announced: Walter Ulbricht, the statesman in modern history most hated by his people, came to take the waters at Karlovy Vary. Dubcek, and the world, could not surmise what was to be scribbled in the margin of a hasty communiqué after the first of the bilateral encounters of the sister parties since Bratislava. It was the hour of destiny. Whistled and booed by other patients at the spa, Ulbricht could laugh in his thin goatee. In

Moscow, military units were already being readied for intervention. As a last test, the Czechs were sent their worst enemy. But Moscow had long ago made its decision.

Impassively, Ulbricht and his advisors dragged out economic negotiations for two days. Political relations were to be, according to the communiqué, "fraternal" and based on "respect for sovereignty."

At home again, the East German leader even delivered an unexpected eulogy on the Czechoslovakian experiment, acknowledging that Prague had embarked on "a historic path important to the building of socialism."

It was August 14. Socialist democracy had still one week to live. *Pravda* appeared in Moscow with a new disguised warning to Prague. But who cared? Briefly quiet after Bratislava, the war on paper and over the airwaves began again in the capitals of orthodoxy.

In Prague, an attempt was made to outline a modality for a half-freedom of the press. The police broke up, without brutality, the crowds of debaters, beatniks, and folk-singers around the statue of Jan Hus in the old square; the municipal council offered them a distant park where they went to sulk. On August 15, the city gave a warm welcome to its other great socialist friend, Nicolas Ceausescu, and *Pravda*, under the byline of the "journalist" Yuri Jukov, asked the Czech leaders "to introduce some elementary order" into their press. New military maneuvers developed on the borders of Czechoslovakia and in East Germany and Hungary.

The Prague which I and most of my colleagues were to leave in mid-August seemed to offer no more page-one stories.

We left the country feeling that, in spite of the regime of supervised liberty which ruled it, Czechoslovakia would be able to pursue its experiment in democratic socialism: "If not Czechoslovakia, where else? If not now, when else?" The most naïve among us thought that Brezhnev, Ulbricht, and Gomulka were in some way jealous of a process which the general conditions of the communist world did not yet permit to proceed elsewhere than in this westernized islet of their empire and that what separated them from Dubcek was the means, not the end. The most pessimistic ones thought that, after a respite of six months or a year, the Muscovite sachems would step on the brakes, forcing new "maneuvers" or economic reprisals. But none among us even thought to imagine the scheme, the monstrous plot, which was being organized before the ink on the Bratislava agreements was dry.

Notes for Chapter 4

1. Josef Smrkovsky's calculated "indiscretion" to the journalists on the eve of the vote of confidence in the Central Committee forced the conservatives into a corner, and, on pain of seeing themselves pilloried, into unanimity. (The old fox repeated this procedure before the Cierna conference.) Kolder, however, gave a vehement speech "against" Dubcek's policy before rallying the ranks with his vote.

2. Jiri Pelikan was one of the organizers of the network of free broadcasters after the Soviet invasion.

3. On that occasion, several press commentators spoke of their "shame" at having to serve as chain-gang guards. A caricature showed Ulbricht, the "madman of the wall," pursuing his good work along the Czech frontiers.

4. Quoted by Michel Tatu in *Le Monde*, July 25, 1968.

5. The dismissal of Prchlik, who was accused by the Presidium of interference in affairs which did not concern him and of which he did not have sufficient information, became even more absurd when Cernik was later ordered by the Central Committee to make a complaint to the six members of the Warsaw Pact against the Soviet violations of three articles of the pact, which had been the exact objects of Prchlik's protest: (1) the Soviets did not inform Prague of the exact numbers of their effective troops on maneuvers; (2) the Soviet troops did not remain in the zones of maneuvers expressly decided and laid out by common accord; (3) the planned date of the beginning and end of these maneuvers was not respected.

6. "The Citizens' Appeal" was addressed above all to the negotiators: "Comrades, it is your historic task. . . . All our aspirations can be summed up in four words: Socialism, Alliance, Sovereignty, Liberty! . . . In the days to come we shall be with you with all our hearts, following your negotiations anxiously, hour by hour. We shall await your news with impatience. We think of you; think of us! You are writing a vital page in Czechoslovakian history for us. Write it with care, but above all with courage! To lose this unique chance would be a disaster for us and a shame for you." The journal invited the people to support the appeal and in three days received several hundred thousand signatures.

7. Conservatives and centrists wanted each member of the Presidium to be allowed to speak and reveal any minor misgiving which would undoubtedly play into Soviet hands. Dubcek required the reading of a single text reflecting the views of the collective.

8. On August 28 and 29, *Le Monde* described the extraordinary brutality with which the Soviets treated Dubcek and his friends when they entered the Central Committee building. In the best gangster-film tradition, Dubcek and his friends were made to line up with their hands raised and their faces to the wall and to stand thus for several hours under threat of machine guns, unable to move or speak. They were then brutally thrown into cars which took them to a secret destination in Slovakia, where they were imprisoned for twenty-four hours, unable to communicate with their families, before becoming "official" guests of the Kremlin in Moscow (according to testimony of Stanislas Budin, editor-in-chief of the Prague weekly *Reporter* and eyewitness at the Central Committee).

9. He told me that he had sent a mission of young agriculturalists to Israel to study poultry farming. I asked him about how severed diplomatic relations affected this matter. He made a vague gesture: "Politics . . . I send my boys where there is something to learn."

10. Without the knowledge of the business committee, and bypassing the party organization which favored Dubcek, a hundred of the three thousand workers from the Auto-Praga factory had sent a letter, through the U.S.S.R. embassy in Prague, which approved the presence of Soviet units in Czechoslovakia. The letter was featured in *Pravda* before becoming the showpiece of the Soviet counterrevolutionary dossier. The black sheep were immediately expelled from the party by the comrades in their cells.

11. Recalling the precedent of the "agrarian party" in Hungary, the Soviets launched strong attacks against the political groups which had developed in Czechoslovakia and had been tolerated by the Dubcek government (Club 231, the Club of Committed Nonparty Members), and they were uneasy about the law on freedom of associations in preparation for the meeting of the National Assembly, which, they maintained, was actually going to permit the restoration of the social democratic party and of other bourgeois leftist organizations of pre-1948 origin. The Czechs reassured Moscow. Club 231 would announce its self-disbanding and its directors would join the official committees which supervise the execution of the law of rehabilitation of former political prisoners. As for the Club of Committed Nonparty Members, it would be assimilated by the National Front and would abide by the discipline of it.

12. At the time of the removal of the Presidium to Moscow, after the invasion, Kriegel, considered to be a "zionist," would be eliminated from the negotiations.

13. See the appendix to this chapter.

Appendix

The Citizens' Appeal . . . July 26, 1968 — Bratislava Communiqué . . . August 5, 1968 — Tass Communiqué . . . August 26, 1968

[The Citizens' Appeal . . . July 26, 1968]

Comrades, We write to you on the eve of your meeting with the Politburo of the Communist party of the Soviet Union, in the course of which you are going to negotiate the fate of all of us. As the history of humanity has often been made, a few men will decide which road millions of their kind are to follow. It is a difficult task and we wish to make it easier for you by our support.

During the last centuries, the history of our country was that of a country deprived of liberty. With the exception of two brief intervals we have been condemned to fashion our national existence in secrecy, and we have even found ourselves, several times, at the brink of extinction. This is why our peoples hailed with such fervor the democracy which the liberation of 1918 brought us. It was an incomplete democracy, for

161

it did not give its citizens security on the political and social level. However, during the Munich crisis, it was the working class which showed most concretely its resolution to defend the state, which was threatened by liquidation. Our peoples welcomed all the more avidly the socialism which brought us liberation in 1945. It was an incomplete socialism for it refused its citizens civil and creative liberty. But we pursued this with an obstinate determination, and we began to come in sight of it last January.

Now the moment is come when, after several centuries, our country has once more become the cradle of hopes, and not only our own. Now is come the moment when we can bring to the world proof that socialism is the only valid choice for the whole of civilization.

We thought that this fact would be hailed with sympathy, in particular by the entire socialist community. Instead of that, we see ourselves accused of treason. We receive ultimatums from comrades, each of whose new interventions proves further their great misunderstanding of our development and of our situation. We are accused of crimes which we have not committed. We are suspected of intentions which we have not and which we have never had.

The threat of an unjust punishment hangs over our heads, but, whatever the form may be, it will strike like a boomerang at our judges as well as at ourselves; it will destroy our efforts, but above all, it will tragically and for many years darken the opinion held of socialism in the world.

Comrades, it is your historic task to prevent such a danger. It is your mission to convince the leaders of the Soviet Communist party that the process of renewal in our country must be followed to the end, according to the interests of our fatherland and the interests of the progressive forces of all continents.

All our aspirations can be summed up in four words: Socialism, Alliance, Sovereignty, Liberty!

Socialism and alliance are proofs given to the sister countries and parties that we shall never permit a development which threatens common interests of those nations with whom we have honestly struggled for more than twenty years in the common cause. In return, sovereignty and liberty are the guarantees for our own country that the grave errors which so recently almost ended in crisis will not be repeated.

Explain to your partners that the extreme voices which make themselves heard here and there in our internal discussions are just the product of bureaucratic and police systems which for so long stifled all creative thought so that because of them many people found themselves thrown into internal opposition. You can convince them, by innumerable examples, that the party's authority and the positions of socialism have never been as strong in our country as at this very moment.

Tell them that we need democracy; we need time and calm in order to become better socialists and more worthy allies than ever! In short, speak in the name of the people who, during these days, have ceased to be an abstract term and have become once more the force which creates history!

Comrades Barbirek, Bilak, Cernik, Dubcek, Kolder, Kriegel, Piller, Rigo, Smrkovsky, Spacek, and Svestka [the titular members of the Presidium of the Czechoslovakian Communist party], Comrades Kapek, Lenart, and Simon, [the substitute members of the same Presidium] it is possible that you are not in agreement on all problems. Certain among you, in spite of participation in the struggles of last January, have been severely criticized for former errors. This is the lot of politicians, and the past seven months have proven that no one dreams of turning this criticism into a vendetta. It would be tragic if your personal feelings were to supersede the responsibility which you bear in this moment for the fate of the 14,361,000 beings who make up the nation of which you yourselves are an integral part.

Negotiate, explain, but defend in unity and without concessions the path on which we have embarked and which we shall not abandon while we live.

In the days to come, we shall be with you with all our hearts, following your negotiations anxiously, hour by hour. We shall await your news with impatience. We think of you; think of us! You are writing a vital page in the history of Czechoslovakia for us. Write it with care, but above all with courage!

To lose this unique chance would be a disaster for us and a shame for you. We have confidence in you!

At the same time, we invite the co-citizens who agree with us to support this appeal.

[Bratislava Communiqué . . . August 5, 1968]

This is the statement of the six Communist parties at the Bratislava conference.

On August 3, in Bratislava, was held the conference of the representatives of the communist and workers parties of the People's Republic of Bulgaria, the People's Republic of Hungary, the German Democratic Republic, the People's Republic of Poland, the Union of Soviet Socialist Republics, the Socialist Republic of Czechoslovakia.

Taking part in the conference, as representatives of the Bulgarian Communist party, were Todor Jivkov, first secretary of the Central Committee of the Bulgarian Communist party and president of the Council of Ministers of the People's Republic of Bulgaria; S. Todorov, member of the Politburo and secretary of the Communist party; P. Kubadinsky, member of the Politburo, and vice-president of the Council of Ministers of the People's Republic of Bulgaria.

As representatives of the Hungarian Socialist Workers Party were Janos Kadar, first secretary of the party; E. Fock, member of the Politburo of the Central Committee of the party, and president of the Hungarian revolutionary workers and peasants government; Z. Komoscin, member of the Politburo and secretary of the Central Committee of the party.

As representatives of the Socialist Unity Party of East Germany were Walter Ulbricht, first secretary of the party and president of the State Council of the German Democratic Republic; Willy Stoph, member of the Politburo and president of the Council of Ministers of the German Democratic Republic; E. Honecker, member of the Politburo and secretary of the Central Committee of the Socialist Unity Party of East Germany; H. Matern, member of the Politburo of the party and president of the Central Control Commission of the party; G. Mittag, member of the Politburo and secretary of the Central Committee of the party; H. Axen, substitute member of the Politburo and secretary of the party.

As representatives of the United Polish Workers Party were Wladyslaw Gomulka, first secretary of the Central Committee; Joseph Cyrankiewicz, member of the Politburo of the Central Committee and president of the Council of Ministers of the People's Republic of Poland; Zenon Kliszko, member of the Politburo and secretary of the Central Committee; A. Starevicz, secretary of the Central Committee.

As representatives of the Communist party of the Soviet Union were Leonid Brezhnev, Secretary General of the party; Nikolai Podgorny, member of the Central Committee and president of the Presidium of the Supreme Soviet of the U.S.S.R.; Aleksei Kosygin, member of the Politburo and president of the Council of Ministers of the U.S.S.R.; M. A. Souslov, member of the Politburo and secretary of the Central Committee; Pierre Chelest, member of the Politburo and first secretary of the Central Committee; B. N. Ponomarev, secretary of the Central Committee.

As representatives of the Communist party of Czechoslovakia were Alexander Dubcek, first secretary of the Central Committee; Oldrich Cernik, member of the Presidium of the Central Committee and president of the government of the Socialist Republic of Czechoslovakia; Josef Smrkovsky, member of the Presidium of the Central Committee and president of the Czechoslovakian National Assembly; Vasil Bilak, member of the Presidium of the Central Committee and first secretary of the Communist party of Slovakia; Jozef Lenart, substitute member of the Presidium, and secretary of the Central Committee. Also on the Czechoslovakian side, Ludvik Svoboda, president of the Republic, was present.

The representatives of the communist and workers parties of the socialist countries, believing that the complexity of the international situation, the undermining activity of imperialism directed against the peace and security of the people and socialism, demanded the continuing cohesion of the countries of the socialist system, believing that the development of socialism brought into being new problems whose solution demanded that unity of the efforts of the socialist states be maintained, judged it necessary to convoke the conference which met at Bratislava.

In the spirit of tradition, in an atmosphere of total frankness, fidelity to principles, and friendship, the parties examined the actual problems of the struggle for socialism, to strengthen the socialist community and to unite the world communist movement. Opinions were exchanged concerning the problems which the actual international situation poses and the support of the battle against imperialism.

The representatives of the communist and workers' parties examined means of strengthening and developing fraternal cooperation of the socialist states.

In the course of the years which have elapsed since the defeat of fascism and the coming to power of the working class, the peoples of the European countries which were engaged in the way of socialism have won victories in all areas of social life. In the course of these years, the parties, overcoming their difficulties and constantly perfecting their work have, in each of the socialist countries, created a powerful industry, transformed rural life, increased the well-being of the people, expanded the national culture. Millions of workers have had access to active political life. The Soviet Union has obtained successes which have been particularly important in the building of socialism and communism. The international influence of the socialist states and their role in the solution of problems of world policy have grown immeasurably.

To sustain, strengthen, and defend these conquests, which were won at the price of heroic efforts, by work accompanied by sacrifices by each of the peoples, is the international duty of all the socialist countries; such is the unanimous opinion of all the participants of the conference who have expressed their immutable resolution to develop and defend the socialist conquests in their own countries and to realize new successes in the construction of socialism.

The parties, on the basis of historical experience, have come to the conviction that one cannot move forward on the path of socialism and communism except by observing with rigor and in a responsible manner the laws of the construction of socialist society, and particularly by reinforcing the leading role of the working class and its avant-garde, the Communist party.

In parallel manner, each party, while creatively resolving questions of socialist development, takes into account national peculiarities and conditions.

The unshakable fidelity to Marxism-Leninism, the education of the masses to the spirit of the ideas of socialism and proletarian internationalism, the unyielding struggle against bourgeois ideology, against all the antisocialist forces, are the proof of the successes in strengthening the positions of socialism and in the defense against imperialist plots.

The parties firmly and resolutely uphold their unshakable solidarity and their very active vigilance against all the plots of imperialism and those of all the other anticommunist forces which try to weaken the leading role of the working class and the communist parties. They will not at any time nor to any person permit the creation of a fissure between socialist states, the undermining of the bases of the socialist social regime. Fraternal friendship and unity in this intention serve the deepest interests of our peoples, constitute the solid basis of the solution of the socio-economic and political tasks which the communist parties of our countries work to resolve.

The parties estimate it to be their duty always to nurture carefully the growth of political activity of the working class, the peasantry, the intellectuals, and all workers, the general progress of the socialist social regime, the development of socialist democracy, and the perfecting of the style and the methods of work of the party and the organizations of the state, on the basis of the principles of democratic centralism.

The different tasks required by the creation of socialist society in each of our countries are much easier to resolve when the countries benefit by mutual aid and support.

Fraternal bonds enlarge and multiply the possibilities of each of the socialist countries. The participants in the conference have expressed the firm will to do everything in their power to deepen the cooperation of their countries in all domains on the basis of the principles of equality of rights, respect of sovereignty and of national independence, territorial integrity, mutual fraternal aid, and solidarity.

The communist and workers parties give importance of the first rank to the fact that, efficiently using the enormous natural riches of our countries, applying the most recent discoveries of science and technology, perfecting the forms and methods of socialist economy, still greater development of the economy shall be realized in the growth of the material well-being of the workers.

The development of economic cooperation of the socialist countries on a bilateral and multilateral basis is the efficient means of attaining these noble ends. The perfecting of the activity of the council of mutual economic aid and the development of cooperation and specialization of production among the socialist countries acquires an always greater importance and this makes even clearer the superiorities of the socialist division of labor.

The urgency of a meeting in the near future of an economic conference at the highest level has been reaffirmed on this basis.

The participants in the conference believe their duty to be to attract the attention of the peoples to the fact that, because of the aggressive policy of imperialism, the international situation remains today both complex and dangerous. In these conditions:

The parties of the socialist countries, taking into account the interests of the struggle for the strengthening of the general peace and the security of the peoples, declare themselves once more ready to agree and to coordinate their actions in the international arena for the organization of a decisive reply to the aggressive policy of imperialism and the affirmation of the principles of peaceful coexistence of the states with different social regimes.

The working class, the peasantry, the intellectuals, all the workers, are thirsty for peace and tranquility for their countries, for all the people of the world. The socialist countries have done, are doing, and will do everything in order that these sacred hopes of the peoples shall be realized. Our parties affirm that they will continue to cooperate, to complete this noble task, with all the workers and communist parties, with all the progressive forces of the world in the battle for total peace, liberty, independence, and social progress.

The communist and workers parties of Bulgaria, Hungary, East Germany, Poland, the Soviet Union, and Czechoslovakia solemnly make known anew their unshakable decision to continue to sustain the heroic people of Vietnam, to bring them indispensable aid in their just combat against the American interventionists.

We are equally concerned with the fact that the situation in the Middle East, by reason of the aggressive policy of the leaders of Israel, continues to remain tense. Our parties will do all that they can to neutralize the results of the Israeli aggression on the basis of the resolution of the Security Council of the United Nations of November 22, 1967, and of the evacuation of the Israeli armies from the occupied Arab territories.

After having examined the situation in Europe, the participants of the conference note that the development of the activity of retaliation, militarism, and neo-Nazism in West Germany directly affect the security of the socialist states and create a threat to world peace. We shall continue to intervene in European affairs in a responsible manner, according to a concerted policy corresponding to the common interests of the socialist countries, to the interests of European security, to oppose every attempt to question the results of the second world war or to destroy the frontiers which have been established in Europe. We shall continue to insist on the nullity of the Munich agreement. We shall resolutely support the Democratic German Republic, the socialist state of the German workers which defends the cause of peace. We shall bring permanent support to the Communist party of Germany and to all forces which struggle against militarism and revanchism for social progress.

The communist parties of the socialist countries express

their resolution to arrive at the realization of European security and confirm the principles of the statement of Bucharest and of the declaration of the conference of the communist and workers parties of Karlovy Vary. They are ready to do everything necessary for the convocation of a congress of the peoples of Europe for the defense of European peace and everything for the maintenance of the peace in the whole world. Our common efforts will be directed toward the realization of this end, which affects the interests of all the peoples.

Today, when the imperialist forces of the United States, West Germany, and other countries exhibit aggressive activity and try stubbornly to weaken the socialist community, the representatives of the parties believe it indispensable to emphasize again the particular importance of the Warsaw treaty.

This treaty, concluded by the socialist states in response to the entry of aggressive Western Germany into the imperialist bloc of NATO, was and remains a strong factor for the peace and security of the peoples of Europe. It is an insurmountable obstacle for all those who would like to revise the results of the second world war. It effectively defends the achievements of socialism, the sovereignty and the independence of the states. It is destined for the reinforcement of European security and for the maintenance of general peace.

The actual situation demands our sustained efforts to increase the defensive potential of each socialist state and of the entire socialist community for the reinforcement of political and military cooperation within the organization of the Warsaw treaty.

The participants in the conference deem it their duty to work in a responsible manner for the reinforcement of the unity of the international communist movement. They note that in recent times great work has been done for the preparation of the new international conference of communist and workers parties.

The parties highly appreciate this work and express the conviction that the conference which will be held will have good results and will make an important contribution to the consolidation of all the revolutionary forces of the contemporary world.

We are fully convinced that the unique conception of the Marxist-Leninist world, the role of the communist and workers parties as the vanguard and the leader of society, and the socialist bases of the economy of our states will continue to be active factors in the maintenance of the cohesion of the countries of socialism, of the unity of their actions in the battle for great common ends.

The parties participating in the conference of Bratislava make the present statement with the profound conviction that the positions and the views which are expressed here are in the interests of all the countries and parties and serve the cause of friendship of the people of our countries and the interests of peace, democracy, national independence, and socialism.

[Tass Communiqué . . . August 21, 1968]

This is the "authorized" statement by Tass Agency, demanded of the U.S.S.R. by men of the Czechoslovakian state and Communist party.

Moscow, August 21 (A.F.P.) — Tass Agency announced that it was authorized to make the following statement:

Men of the Czechoslovakian state and Communist party have asked the U.S.S.R. and the other allied states to come to the support of the Czechoslovakian people by bringing them military aid.

This appeal has been occasioned by the threat from counter-revolutionary forces, acting in accord with forces which are enemies to socialism, against the socialist regime existing in Czechoslovakia as established by the constitution.

The events in Czechoslovakia have several times given place to exchanges of views between the leaders of the socialist countries, including the Czechoslovakian leaders. These countries are unanimous in considering that the support, the reinforcement, and the defense of the achievements of socialism are an international duty of all the socialist countries. This common position of the socialist countries has been solemnly proclaimed in the Bratislava statement.

The recurrence of tension in Czechoslovakia affects the vital interests of the U.S.S.R. and the other countries of the socialist community, the security of the socialist community. The threat to the socialist regime in Czechoslovakia at the same time represents a threat to the very foundations of peace in Europe.

The Soviet government and the governments of the allied countries (People's Republic of Bulgaria, People's Republic of Hungary, Democratic Republic of Germany, and People's Republic of Poland) in conformity to the principle of indissoluble friendship and cooperation arising from the obligations owed to established treaties have decided to accede to the urgent demand for help for the Czechoslovakian people.

This decision is clearly in conformity with the right of the states to individual and collective defense as set forth in the treaties of alliance concluded between socialist countries. It also corresponds to the vital interests of our countries in defense of the peace in Europe against the forces of militarism, aggression, and retaliation which have more than once provoked wars between peoples.

Soviet military units accompanied by units from the allied countries cited entered Czechoslovakian territory on August 21. They will leave it as soon as the threats to the achievements of socialism in Czechoslovakia, to the security of the socialist community, are removed and when the legal powers consider that the presence of these troops there is no longer necessary.

This action is not directed against any state whatever and does not in any way undermine the interests of the state of anyone at all. It serves the cause of peace and is dictated by the concern for reinforcement of this peace. The sister countries align themselves firmly and energetically against all threats from the outside. They will never permit anyone to remove a link from the socialist community.

5

Invasion . . . August 20–26, 1968

Midnight at Ruzyne Airport — Betrayal and Confusion — The Reports of Ambassador Chervonenko — A Journey to Moscow — The Curtain Falls — Appendix: Proclamation by the Government of Czechoslovakia to All Czechoslovakian People — Proclamation of the Special Meeting of the Fourteenth Congress of the Czechoslovakian Communist Party to the Citizens of Czechoslovakia — The Protocol from Moscow — The November Resolution of the Central Committee

[Midnight at Ruzyne Airport]

It is seven o'clock on the evening of August 20, 1968, at the Prague-Ruzyne International Airport; the night crew is taking over in the control tower. The night promises to be a calm one. Except for two couriers from Belgrade and Sofia and one mail plane, no traffic is anticipated.

Crew Chief Jan S. and his companions have brought sandwiches, Thermoses of coffee, and a good supply of newspapers. For eight months there has been much to read in Czechoslovakia's newspapers. In the dilapidated departure terminal (the bright new buildings rising a few miles away have not yet been officially dedicated and so are closed to the public), travelers wait for the night planes, among them a Britisher who missed a previous flight. Something is unusual: normally at this late hour only the cleaning women of the night shift are moving

175

about; tonight the customs department is brightly lit and peopled with feverish figures coming and going behind its doors. Jan S. is aware of nothing.

He is surprised when at eight o'clock he receives a request for landing instructions from a special Soviet plane from Moscow. The plane lands and taxis to the end of the runway; no one gets out. Later it will be learned that this machine is a small electronic miracle, a laboratory plane that is to take over the control tower if necessary . . . even if the tower has to be destroyed. One hour later, two other "special" planes from L'vov in the Ukraine seek landing instructions. At midnight a voice arrogantly signals the control tower to authorize no further landings or take-offs. The tower technicians understand this order as little as they understand the unusual activity in the airport buildings; they speculate an unscheduled arrival or departure of some official dignitaries. Military maneuvers? Even in Czechoslovakia, a country "on the road to democratization," it is wise not to ask too many questions. By the time Jan S. and his friends begin to wonder if something is truly wrong, it is too late. Small groups of Russian and Czech henchmen have landed in the "special" planes or in planes coming from Prague; they have taken over control of the airport.

What could the technicians have done? The visitors were warmly and very officially welcomed by two officers in full dress uniform: Lieutenant Colonel Stachovsky, the head of passport inspection, and Colonel Elias, both responsible for airport security. At one o'clock in the morning they were joined in their still brightly lit offices by a Soviet colonel and the Prague Aeroflot representative.

At 1:30 A.M. the first AN24 transport plane, guided by the laboratory plane, landed in Ruzyne. A Russian commando and some technicians debarked and joined the agents already there. Together they took over the control tower, ending the perplexity of the Czech operators. Replaced and told to go home, Jan

S. and his companions had time only to glimpse the arrival in wave after wave of the Antonovs. Some spinach-green uniforms blended with the khaki fatigues of the Russians; the green ones belonged to East German soldiers, the first helmeted, booted, machine-gun-bearing German soldiers the Czechs had seen since 1945. They were Walter Ulbricht's troops.

The betrayal was perfectly executed. Brutally evicting travelers and employees from the airport, the commandos searched every nook and cranny of Ruzyne but overlooked the telegraph room. All morning the Ruzyne telegraph operators tapped out, under the noses of the occupants, messages calling for help and announcing the stupefying news to the nation: Czechoslovakia has been invaded by the Red Army.

[Betrayal and Confusion]

The perfection of the actual military operation was admired in the West. But the seven-day occupation was not the six-day war. An army undermined by betrayal at every level was neutralized from the start.

The Warsaw Pact troops appeared at Czechoslovakia's borders on Tuesday, between 11 and 12 P.M. By one o'clock on Wednesday morning, although vigorously protesting an act "contrary not only to the fundamental principles of relations between socialist states . . . denial of international rights," Dubcek and the presidium members of the Central Committee gave the imperative order not to defend the country:

> The Presidium of the Central Committee of the Czecho-slovakian Communist party appeals to all the citizens of the Republic to maintain calm and not to resist the troops, as the defense of our national borders is impossible

at this time. Therefore, neither our army nor the security forces nor the peoples' militia have received orders to defend the country.

The officers of the intervention forces had previously received "briefings" to the effect that the Czechs would not budge. Although sabotage might have hindered the invaders' activity, Dubcek's instructions and the "complex of abandon," the historical tragedy of the armies and the people of Czechoslovakia, weakened even the most fearless. Under the circumstances, to speak of the military prowess of the U.S.S.R. and its allies is to say too much. The Soviet invasion was a military parade carefully guided by treason.

And yet by the fourth day of the invasion the Russians still had not "discovered" vital installations located throughout the country; some of their maps dated from World War II. Their logistics were pitiful; troops were without food or water (in Prague water taken from the muddy bed of the Vltava caused a dysentery epidemic) and were even ignorant as to where they were. Most of the soldiers thought they were in West Germany — some thought they were in Vietnam. Their lack of sangfroid often bordered on hysteria. The most striking example is perhaps the incident which occurred in the early afternoon of August 22 in Wenceslas Square, which at the time was crowded with passersby: the antenna of a tank brushed against a trolley cable and wild rifle fire ensued, resulting in numerous injuries. The traces of this incident can still be seen on the front of the National Museum, which is riddled with hundreds of machine-gun bullets and chipped from 85 mm. blows.

The deployment of troops was massive and impressive, to be sure: 700,000 men, a thousand armored tanks, heavy artillery, and even several battalions of rocket launchers; hundreds of planes and heavy helicopters were unloading, especially over

Prague, the elements of the Soviet *force de frappe*, the para-troopers with their multicolored berets who had been exhibited by Moscow for the first time on the fiftieth anniversary of the October revolution. But the morale of these troops was hardly any higher than their intelligence, which was cause for concern even among the officers. Even the officers who did not refuse to converse with the passersby in the early hours of the invasion spoke only in clichés: "Dubcek is a capitalist and a nationalist. The true communists have asked us to protect them . . ."

Those who witnessed the initial days of the invasion were surprised by the brutal, almost feudal, nature of the hierarchical relationships within the Red Army. Despite their ultra-modern matériel, the Soviet invasion army gave the impression of a force singularly lacking in the tactical and operational sophistication necessary to modern war. In a different political and international environment the Czechoslovakian army, though without significant traditions or war experience, could doubtless have inflicted a series of strong blows on an invader more vulnerable than was at first apparent. The workings of the treason which permitted the Soviet invasion are now known. The signers of the famous letter from the "high party and government officials" calling on the U.S.S.R. to invade the country consisted of a small group of obscure, embittered people — employees of the secret police and second-rate Stalinite bureaucrats — so unrepresentative that the Soviets have not dared until now to reveal their identity. The most notorious of these individuals are Pavel Hausberg, the secretary of the dogmatic publication *For Peace and Socialism*; Bohus Chnoupek, vice-minister of culture; Karel Hoffman, former communications director for the post and telecommunications; and Miroslav Sulek, former editor of Ceteka, the official press agency. Their task accomplished, they have returned to obscurity.

[The Reports of Ambassador Chervonenko]

On August 16 during a special session of the Politburo of the Soviet Communist party, intervention in Czechoslovakia was *unanimously* accepted. The existence of a "progressive" group led by Kosygin in opposition to Brezhnev and the military was just one of the pathetic myths which originated at the time of the invasion; when the Czechoslovakian population was despairingly clutching at the slightest straw, there was even talk of Kosygin's resignation. A similar hoax was an alleged ultimatum from Lyndon Johnson to the U.S.S.R.; actually, in the name of Yalta and peaceful coexistence, the United States and the other Western powers tacitly yielded to the aggression shortly before it began. It is true that Chelepin and Souslov, concerned with maintaining ties with the communist world, expressed some reservations, but they agreed basically that the evolution of events in Czechoslovakia presented a growing danger "for the political, strategic, and military cohesion of the socialist camp."

The view of the Soviet military was the most alarmist. These leaders insisted that the planned and partially initiated overhaul of the Czechoslovakian armed forces and the purge of the security forces — some fifteen Czech K.G.B. agents who operated within the security forces of the army, the S.T.B., and other departments had been discreetly dismissed — were destroying the Soviet surveillance machinery which had been solidly entrenched in the country since 1945 and was considered invulnerable. The Soviet military leaders listed the advantages of the operation from a strictly strategic point of view: the strict control of some three hundred kilometers more of a vital portion of the Western "front," the strengthening of the Warsaw Pact, and a simultaneous increase of strategic and tactical "options," particularly nuclear, vis à vis the NATO forces.[1] Marshal Yakubovsky, commander-in-chief of the Warsaw Pact troops, had seen — in the vigorous refusal of the Czech chief of staff, Prchlik, to authorize the stationing of Soviet troops at the western border of the country and in his previous request for a revision of the pact — a veritable treason heralding an evolution "in the Rumanian style" and possibly leading to the complete disruption of the alliance. Another vigorous champion of intervention was the secretary-general of the Ukrainian Communist party, Pierre Chelest; he claimed that his region was being contaminated by Czechoslovakian deviation via Radio Kosice (in eastern Slovakia) broadcasting in the Ukrainian language. These broadcasts intended for the Ruthenian minority living in Slovakia were appropriated throughout the Ukraine as B.B.C. had been by the Europeans under Nazi occupation.

The reports sent by Stepan Chervonenko, Russian ambassador to Prague, and, independently of him, by secret-service agents and high-placed "friends" finally swayed the balance. Soviet leadership took on faith the declarations that Dubcek was an isolated man who enjoyed popularity only with a minority composed of intellectuals and student "revisionists." Ambassador Chervonenko spoke of the "intellectual terror" that a handful of journalists wielded over the country, preventing the still "healthy" working class from expressing its groundless love for the Soviet Union. The alternately Zionist and German-revenge conspiracy myth was undoubtedly taken less seriously by the Kremlin than were certain detailed reports asserting that civil and military party structures had remained loyal to orthodoxy but risked coming under the control of "rightist elements."

For those for whom, by principle, mass "spontaneity" does not exist, the idea that the solid majority of the Czech and Slovak peoples stood behind the new course of events could not for a moment be entertained. In order to return to the status quo, the Soviets considered as sufficient the prevention of the revisionists from taking control; the masses did not count. On the basis of the Chervonenko reports, which served only to reinforce preconceived ideas, the Soviet leaders believed the invasion would be merely a "surgical operation" which in a few hours' time would produce the liquidation of a "clique" of "renegade traitors" and the installation of a "worker and peasant" government. Indeed, the invasion troops, in good working order following the summer maneuvers and probably ready for the invasion for several months, rushed into Czechoslovakia with only a two days' supply of fuel and provisions.

In Prague the Soviet invasion, heralded by the letter written by "high officials," was supported primarily by members of the conservative bloc within the Central Committee of the Communist party Presidium and the state security service, the S.T.B., whose director, vice-minister of the interior Viliam Salgovic, was a Russian agent. Dubcek paid in just one night the price for not being tough enough during the eight months of the spring purification of vital government institutions.

Twenty-four hours before the Warsaw Pact armies stationed themselves along the borders of the Republic, Salgovic had already assigned tasks to his accomplices at the S.T.B. On August 20, 1968, at 4 P.M., in the regional management building of the S.T.B. on Bartolomejska Street, which was being closely guarded in order to avoid any indiscretions, Viliam Salgovic gave his orders. The second section was instructed to isolate both Western diplomatic institutions and the Rumanian and Yugoslavian embassies in order to prevent Czechoslovakian citizens from taking refuge in them. The seventh section was directed to take control of all means of communication, including radio and television. The group under Lieutenant Colonel Molnar assumed the heaviest responsibilities of the putsch: it paved the way directly for the invasion by assisting the Soviet

K.B.G. agents in the take-over of Ruzyne airport immediately after the planes landed and it led the Soviet troops and agents to the proper official buildings that they might kidnap the leaders.

While the secret police, aiding the enemy, planned its attack, the conservative bloc in the Presidium "amused the gallery" throughout the day of August 20 and the fatal night of the 21st. In these hours supposed crucial to the future of the party and the country, Indra and Kolder insisted on discussing the long-drawn-out report of a certain Kaspar, a conservative politician. The report, presented as a scientific attempt to analyze the situation in Czechoslovakia since the Bratislava agreements, was in fact an outlandish accusation of Dubcek and his staff. Red-eyed from lack of sleep, the progressives, inspired by Frantisek Kriegel, president of the National Front, blocked the scheme of Indra and Kolder to make a new majority of the ten members of the Presidium who staunchly backed Dubcek, with the votes of the conservatives and the undecided (Bilak, Svetska, Piller, Frantisek Barbirek, and Emil Rigo). This new "majority" would have called the Russians to the rescue and lent their putsch an appearance of legality. The lucidity of the progressives who anticipated the maneuver prevented the Dubcek group from becoming a minority. Undoubtedly this frustration of the cushion of legal pretext for invasion explains why the letter written by the "high party and government officials" was signed only by the backers of the plot and ultimately excluded from the arsenal of Kremlin propaganda.

[A Journey to Moscow]

Despite the perfectly organized treasons, the early take-over of the executive branches, and the introduction of an expeditionary force greater in number and more heavily armed than that of the Americans in Vietnam, the Soviet Union met with a complete political breakdown in forty-eight hours. The "worker and peasant" government could not be organized; the Soviet Union's most faithful ally had been transformed into an occupied and irredeemably hostile country. In the face of the mass uprising, even the initial plotters still deny their part: two years after the invasion, Bilak, Indra, and Kolder still remain a small group scorned even by their Soviet masters.

The great moments of this peaceful but determined seven-day resistance did not save the country but retrieved at least its honor and enabled the preservation of something from January, if only a brief respite.

The extraordinary exploits of the press, radio, and television journalists changed the course of events from the start. When the occupation troops and S.T.B. agents began taking over installations, the printing presses and the studios organized clandestine shifts and, improvising, gave a people who had become adult free access to information, which frustrated Soviet propaganda and political objectives.

By removing Dubcek and his principal collaborators and by isolating President Svoboda in his Hradschin castle, the occupants had hoped to interrupt all communication between the government leaders and thus to "legalize" their presence. After the failure of the worker and peasant government, they turned to the National Assembly, the only institution they permitted to function, probably because they hoped to find in this Assembly, whose members had not been renewed since the Novotny era, those blocs which had escaped them in the party presidium, the labor unions, and elsewhere. But on the morning of August 21 Deputy Polednak of the National Assembly succeeded in communicating with President Svoboda through the technical skill of a Hradschin telephone operator; he beseeched him not to yield to any blackmail and warned him of the determination of the National Assembly, which was to be convened in a plenary session, to vote on a resolution heartily condemning the invasion. Polednak's cleverness was repeated throughout the day. Other politicians, including the brilliant young law professor Zdenek Mlynar, the president of the judicial commission of the Central Committee, even succeeded in entering the presidential dwelling by presenting forged passes to Russian sentinels. The conversations they had permitted President Svoboda, to whom the Soviets had falsely announced the resignation of the Cernik government, to expel a delegation composed of Soviet Ambassador Chervonenko, Indra, and Ivan Pavlovsky, former Prague representative to Moscow who had come to present for his approval the list of a worker and peasant government which was to save the country.

At noon the free radio announced an hour-long general strike which was widely followed; an hour later it broadcast a statement from "those members of the government who had been able to meet freely," condemning the invasion and reasserting that they represented the only legality of the country.

At the ministry of the interior, Josef Pavel was taking the security service in hand and the pro-Soviet S.T.B. agents took flight, hunted down by the people, who had been warned by underground radio of the license-plate numbers of the cars with which they were to make their arrests.

The final blow dealt to Moscow was the rapidly called meeting of the Fourteenth Congress of the Czechoslovakian Communist party. Ignoring all the ambushes and roadblocks, nearly a thousand elected delegates met secretly in the C.K.D. factory in Vyscocany, a suburb of Prague. Guarded by the people's militia, those one-time neo-Stalinist groups, the Congress not only denied the supposed divisions in the party and in the working class but made them spearheads of resistance against the occupant. Since then and to this day, the struggle for democracy has become the affair of the workers, the same Czech and Slovak workers who had been so hard to convince during the feverish days of the spring.

As early as the second day of the occupation the Soviets had to bow to the facts. The evaluations based on information supplied by Chervonenko proved to be inexact. President Svoboda was refusing all contact with the Russian ambassador and all *missi dominici* sent by the Kremlin. On August 23 at 9 A.M. some Russian officers brought the Czechoslovakian chief of state to the Prague air terminal, where a special plane took him to Moscow.

In a remarkable series of articles Kremlinologist Pavel Tigrid,[2] relying on unpublished accounts whose accuracy, with the exception of a few minor details, was confirmed for me in Prague, has skillfully restored the film of President Svoboda's trip to Moscow, as well as the three tragic days prior to the signing of the veritable "dictate" which is the Moscow protocol. He also describes the arrival of the general, "hero of the Soviet Union": "The reception reserved for President Svoboda at Vnoukovo was grandiose, but once the Kremlin doors were closed behind him he watched his smiling hosts turn into wild beasts."

For an hour, despite the fatigue of the trip which, added to the tension of recent days, had physically exhausted this old man of seventy-three, Svoboda confronted the unruly mob with superhuman courage. He made it clear that he would not deal with them as long as the other members of the Presidium (Dubcek, Cernik, and Smrkovsky)[3] were not at his side. No threat could shake him; the tension was such that Svoboda broke an ashtray in his clenched hands. He then retired to a heavily guarded apartment in the Kremlin, telling his "hosts" that they could kill him, that at his age life was not so precious, but that he would not deal with them as long as he could not see his friends.

Throughout the day of August 23, the Politburo of the Soviet Communist party met without intermission. From time to time Brezhnev communicated with President Svoboda in letters which were alternately threatening and conciliatory. Toward the end of the afternoon Brezhnev, after several refusals, finally authorized Svoboda to phone his wife to give her news of his health: alarm was at that time spreading through Prague; Svoboda and the other members of the Presidium were already imagined shot down in the Caves of Lioubanka. It was good strategy to dispel these rumors. But once communication with the Prague château was assured by military line, Mrs. Svoboda begged her husband to stand firm.[4]

On the evening of August 23, the ousted Czechoslovakian leaders were escorted to Moscow. Taken under the threat of machine guns, made to separate, and some of them (Dubcek and Kriegel) severely beaten,[5] they were cordially welcomed by a Brezhnev who asked after their health. Dubcek and Cernik had hardly had time to restore themselves and change clothes when they realized that they were to "share a room"; Brezhnev and Kosygin were attempting the same isolation maneuver they had tried on Svoboda. Despite his state of near physical collapse, Dubcek refused to negotiate in the absence of Svoboda and the other members of the Presidium, repeating in turn that he would not betray the confidence of the people and that he was not concerned with his own fate.

The conversations were resumed in plenary session, on August 24, 25, and 26. At the outset President Svoboda had sent a radio message to Prague requesting that the two countries "not do anything that would make the Moscow conversations more delicate." The second day of the discussions, on the evening of August 25, a broken General Svoboda, influenced by Husak, the future secretary of the Slovak Communist party, who was already showing the first signs of "realism," opposed Dubcek and especially Smrkovsky, both of whom refused to sign the fifteen-point dictate proposed by the Russians. The Soviets pointed out that the Czechoslovakian delegation, whose composition was purely fortuitous, had no mandate to sign and that it had to submit the text to the government and the National Assembly.

This division was heavy with consequence. It now seems certain that, considering the impasse confronting the Soviets, they might have been more accommodating. Svoboda's attitude disarmed Dubcek and isolated Smrkovsky — decidedly the only strong man of the spring group — in a desperate refusal which the Soviets were to remember.

At midnight on August 26, the document called "Moscow Protocol" was signed by the Czechoslovakian delegation, which then was granted permission to return home but not without a final and painful incident. When they arrived at the airport, the Czechoslovakians saw that Kriegel was missing. They refused to take the plane. Several hours of bittersweet discussion were necessary before the "Jew from Galicia," who was undoubtedly being kept in reserve for a future "Zionist" trial à la Slansky, came to join them.

[The Curtain Falls]

The Czechoslovakian delegation returned to Prague in an atmosphere of sadness and discouragement, without fanfare, almost furtively, at dawn on August 27, after having signed as degrading a capitulation as President Hacha's at Berchtesgaden. With a thirty-year interval, this was for the Czech and Slovak peoples a new Munich.

The Moscow protocol, the fourteenth article of which stipulates that it, the protocol, will remain a state secret,[6] nevertheless gradually became known to the Czech people and the world; it still has not been published in Prague or Moscow. From the start, instinctively, the man in the street in Prague and Bratislava understood that the January victories were going to be eliminated. The Moscow ukase was going to destroy the internal democracy of the Communist party by making the Fourteenth Congress void; it would gradually reestablish censorship; it would impose the presence of occupation troops on Czech territory for an indefinite period until a problematic "normalization," left to the discretion of Moscow, was reestablished; it would align Prague unconditionally with Moscow's foreign policy; and it would brutally return the country to the Comecon and Warsaw Pact choker, reducing to dust all hope of an improvement of economic problems.

Pavel Tigrid quotes the account of one of the participants in the negotiations:

> We will always be able to ask ourselves if we really conducted the Moscow talks last August with the greatest effectiveness. For it is undeniable that we could have gotten much more out of the Russians than we finally did. For example, Brezhnev was obviously ready to bargain in regard to Bilak, Indra, and company: we could therefore have gotten something substantial in exchange for our agreement to Point 7 of the protocol,[7] an assurance of the permanent elimination of the conservatives. We certainly all realized that we would have to yield to Soviet demand number one — the presence of their army on our territory — but it should have been essential to know at what price. It is now clear that our initial concession was too modest, according to an old proverb so much a part of us which says that there are no small gains.

President Svoboda for his part justified his action at a meeting of the Central Committee of the Communist party in these terms:

Throughout this crisis I held to three principles. First of all at no price did I want to see blood spilling and bodies piling up. I also felt that the situation demanded a political solution which had as its condition the restoration of legal power. And finally I wanted the people to be able under the aegis of the party to continue the policy inaugurated in January. Our Soviet comrades will therefore not intervene in our internal affairs. I am giving you an account, Comrades, of what I had undertaken to do, not as president of the Republic but more as one who above all wanted our party to keep a spotless image.[8]

The little gleaned from Dubcek's confessions indicates a pathetic candor and incurable optimism. Understanding and confidence are still the key words of his public statements — words which signify that in the end "they" will understand, in the end "they" will have confidence in us, the Czechoslovakians. After the Moscow protocols Dubcek and Svoboda ceased being heros and became martyrs.

Confidence and understanding were once again to be put to the test during further discussions in Moscow on October 2, 1968. The Soviets did not make the slightest concession but rather showered the Czechoslovakian delegation (Dubcek, Cernik, and Husak) with bitter reproaches: the "counterrevolutionary" forces would once again raise their head; the press, radio, and television were continuing to denigrate the Soviet Union and authentic communism; the party had not yet been "purified" etc. . . . Another session of the Presidium took place upon the return of the delegation in the middle of the night. Even Husak, beaten and discouraged by Soviet intransigence, had come around.

This night and the following day rumors of Dubcek's resignation spread throughout the country, inspiring further panic in a population which had already suffered so greatly and causing a few thousand additional intellectuals to seek exile. But Dubcek did not resign. He was to drink the cup of sorrow to the dregs. On October 18, 1968, the "pact on the temporary stationing of Soviet troops" was ratified, after government approval, by the National Assembly in a funereal atmosphere. The pact finally legalized what a statement from the Socialist Republic of Czechoslovakia had termed, on August 21, 1968, "an act of aggression perpetrated for the first time in the history of the international communist movement by the allied armies of the socialist countries against *a state controlled by the Communist party.*" The outcome was unanimous, with the exception of three votes: that of a woman deputy who was so moved she could hardly be heard; that of the courageous Frantisek Kriegel, the "Galician Jew" who refused exile despite the pleas of Dubcek, who, it is said, still fears for Kriegel's security and his life; and, finally, that of old Frantisek Vodslon, who had previously been the first to rise against Novotny's dictatorship prior to the Prague spring. Amid world indifference, the curtain had just fallen on the most tragic chapter of European history since the end of World War II.

Notes for Chapter 5

1. See the study by Lawrence L. Whetten, "Military Aspects of the Soviet Occupation of Czechoslovakia," *The World Today* (February 1969).
2. "Entre Prague et Moscou," *Le Monde* (March 24–26, 1969).
3. Faced with the fervent anti-Semitism of the Soviets, who hurled insults at Frantisek Kriegel, calling him a Galician Jew and a Zionist, he did not insist on the presence of the president of the National Front at the negotiations, but he did demand guarantees for his security.
4. An anonymous leaflet distributed the next day in Prague gives this dramatic version of Mrs. Svoboda's appeal: "They're shooting here in Prague; it's a blood bath, but the people are with you. Ludvik, don't be afraid, don't give in an inch. Everyone loves you but it all depends on you now and you must help us!"
5. When he first appeared in public in Prague, Dubcek had a large bandage on his head.
6. See the text of the protocol in the appendix to this chapter.
7. No sanctions against those who collaborated with the Soviets at the time of the invasion.
8. From the minutes of the meeting.

Appendix

Proclamation by the Government of Czechoslovakia to All Czechoslovakian People . . . August 21, 1968 — Proclamation of the Special Meeting of the Fourteenth Congress of the Czechoslovakian Communist Party to the Citizens of Czechoslovakia . . . August 23, 1968 — The Protocol from Moscow . . . August 26, 1968 — The November Resolution of the Central Committee . . . November 14–17, 1968

[Proclamation by the Government of Czechoslovakia to All Czechoslovakian People . . . August 21, 1968]

This proclamation was circulated by radio broadcast and leaflets.

Czechoslovakia has been occupied by five Warsaw Pact nations against the wishes of its government, its National Assembly, the leadership of the Czechoslovakian Communist party, and its people.

For the first time in the history of the international communist movement, allied armies of socialist countries have perpetrated an act of aggression against a country directed by the Communist party.

The crisis began in the early morning hours. The functioning of the Republic's constitutional organs has been disrupted: the members of the government, the National Assembly, the Czechoslovakian Communist party leadership, the National Front, and other organizations can establish no agreement with one another nor can they communicate with this country's population, which these past months has so spontaneously demonstrated its confidence.

Numerous members of the government and the party leadership, officials of the National Assembly, and others have been interned; the only channel of liaison and communication remaining is the semiclandestine Czechoslovakian radio, which is itself gradually being silenced in spite of the extraordinary efforts of its workers.

Even under these circumstances the government and the Czechoslovakian constitutional organs, as well as the party leadership, wish to insure the normal life of our country, to exercise the duties for which they have been elected.

We address you, Czechs, Slovaks, members of national minority groups, all citizens of the Czechoslovakian Republic:

1. We demand the immediate departure of the troops of the five Warsaw Pact countries, adherence to the terms of this Pact, and full respect of the sovereignty of the state of Czechoslovakia.

2. We urgently request that the governments of the U.S.S.R., Poland, Hungary, Bulgaria, and East Germany order the cessation of the armed operations which are causing bloodshed and destroying the material well-being of our country.

3. We demand the restoration of the normal working conditions of Czechoslovakian constitutional and political organs and the release of the various members of these organizations in order that they may resume their functions.

4. We request the immediate convocation of the entire National Assembly, in the presence of which the complete Czechoslovakian government would consider the solution to the current situation.

To all citizens:

We ask you above all to support these government demands

1. By upholding, as you have so often in the past, the infallible wisdom of the state and by uniting your forces around the duly elected Czechoslovakian government, to which you have given your support.

2. By refusing to tolerate the installation at the head of our Republic of any government other than one elected under those free and democratic conditions which maintain the principles of our constitution.

3. By asking the personnel of our factories, agricultural cooperatives, and other places of work to address to the commanders of the occupation units and to the governments of the five Warsaw Pact countries declarations supporting the views of the Czechoslovakian government.

4. By creating conditions permitting the maintenance of order; by abstaining from any spontaneous action against the members of the occupation troops; by insuring through your own means the indispensable supply of food, water, gas, electricity, to the population in every region; by providing for the defense of factories and important installations; and by averting any further economic loss.

Dear fellow citizens!

These are difficult moments for us. Only the people can insure the happiness of this country in which they live and work.

We are convinced that in these times you are giving your

full support to your government and to the service of our socialist Republic.

Citizens!

It is still in our power to bring about, with your help, the great rebirth which we undertook in January. The government believes firmly that with your help it will succeed in bringing it about without bloodshed, without needless sacrifice.

[Proclamation of the Special Meeting of the Fourteenth Congress of the Czechoslovakian Communist Party to the Citizens of Czechoslovakia . . . August 23, 1968]

Comrades and Citizens of Czechoslovakia:

Today, August 22, 1968, the special congress of the Czechoslovakian Communist party convened. It adopted the following introductory proclamation.

Czechoslovakia is a sovereign and free state, founded on the will and support of its people. However, its sovereignty has been violated; on August 21, 1968, its territory was occupied by troops from the U.S.S.R., Poland, the German Democratic Republic, Bulgaria, and Hungary.

Some try to justify this act by saying that socialism was being threatened and claiming that this intervention was called for by some of the Czech leaders. However, as it was disclosed in yesterday's declaration by the Central Committee of the Czechoslovakian Communist party, in the second radio broadcast of the president of the Republic, in the joint declaration of the National Assembly and government of the Republic, and in the proclamation of the president of the National Front, not one qualified constitutional or party organization has asked for this intervention.

There was no counterrevolution in Czechoslovakia; its socialist evolution was not threatened. The people and the party were fully capable of solving any problem; witness the immense confidence enjoyed by the new party leadership headed by Dubcek. Moreover, the fundamental ideas of Marx and Lenin on the evolution of socialist democracy were being carried out. Nor had Czechoslovakia violated its agreements with and obligations to its allies; and as for the future it had not the least interest in modifying the friendly relations with the other states and peoples of the socialist countries. Nevertheless, these relations were violated by the troops of the occupying countries.

Czechoslovakian sovereignty, along with the provisions of the Warsaw Pact and the Cierna and Bratislava agreements, was trampled underfoot. Government and party officials were illegally arrested, isolated from the people, and deprived of the possibility of exercising their powers; many official government buildings were occupied. Grave injustices were committed.

The Congress expressly demands that there be created immediately the conditions necessary to the resumption of the activity of all constitutional and political organizations, demands that the detained workers be freed without delay.

In this crisis, unity of the people, the unity of our nations, and loyalty to our party become most urgent. Even after this armed intervention, the Czechoslovakian people have not ceased to be the sole legitimate and sovereign leader of the country. The defense of freedom in this socialist country is the concern not only of its communists but of all Czechs and Slovaks, members of national minorities, workers, peasants, and intellectuals, of youth, of all those who desire a dignified and free life for our socialist country. Communists can fulfill their leadership role only by becoming as devoted as possible to achieving the departure of the foreign troops. They can accomplish this goal only in closest union with all patriots and with all active democratic forces of our society.

The situation created in our country on August 21 cannot

endure. Socialist Czechoslovakia will never accept administration by either military occupation or an indigenous collaboration force supported by the occupation powers.

The special Fourteenth Congress of the party proclaims that it recognizes only the constitutionally elected leaders of the country: the president of the Republic, Ludvik Svoboda; the president of the National Assembly, Josef Smrkovsky; the president of the government, Oldrich Cernik; and others, just as it recognizes only Alexander Dubcek as the leader of the party. It does not recognize as party members those of the current Central Committee who have not resisted in these difficult times. Fundamental is the demand for the departure of foreign troops. If the demands are not satisfied, particularly if negotiations for the departure of the troops are not begun with our free leaders within twenty-four hours, and if Comrade Dubcek does not make a proclamation to the nation in time, Congress invites all workers to stage on Friday, August 23, at 12 A.M. a Communist-led protest strike lasting one hour. If the demands are refused, the Congress has decided to take further unavoidable measures and, following the election of the Central Committee, to entrust this newly elected body, the sole legal representative of the party, with the execution of these measures.

The Congress addresses itself to all communists and to all citizens and asks them to continue to insure calm, order, and discipline, to refrain from acts which could lead to grave consequences for this country and its citizens.

The Congress charges all party agencies and organizations with the full execution of this decision.

[The Protocol from Moscow . . . August 26, 1968]

The protocol was signed by the members of the Politburo of the Soviet Communist party and by the members of the Presidium of the Czechoslovakian Communist party.

During the course of the meetings, questions related to the defense of the conquests of socialism were dealt with, and also taken into consideration was the situation which had developed in Czechoslovakia, as well as the priorities of measures called for by this situation and by the stationing of allied troops on Czechoslovakian territory. In keeping with the universally recognized standards concerning relations between socialist parties and countries, and in accord with the principles agreed upon in advisory documents from Cierna nad Tisou and Bratislava, the two parties reaffirmed the mutual bonds among socialist countries, the goal of which is to maintain, consolidate, and defend socialism and to combat without mercy counterrevolutionary forces — these constituting the international responsibilities shared by all socialist countries. Further, the two parties maintained with determination that, in the present situation, their major task was the concrete and effective realization of the principles and obligations resulting from the conference of Bratislava and from the agreements reached at Cierna nad Tisou.

The Presidium of the Central Committee of the Czechoslovakian Communist party declared that the independent Fourteenth Congress of the Communist party, which reconvened on August 22 of this year without the Central Committee's authorization, represented a violation of the statutes of the party. This congress, having continued without the participation of the members and secretaries of the Presidium, without the secretaries of the Central Committee of the Slavic Communist party, as well as without the majority of military and numerous other delegates, is to be considered meaningless. Upon its return to Czechoslovakia the Presidium of the Central Committee of the Czechoslovakian Communist party will take the measures appropriate to this subject. A special congress will be called after the situation in the party and in the country has returned to normal.

The delegation of the Czechoslovakian Communist party announced that the plenum of the Central Committee of the party will reconvene within the next six to ten days, along with the participation of the Control and Revision Commission of the party. The purpose of this session will be to evaluate the normalization process within the country, to take measures conducive to the improvement of the function of party and state organizations, to examine the economic and standard-of-living issues, to consolidate on all levels the visible workings of the party and of the state, and to free from these organizations the persons whose present activities no longer conform to the imperative of strengthening the directive role of the working class and of the Communist party. This plenum will, in addition, implement the resolutions adopted in the January and May [1968] sessions, which are concerned with the consolidation of the positions of socialism with the country and with the development of external relations between Czechoslovakia and the other countries of the socialist community.

The representatives of the Czechoslovakian Communist party affirmed the necessity of a rapid implementation of a whole series of measures aimed at reinforcing the socialism and the government of the workers, notably in the area of priority measures to control the information media so that they might fully serve the cause of socialism and end the antisocialist manifestations on radio, on television, and at the heart of certain organizations which have assumed distinctly antisocialist positions. The resurgent activities of the social democratic, anti-Marxist party are not to be tolerated. All appropriate measures will be taken in the interest of effective realization of these objectives. The party and state organizations will supervise the coverage of the situation in the press, on the radio, and on television by means of new laws and ordinances. In view of the abnormal situation, the execution of these plans will impose certain temporary measures so that the government might repress without hindrance all antisocialist, individual, or collective forms of interference. A reform of the guiding structures of the press, of radio, and of television has emerged as inevitable. As at Cierna, the representatives of the Soviet Communist party have now reaffirmed their full support of such measures which correspond equally to the fundamental interests of the socialist community, its security, and its unity.

Both delegations dealt with the question concerning the presence of troops from socialist countries and notably have made clear the common agreement that such troops will not interfere with Czechoslovakia's internal affairs. As the impinging menace to socialism in Czechoslovakia and to the security of the socialist community is being dissolved, the allied armies will be withdrawn in stages from Czechoslovakian territory. The commander of the allied troops will immediately confer with a representative of the Czechoslovakian army on the tactics of withdrawal and about the new quarters of the united allies in the villages and rural districts where the local authorities will be in a position to guarantee public order. The distribution of allied forces will take place in the barracks, on the training fields, and at other military sites. The problem of security along the West German border will be given special attention. The number of men on active duty, their organization, and their relocation within the country will be determined in collaboration with the representatives of the Czechoslovakian army. Questions in the spheres of supplies, methods, and sanitation, as well as other problems pertaining to the provisional troops in Czechoslovakia, will be settled by means of separate agreements from the ministers of the departments of defense and foreign affairs. The examination of fundamental areas of litigation will be left to the respective governments. The conditions of stationing and withdrawal of the allies will be set by agreements between the Czechoslovakian government and the governments of other involved countries.

The Presidium of the Central Committee of the Czechoslovakian Communist party and the government will adopt, with reference to the press, radio, and television media, all measures conducive to eliminating from the start the possibilities of conflict between the allied troops and the Czechoslovakian population.

The representatives of the Czechoslovakian Communist party have declared that they will not allow any exercise of sanctions, much less any acts of violence, in the encounter with the officers or representatives of the party who have fought for the consolidation of the socialist positions, against the antisocialist forces, and who have been in favor of friendly relations with the Soviet Union.

An agreement has been reached on the subject of the different committee members who must soon reveal their thoughts on the numerous questions concerning economic order, with the intention of enlarging and intensifying economic, scientific, and technical collaboration between the U.S.S.R. and Czechoslovakia, especially in the areas that concern the external needs of the national economy, so that the plan of economic development conforming to the resolutions of the Central Committee of the Czechoslovakian Communist party might be implemented.

Complete unity of views has led to the judgment that both the economic evolution of the international situation and the aggressive schemes of the imperialists, contrary to the peace and security of nations and contrary to socialism, demand constant reinforcement and increased activation of the defensive system of the Warsaw Pact, as well as of the other organizations and forms of cooperation among socialist countries.

The leaders of the Soviet and Czechoslovakian Communist parties confirmed their determination to scrupulously respect the principle of coordinating their activities in the area of international relations, with the aim of reinforcing the unity of the socialist community, peace, and international security. The U.S.S.R. and Czechoslovakia will pursue, in European affairs, the policies which they have practiced up to now and which correspond to the particular and common interests of the socialist countries, as well as to those of European security; they will resolutely oppose the militaristic, anti-Soviet, and neo-nationalistic forces whose policies aim at revising the results of the second world war and the boundaries which presently exist in Europe. The two parties have firmly declared their determination to fulfill all the obligations which stem from the bilateral and multilateral agreements among the socialist countries. They will pursue, in close collaboration with the other countries of the socialist community, their battle against the aggressive schemes of imperialism and will support the movements of national liberation and will work for the relaxation of international tensions.

Concerning the topic of the supposed Czechoslovakian affair at the Security Council of the United Nations, the directors of the Czechoslovakian Communist party stated that their country had never asked the Security Council to deal with this question. The representatives of the Czechoslovakian Communist party added that their government had instructed the Czechoslovakian delegation at New York to categorically protest the discussion of the Czechoslovakian affair both in the Security Council and in the other organizations of the United Nations and that the government had firmly insisted that the point be withdrawn from the day's agenda.

Invasion

The Presidium of the Central Committee of the Czechoslovakian Communist party and the government have declared that they will investigate the attitudes of its officials who, finding themselves abroad, have taken a position in the name of the government of the Czechoslovakian Socialist Republic on domestic and foreign questions, especially concerning the execution of the policies of the Communist party and of the government of the Republic. Appropriate measures will be taken in light of the results of this investigation. In this area, the representatives of the Central Committee of the Czechoslovakian Communist party deem it necessary to bring forth new, structural changes at the heart of different organizations of the party and of the state in the interest of the general solidification of the situation within the party and within the country. These questions will be studied from all aspects upon the return of the delegation to Czechoslovakia. Similarly, there will also be a profound investigation of the activities of the department of the interior, the results of which will determine the measures to be taken proper to the strengthening of the direction of this office.

The two parties mutually agreed to soon begin bilateral encounters, between the delegations of the two parties and governments, the aims of which would be to examine in detail and to resolve the problems arising from mutual relations, as well as to discuss current international issues.

The two delegations reached a common agreement, in the interest of the two Communist parties and in the interest of Soviet-Czechoslovakian friendship, to consider all contacts between the representatives of the Czechoslovakian and Soviet Communist parties after August 20, 1968, as strictly confidential. The discussions which have just been terminated are consequently covered by this agreement.

The two parties have both committed themselves, in the name of their respective parties and governments, to implement all the efforts of the two parties and governments in order to intensify the traditional friendship between the people of the two states and their fraternal friendship forever.

[The November Resolution of the Central Committee . . . November 14–17, 1968]

These are the conclusions of the resolution of the plenary session of the Central Committee of the Communist party of Czechoslovakia. The text of this resolution is ambiguous enough so that the progressives as well as the neo-Stalinists can both claim it, the former in the name of the post-January political policy, the latter in the name of realism, normalization, and submission to Soviet demands.

After critical examination of the evolution of party policy in recent years, including the period after January 1968; after examining the present condition of society and of the party; and after specifying the principal tasks of the coming period, the Central Committee of the Czechoslovakian Communist party considers as a major objective the unification of the party in its entirety along the positive lines of the post-January political policy.

The principal task of the Czechoslovakian Communist party, of its branches and organizations, is to reinforce and multilaterally to develop socialism in Czechoslovakia: to develop the economy and the defense capacity of the Czechoslovakian Socialist Republic, to strengthen the mutual struggle of the socialist camp against international imperialism, and to insure the leadership of the Czechoslovakian Communist party throughout the political system by developing social democracy.

The Central Committee of the Czechoslovakian Communist party and all party branches and organizations must strive for a unity within the party regarding Marxist-Leninist principles.

At the present time the Central Committee of the Czechoslovakian Communist party especially stresses the application of the principles of democratic centralism, party discipline, and responsibility. There will be no support of the activity of any group which violates the Leninist principles of the work of the party or which strives to impose its own political policy outside the party.

On the basis of the analysis of the preceding period, the party will firmly oppose all opportunistic and rightist tendencies. It will also act on sectarian and dogmatic tendencies.

The Central Committee of the Czechoslovakian Communist party considers it indispensable to consolidate the leadership role of the party, to strengthen its functions of initiative, organization, criticism, and control throughout the political system, and to require that those communists who fail to carry out, elude, or violate the decisions adopted by the party, as well as those who repress democracy within the party, be held responsible before the party.

The Central Committee of the Czechoslovakian Communist party fully supports all the decisions and documents of the January plenary session and under no circumstances will permit a repetition of the violation of socialist legality or the deviations which have gravely compromised socialism. It will pursue the righting of wrongs toward communists and other citizens.

With regard to the economic domain and state agencies, mass organizations, and organizations making up the National Front, in all forms and at all levels of leadership within party organs and the components of the central council of the trade unions, the Central Committee of the Czechoslovakian Communist party deems it indispensable that they return to their own programs of action and that they verify the execution of these programs and note their results.

Communists will work actively and with initiative in the National Front and in mass organizations, thus contributing, in the interest of the workers, to the accomplishment of their tasks and to the strengthening of the leadership role of the party within the political system of the National Front.

The Central Committee of the Czechoslovakian Communist party fully upholds the principles contained in the resolutions on the Moscow discussions of August 26, 1968, and in the communiqué on the discussions between the Communist party of the Soviet Union and the Czechoslovakian Communist party of October 3 and 4, as well as the principles of the six-sided Bratislava declaration of August 4, 1968. It stresses the responsibility of all communists, particularly on the national level, for the practical realization of the principles stated in these documents.

The Central Committee of the Czechoslovakian Communist party invites all communists to consider as the principal strength of the party its alliance with the socialist forces of both nations and to constantly and effectively act on any attempt at provocation or abuse of the national viewpoint of workers which is not in the interest of sovereignty, socialist democracy, or the entire post-January political policy in our country. Every Communist should be the guardian of party unity, legality, the constitutionality of our development, and the close union of the party with the people. However, the Czechoslovakian Communist party will not permit anyone to oppose, contrary to party rules, the political policy of the party. Nor will it permit the organization of pressure groups, provocation, publication of political propaganda, mass distribution of resolutions, or the like. It is the duty of all communists to conduct a campaign to this effect in all sectors, in every place of work, in cities, districts, regions, and within national or federal organs.

The Central Committee of the Czechoslovakian Communist party, having at interest the peaceful future development of our country, intends that this resolution, which will unite the healthy forces of the party, should motivate the activity of all state, economic, and mass agencies and organizations and that of every citizen of our Czechoslovakian Socialist Republic.

The Czechoslovakian Communist party is capable of creating the conditions necessary to general development and initiative, to application of the capacities and creative forces of all workers and of every citizen willing to work for the edification of socialism and the well-being of our socialist country.

II.

Heritage and Hope

Notes on the Prisons, the Peoples, and the Problems of the Future

1

Nightmare

Ruzyne — Kolodeje — "Report on the Violations" — *Deportation Journal* — Jachimov — Reading the Statistics — Remember . . . — The Shadow of the Terror

[Ruzyne]

On the minithruway that leads to the Prague airport, an exit sign points to Ruzyne, a petit bourgeois section of apartments, villas, and gardens. Families of pilots and employees of C.S.A. — the Czechoslovak Airline Company — live in Ruzyne. In the midst of this complex rises the "model" prison of the socialist bloc. The twelve-story building boasts a thousand cells.

In 1949 Soviet experts came to help local architects; Beria's men came to help "interrogators" of the Czech police. Later a *Manual for the Interrogator* was generously distributed. The most refined methods of torture, developed by experts at Lubianka prison, were to be zealously applied. Indeed, the cells, or rather the caverns on the five underground floors, were themselves instruments of torture; their inmates could only crouch. The cells on the seven upper stories were more reasonable.

An economist, Dr. N., described an "ordinary" cell into which he moved in 1953:

> I was in a space four meters square. In one corner stood a Turkish-style toilet; built against the wall were a little table, a stool, a bed. One could use the table and the stool only during meals and the bed only at bedtime. The rest of the time they were folded back against the wall. From five in the morning to nine in the evening, I had to pace the cell — four steps in one direction, four in the other. We were constantly watched through the Judas window and cursed even if we stopped to attend to natural needs.
>
> Twenty-four hours a day a powerful light shone in the cell. In any case one could not have enjoyed the six hours of sleep theoretically possible. We had to keep our hands flat on top of the covers. If we didn't, we were cursed or struck. The fear of unconsciously putting my hands against my body, especially in winter when the cold in the cell was unbearable, made me so anxious in the beginning that I could not close my eyes. Every ten or fifteen minutes — thirty times and more a night — the guard knocked at the door. I had to jump to attention and recite: "Prisoner Number X reporting: the prisoner is in his cell, nothing to report." From the other side of the door the guard repeated this litany which echoed down the corridors. I was finally in such a state of exhaustion that between each "report" I did fall asleep. When knocks on the door and shouts didn't waken me, the guard would enter and brutally rouse me.

When it was not lack of sleep, it was hunger that tortured the prisoners of Ruzyne. The interrogators purposely prolonged their sessions into the meal hours. When they released the prisoner, he returned to his cell to be told by the guard that it was too late to eat.

Preventive detention at Ruzyne could last for months, years. Eugen Loebl was held secretly for three years before coming to trial.

In *The Age of Distortions*,[1] the first book which appeared during the thaw, Loebl describes his first weeks of detention:

> Tortured by hunger, brutally dragged from the depths of sleep, and always standing on feet squeezed into stiff leather boots, I was ever prey to unbearable physical torture.
>
> At the end of two or three weeks I had swollen feet; my entire body had become very sensitive: to get up was anguish; I suffered horribly with each step. Interrogation — during which three policemen relayed each other — consisted of an endless succession of insults, obscenities, and threats. Sometimes I had to stand all day with my face to the wall. I was exhausted by the endless repetition of the same questions. If interrogation brought no results, the detainee was sent to the "fridge," confined to his cell all day long. There I was tormented by a deep boredom. I could never sit down. I ate my meals standing. I stood to use the Turkish toilet. I walked sixteen hours a day and even walking very slowly averaged twenty or thirty kilometers on swollen feet. Days dragged out in an endless wait for evenings. But once in bed I suffered the change of position of my stiffened legs, and it often made me cry out in pain. The regularly timed "report" exacerbated physical and nervous suffering.

One must add to this nightmare of individual suffering the atmosphere of communal anguish in which the prisoners lived.

The building was not — by design — soundproof. All day and all night one was haunted by the screams of the men and women being interrogated, the shouts of the torturers and guards. "Drugs" and "scientific conditioning" complemented beatings. Loebl, speaking of the drugs that were added to prisoners' food and water, said he believed he was going mad: "It was worse than the fear of losing one's life. I finally cursed the providence that commuted my death sentence to perpetual detention . . ."

[Kolodeje]

One of the high dignitaries of the Slovak Communist party accused of "nationalism," Gustav Husak, described the procedure of the political police in the castle of Kolodeje, near Prague, where he was held during the first months of his imprisonment:

> The interrogated prisoner, in his underwear, was left in a room at a temperature of minus twenty degrees. After a time, dressed very warmly, he was transferred to a higher floor and a windowless room whose ceiling and walls were completely wallpapered; there the temperature was forty degrees. The victim soon lost all sense of space and began to feel that the walls and ceiling were moving toward him and threatening to crush him. The interrogators, who entered by a door concealed in the wall, wore only shorts and light shirts and relieved each other every five or ten minutes. At the end of thirty or forty of these sittings the prisoner would sign a confession prepared in advance.[2]

["Report on the Violations"]

Infamous moral blackmail was added to physical torture. Anything and everything became a weapon: family, fatherland, party. In the "Report of the Central Committee of the Czechoslovakian Communist Party on the Violations of Party Principles and of the Socialist Legality in the Era of the Cult of Personality," [3] a highly confidential and fairly sugar-coated report which Anton Novotny must have read on April 3 and 4, 1963, these practices were described as follows:

> Certain victims report that the moral torture was perhaps worse than the physical torture. In principle there were two methods of persuasion employed by the security police. According to the first, the victims were told that if they confessed, their families would be spared — otherwise, no one could guarantee what would happen to them. In reality only the cruelest treatment was reserved for the parents, wives, and children of the accused — even before the trial. They were driven from their homes and lodged in abandoned slums. The children were not allowed to go to school. All were refused many of the medical services. None could earn even a meager pittance. The second method was reserved for formerly high functionaries of the party: they were given to understand that everybody, including the leaders, knew the accusations to be fabricated. However, in the intensified class struggle the party needed the confession of hideous crimes committed "against socialism." The accused should admit to having committed them; the accused could render a great service to the party. In return they could hope for a lighter sentence.

And Loebl reported: "Thus, added to the brutalities of the guards were the sensations of innocence and of absolute powerlessness and, perhaps the worst, the knowledge that one was victim of one's own party, for which one had lived, and to which one had sacrificed everything."

[Deportation Journal]

In his *Deportation Journal* [4] the writer Jiri Mucha described those

little sterile cubical cells — like test tubes — where the detained awaited trial. The detainees waited. They were embryos in glass jars. They were fed just enough to permit their bodies to function. Ten, a hundred, a thousand embryos, tagged and dated. In silence they waited. For what? Birth? Death? In their gray uniforms the dead marched silently in the corridors, like blind men . . .

Today a political prisoner occupies the lowest rank in the hierarchy of beings. Preventive detention is such a horror that each awaits the moment of judgment as one of the most beautiful days of his life.

The breakdown of the prisoner's nerves was not the only aim of solitary confinement. It permitted the comedy of confession to be played out with maniacal precision:

When a man has himself gone through the experience of a grand trial, he reads the accounts of others like a chessplayer following a game in progress. Only a connoisseur can appreciate the difficulty there is in rehearsing a role as demanding as that of the accused, can know the exactitude which must be brought to the art of making the depositions agree with one another, of adjusting them all like clockwork. People say they cannot understand how these confessions can flow so freely, be so neatly formulated. As if the ones who confessed cared. Their fate is decided. All they can hope for now is to play their parts without mistakes, in order not to make things any worse for others. And there is always a hope; therein lies the mystery of the trials. The rehearsals are played out to the accompaniment of good food, American cigarettes, well-pressed clothing, the carefully knotted tie — the kind of care taken of a film star shooting a key scene. Every theater should rehearse its performances so seriously.

[Jachimov]

The caverns of Ruzyne were walled up after the thaw by order of one of their former residents, the minister of the interior, Josef Pavel, and Ruzyne was made a really model prison for common-law prisoners tended by psychologists and social workers. Its past is as unrecognizable as that of the discontinued uranium mine of Jachimov. In this little watering place in northern Bohemia, it is almost impossible to imagine that tens of thousands endured one of the most terrible concentration camps since Hitler. Jachimov is one long street which climbs interminably. At the bottom of the street a gigantic hotel houses patients enjoying thermal baths of radioactive water taken from the mine. The mine lies above on the flank of the mountain. A half-dozen gloomy-looking workers keep up its kilometers of tunnels, now occupied only by awkward tourists, vaguely nervous in their borrowed equipment — plastic helmet, yellow overalls, and miner's lamp.

But as the thick walls of Ruzyne disguised "scientific" cells, so in Jachimov the simple concrete building covering the cages of two elevators, the admissions barracks, and the mountain dotted with peacefully grazing cows scarcely permit one to imagine the hell of the uranium mines. The smallest traces of a concentration camp had been effaced. The last detainees' barracks, hidden in the mountain and invisible from the road, had been torn down after the thaw. The brochure distributed among tourists contained no allusion to the camps. The guides discouraged questions. The waiter in the Jachimov restaurant and the natives in the streets had lost their memories. Was this a spontaneous conspiracy of silence among the inhabitants of a little town ashamed of its past, or official instruction? It makes no difference for the tens of thousands of Czechoslovakians who went through Jachimov.

Jiri Mucha was a miner for several years and then a nurse at Jachimov. On the tablecloth of the restaurant where we dined he drew for me the rolls of barbed wire which began at the entrance to the mine, climbed the flanks of the mountain, branched out, and reached the twenty camps where the detainees stayed at night: "It was like the circus passageways which lead the lions from their wagons to the cages where the tamers work with them."

For a space of nearly a hundred square kilometers, the top of the mountain was illuminated all night from control towers: "Jachimov at night was as beautiful as New York from an airplane. Everything was lit up; the camps with their two-story barracks seemed to be great cities. Loudspeakers woke us with music at five in the morning. We gathered shivering under the howling wind and the mangled music of Beethoven's *Eroica*."

The concentration-camp rule at Jachimov was both fierce and capricious. The guards did not systematically beat the detainees, but absurd rules caused the loss of numbers of human lives: "After 9 P.M. they fired on us like rabbits if we left the barracks. To go to the toilet — you had to go forty meters — became a dangerous game. Every night was punctuated with

machine-gun fire . . . Our guards were haunted by the thought
of a revolt. They read and reread to us the Byzantine rules
which were nearly impossible to follow to the letter. We had
to walk in groups of five abreast in the corridors of barbed
wire. The guards ran outside the barbed wire on either side
with their machine guns and their dogs; the smallest break or
irregularity in the line was treated as an insurrection. The
guards fired, wounded, and killed."

Most of the losses among the detainees of Jachimov were
caused by the inhuman working conditions in the mine. Without helmets, driven at a breakneck pace — in five years the
frenetic overexploitation of Jachimov by Soviet engineers was
to despoil mines with fifty years of reserves — the prisoners followed the uranium-bearing vein by hollowing out chimneys
which sometimes were fifty meters high. The smallest rockfall
fractured their skulls.

Mucha continued: "During the time I was a nurse, I treated
serious injuries and saw dead men every day. When I first
started the job, the infirmary possessed one pair of scissors, a
little box of sulfanilamide, and some absorbent cotton. A team
of dynamiters had calculated badly. I had on my hands a dead
man who was brought to me in pieces, one fellow who, scarcely
better off, was riddled with a hundred wounds, and three other
seriously wounded men."

L. T. was sixty years old. He was a rare bird. A veteran of the
International Brigades, he not only was one of the old-timers
of Jachimov, but he had previously known Nazi concentration
camps and Soviet "solitary confinement" in Siberia. To this
"expert" the Czech concentration-camp system astutely combined the sadism and *Gründlichkeit* of the Germans with the
capricious brutality of the Soviet convict gangs: "But thank
God there is a Schweik sleeping in the heart of every Czech,
even when he is a concentration-camp guard."

For Jiri Mucha too the regime that had been so rigid in the beginning degenerated into a Schweikade: "Where I was interned the detainees were already being paid and earned a good deal of money — sometimes much more than their guards. Vodka transformed us into one big happy family."

[Reading the Statistics]

Ruzyne and Jachimov are symbols, fairly well known names. But no one in the West has ever had any idea of the real dimensions, the horror, of the Czechoslovakian concentration camps. Little Czechoslovakia was the best disciple of its Soviet Big Brother: Club 231[5] held a reunion of victims of the age of distortions; more than 150,000, or 1 percent of the population, women and children included, attended. Official statistics gave the figure as 130,000 persons condemned since 1948, of which 50,000 were sentenced to more than ten years of prison and forced labor. The network of prisons and of T.N.P. ("obligatory work camps") covered the entire surface of the country. Around the black star of Ruzyne, the central interrogation prison, detainees collected at Pankrac, the historic prison of Prague, at Mirov in Moravia, at Bory, Valdice, in Bohemia, and even in the old fortress of Leopoldov in Slovakia. Although Jachimov, with its twenty satellite camps, took the doubtful honor of publicity, more than fifty other T.N.P.'s were clustered throughout the Republic, especially around mines — Pribam (uranium) and Kladno (coal),[6] both quite near Prague, Rtyn-Tmarydul (lignite) in Bohemia, and others.

The social composition of the detainees is indicative of the destruction of the economy of a developed and prosperous country within two decades: nearly 50 percent peasants, 30 percent government workers and intellectuals, 15 percent laborers, and 5 percent various occupations.[7]

The curve of arrests and its fluctuations from 1948 to 1960 is instructive. The communist takeover in 1948 is represented by a wave of arrests of the soldiers and officers (3,000 to 4,000) who fought in Western Europe under the orders of Benes' "government in exile." A great number of these married Western women; the wives were brutally expelled. The "Westerners" later could pursue their quarrels with their opposite numbers on the Eastern front — the troops which fought in the ranks of the Soviet army under the orders of General Svoboda. The "Easterners" were accused of failing to fight until after the denunciation of the Nazi-Soviet pact.

Arrests reached their height in the years from 1950 to 1953, when the conflicts between Russian demands and the existing social structures became acute in all areas (forced collectivization of land, consolidation to the profit of heavy industry and the destruction of light industry, constrainment of the intellectuals and artists). The "great trials" were nightmarish carbon copies of the trials of the 1930's in the U.S.S.R. The practice of "amalgamation" permitted the mass hanging on December 3, 1952, of eleven condemned men, of whom Rudolph Slansky was one among an anomalous assembly of his protégés, his adversaries, and his victims.

The curb on arrests came in 1953 with the deaths of Stalin and Beria. The Soviet "specialists" were sent home. Within the party the Communist detainees were gradually and discreetly rehabilitated after the meeting of the Central Committee. In 1956, after the Budapest uprising, the liberations were interrupted by a new wave of arrests. But the repression was much less fierce and the use of torture practically unknown. A limited number of detainees was released from 1956 to 1960, when an extensive amnesty freed most of the "state criminals." [8]

State crimes covered a variety of misdemeanors, particularly economic misdemeanors, which are fiercely repressed behind the iron curtain and include acquisition of Western currency — the possession of which naturally indicates plans for flight abroad. So great was the economic fiasco, so general the corruption which assumed proportions of a nationwide plague, that "true" economic delinquents did finally constitute the majority of detainees, despite the often indiscriminate application of the charge.[9] New amnesties marked 1962, 1964, and 1965. With Dubcek's accession to power the last political prisoners were freed. In the prisons, there remained only a thousand common-law prisoners.

[Remember . . .]

The world of the concentration camps became a major theme of the Czech writers and film-makers. I remember watching on Prague TV a strange psychological drama, shot against the actual background of the Mirov prison in Moravia. The director posited a confrontation between a former political detainee and his guards and interrogators. The ex-convict and his tormentors seemed to understand each other beautifully; the former forgave and the latter rationalized — with the air of Boy Scouts who had broken the tenth commandment. The impact was so false as to be almost obscene, as were many other manifestations of this feast of forgiveness promoted by the new team.[10]

Original sin of the second Czechoslovakian Republic, the Slansky trial continued silently to overshadow political life. "It will be the Dreyfus affair for several generations of Czechs and Slovaks," General Vaclav Palecek told me. A man of sixty-four, this ex-diplomat had been condemned to thirteen years of prison for "Titoism." He told me an anecdote which illustrated the irrational quality of the arrests and the tragicomic episodes which detainees experienced. In 1951, the prisoners of Jachimov learned that the ambassador from Czechoslovakia to the United Nations, Vavro Hajdu, had solemnly declared that there were no concentration camps in his country. It was an invention of the instigators of the cold war, he stated with tears in his eyes, and even swore by all he held most sacred that this rumor was totally without truth. His statement filled the detainees with fury; several of them took an oath to kill him with their own hands at the first opportunity. One year later, Hajdu, recalled to Prague and caught in the whirlpool of the Slansky trial, was condemned to life imprisonment. He left, suitcase in hand, for the Jachimov camp.

"I had a great deal of difficulty in keeping him from being lynched," Palecek related. "I had seniority in the camp at that time and finally was obeyed. He was one of my long-standing friends. He assured me that he had been sincere in his statement to the United Nations. Neither he nor any of the members of the Central Committee knew of the existence of the camps."

Other ex-detainees were more skeptical. An engineer from Brno told me: "Every day we saw a friend or relative disappear. We doubted that they had left for the Côte d'Azur. But, as in the time of the Nazis, to worry about a loved one was to put a noose around one's own neck."

The stories of communist detainees attacked by fellow prisoners were distressing, but the sordid complicity which united the guards and the Soviet "specialists" with the former Nazi S.S. remains the most infamous page of recent Czechoslovakian history.

According to General Palecek: "The most horrible thing for those of us who had already suffered in the Nazi camps was to be handed over to former torturers from the Gestapo S.S., who, after capture, were taken into the confidence of the new political police. We heard them carousing and getting drunk on slivovitz and Crimean champagne in their barracks and we said to each other: 'It isn't possible. Not that. Not here.' "

The agents of the Czech secret police assimilated not only the methods but the mentality of the Nazis, including — with relish — a furious anti-Semitism. In her house in Bratislava, Eugen Loebl's wife recalled her first interrogation at Ruzyne:

> I was standing in front of a lout who blew cigarette smoke in my face. He asked me my nationality in a sanctimonious voice.
>
> "I was originally Austrian, but I am Czechoslovakian by marriage."
>
> He acted as if he had not heard and repeated his question. I gave the same answer. This little game went on for at least ten minutes.
>
> Abruptly, he straightened up and spat in my face. I can still feel that spittle on my cheek.
>
> "You're neither an Austrian nor a Czechoslovakian. You're a kike, a kike. And your husband isn't a Slovak but a kike, nothing but a dirty kike."

This delicate and smiling woman told me what she had undergone: prison, then four years at hard labor in a factory in Bohemia. Her son, age twelve, was deported to Russia to a reform school for young delinquents. When he returned to Prague two years later, the boy was not permitted to continue his studies. He was put to work unloading wagons of coal. The house in Bratislava was stripped bare of every possession.

Hundreds of similarly nightmarish and duly authorized documents were to be found in the Club 231 archives. The hours I spent in the club's modest quarters at 17 Karlovo Namesti reminded me of the horrible days when I was in Koblenz preparing my thesis on conditions among detainees in Nazi Germany — by going through the hideous archives of the Gestapo.

Pavel Tigrid, specialist on Czechoslovakian issues, is right when he says in a recent work:

> The arbitrariness of justice, the legal assassinations, and, in a general way, all the complicated machinery of terror which the party set in motion soon after taking power were essentially the reasons for the end of the Novotny regime; to date they represent the gravest accusation against him and perhaps have shaken the very roots of not only "Czech model of socialism" but also the international communist movement. All studies dealing with postwar Czechoslovakia will have to deal seriously with this history of terror which is so surprising in a people like the Czechs who never counted bellicose sentiments or cruelty among their predominant character traits.[11]

[The Shadow of the Terror]

The nightmare of the past disturbed Dubcek's experiment and it will poison that of his successors, whatever the destiny of the Czech and Slovak peoples.

I watched the ebb and flow of hope in the improvised offices of Club 231, an organization with neither resources nor legal status. I watched housewives and students enter furtively to put down a little gift. In the room where the evidence was collected I rediscovered the feverish climate and the stubborn will to obtain reparations which I had known in deportee organizations, with this difference: neither organizers nor "clients" of the club had the feeling that the bad days were forever behind them. They could not forget that fifteen years after the era of the "great trials" they were still taking risks.

Club 231 opened its doors in January. By July, it had not only gathered three hundred documents from survivors of prisons and camps but had also received thousands of telephone calls and letters, often anonymous, from other victims of Stalinism. These said, in effect: "We will come to bear witness later, when we are sure that democratization is assured. We are still afraid."

Brodsky, the secretary of the club, explained how the scarcity of witnesses was a function of events: "There were a great many of them when things seemed to be going well, but they dried up when the political climate changed. During the period of June and July 1968, between the threatening letter of the Warsaw five and the communiqué from Bratislava, we received almost no more testimonials. People were too frightened. They thought that the bad days could come back, in one form or another."

However, the course of the new socialist justice did not seem much influenced by the war of nerves loosed against the Dubcek team on an international scale. On June 25, 1968, the rehabilitation law was passed (unanimously except for one vote) in the National Assembly. This law, which had been more or less in effect for several months, and that suppressing censorship were ratified several days later, the first important legislative act of the "renewal." The rehabilitation act covered the period from October 24, 1948, to July 31, 1965; it was to be put into effect on August 1, 1968.

The text of the statute stipulated that each person who felt he had been unjustly condemned could, during the year following that date, introduce a request for rehabilitation. These citizens could also make appeal against judgments previous and successive to the period covered by the law, but only in the frame of reference of the legislation already existing. It was the first time that a socialist country had attacked in a total and systematic manner the original sin of all the popular democracies.

The historian Charles Nigrin, president of Club 231, told

226

me that he believed the law was on the whole satisfactory. Of course, it did not include the suggestion of the noncommunist ex-detainees — 80 percent of the total number of political prisoners — to annul judgments and to punish those responsible:[12] "In the context of reality this was plainly impossible; for the 'new men' still retained those directly or indirectly responsible for atrocities, and gilded stucco replicas of Gottwald, under whose reign the worst acts were committed, still adorned the seats in union party cells."

In the confusion of responsibilities, God rewarded his own. It was decided that cases would be examined individually and that action would be taken against torturers within the measure of the possible. But in nine months, only six avowed assassins had been "found" and locked up.

According to Vaclav Palecek: "Most of the torturers from the camps still had very good positions. Only the highest functionaries on the ministerial level had been replaced.[13] Among the people who had personally interrogated and tortured me, one was still the secretary-general of the party in a district in the Prague region; another whom we had nicknamed "The Butcher of Jachimov" was in the diplomatic service in a post at Djakarta; still another, who had enjoyed throwing me into the camp sewers to 'refresh my ideas,' was police chief at Lany; and the last, who forbade my son to continue his studies at the high school, became the rector of the Pedagogical Institute of Charles University . . .

"It was a very slow process and explains why the government and the party refused to recognize our organization officially. They knew that if we had a legal existence, day after day we would bring out our index cards and publish our documentation of the crimes of the past, our lists of criminals and their accomplices."

The heritage of totalitarian regimes is heavy. One cannot help making the comparison with West Germany, where all sorts of "objective" and "subjective" reasons thwarted the pursuit and arrest of criminals. Adenauer was an authentic anti-Nazi who nevertheless kept the sinister Globke at his side and covered thousands of functionaries with the mantle of Noah. Dubcek and his friends, of whom a certain number had been in the camps themselves, for similar reasons of state feared to attack the machine in which the conservatives still had so much power.

As in West Germany, there was more promptness in the area of financial compensation. For one year passed in the prisons or the camps, ex-detainees could receive up to 20,000 crowns. Compared to ordinary salaries — 10,000 to 15,000 crowns — this seems reasonable.[14]

Otherwise, however, it was less the example of West Germany than that of the U.S.S.R. which comes to mind. In Germany the guilty could at least be freely denounced, even if the victims shouted themselves hoarse in a desert of an indifferent public opinion, and they could strike out at the distorted and scandalously indulgent tribunals. In the U.S.S.R., however, although Stalin was expelled from the mausoleum of the Kremlin, the story of Alexander Solzhenitsyn, *A Day in the Life of Ivan Denisovitch*, burst forth like a bombshell. Two years of confused argument reduced to nothing the wholesale terror; Stalin and Beria were the only guilty parties. The truth emerged: those who led de-Stalinization had in their time been accomplices to the dictator. In 1963 Khrushchev reduced the whole matter to some "excesses." The leadership succeeding him maintained this fiction and no concentration-camp accounts turned up to trouble the good conscience of the Soviets.[15] For failing to play the game, and publishing texts abroad, though they were blander than Solzhenitsyn's novel, the Czechoslovakians Yuli Daniel and Andrei Sinyavsky went to prison.

Such was the dilemma of Dubcek and his friends in yesterday's Czechoslovakia. It was impossible to call Novotny the only one responsible for Ruzyne and Jachimov. And Josef Smrkovsky must have met often some of his former denouncers and jailers in the corridors of the National Assembly over which he presided. So assassins and victims rubbed elbows, whether they liked it or not, under the banner of democratic socialism.

By what sinister perversion of the mind did the Communist party, that of Dubcek and the thaw, have the impudence to decorate the widows and orphans of martyred officials with the order of Klement Gottwald, who had presided over the execution of their husbands and fathers? [16] The strangest thing is that to my knowledge none of these decorations were refused.

On the eve of the Russian invasion, I was, as often happened during my trips to Prague, in the office of a journalist friend. I was present at a scene whose significance would later be revealed. The chauffeur of a Novotnyan member of the Central Committee came to make a deposition. He intended to speak confidentially to my friend, and to him only, to denounce his employer's actions. This latter frequently took other Novotnyans in his car, had the vehicle driven out in the country, stopped there, and plotted with these men against the government. The chauffeur gave dates, named names.

"Why don't you go to the police?" my friend asked him. The chauffeur shrugged his shoulders. He had recognized eminent members of the criminal investigation department among the plotters. The man seemed frightened: "Don't give my name, not yet. Later, if there's a trial, I'll give evidence. But I don't trust anyone except you people, the journalists."

My friend laughed kindly at this brave man: "The bad days are over. They won't be back." The deepest instinct was closer to the truth than the reasoned optimism of the intellectual.

Notes for Chapter 1

1. The work edited in Bratislava under its German title, *Die Revolution rehabilitiert Ihre Kinder*, was later published in Vienna by Europa Verlag.
2. Quoted in *Le Contrat Social* (Paris, July–August 1967).
3. This stupefying document, full of elisions and confused and embarrassed explanations, was the first manifestation of de-Stalinization of Novotny's regime after the Twentieth Congress. It was classed as a state secret and circulated in a mimeographed, limited (and numbered) edition within the party in two versions, one of a hundred pages for the upper ranks of the party, the other reduced to twenty pages for the subordinate functionaries. The lowest orders could only hear "selected extracts" read aloud from it by the responsible members of their cells. Party functionaries of liberal tendencies succeeded in making a photocopy of the "abridged" version, which they sent to the West where it was published in, among other journals, *Le Monde* on May 29, 1966, with notes and comments by the senders which indicated its omissions and its lies.
4. Published in France under the title *Ce Soleil sans chaleur*.
5. The "club" took the number of the statute which was invoked against political offenses.
6. As an ironic tribute, the detainee's camp at Kladno was officially called T.N.P. Fierlinger, after the social democratic leader who joined the communists in 1948.
7. Among these last were 2,000 Catholic priests and 3,000 Jews (10 percent of the Jewish population which survived the Nazi occupation).
8. Among the former detainees of the government staff and of the actual party, Josef Pavel, minister of the interior, and Josef Smrkovsky, president of the National Assembly, were freed in 1955; Gustav Husak, vice–prime minister, was freed only in 1960.
9. The term "political prisoner" did not appear at all in the codex of the new democratic-socialist justice. But if the premise had changed there was still the attempt to keep the forms of an orthodox communist regime — whence the embarrassment in party circles, in the National Assembly, in the ministry of justice, in finding a name for the former, political, detainees. Various paraphrases were tried: "Victims of the age of distortions," "of the cult of personality," "of the dark days," and the like.
10. In connection with the telecast, Jiri Pelikan told me that in his zeal,

the producer, as representative of the detainees oppressed by the former system, went looking for an authentic C.I.A. spy, whereupon there was a double outcry, from authentic former political prisoners on the one hand, communists, socialists, or Christians, and from the Stalinists on the other.

11. *Le Printemps de Prague* (Le Seuil, 1968).

12. On these two points the government position was the following: (1) Total annulment would have led to acquitting authentically counterrevolutionary delinquents, whose sentencing was "just." But how was the distinction to be made between those falsely accused and the true miscreants? Where was the line between the "necessities of the revolutionary struggle" and "abuses"? (2) Short of completely disorganizing police and judiciary machinery, and taking into account the regulation, the only "possible" sanctions — except for individuals having caused the death of a man — were administrative sanctions, demotions, or early retirements.

13. Officially three hundred persons should have been demoted or discharged by the ministry of the interior, which was responsible to the police. But at the time of the Soviet invasion one saw a group of the "new men," with the reputedly progressive vice-minister of the interior at their head, offering their services to the occupiers.

14. Up to 1953, the prisoners who performed forced labor in the mines and factories were not paid. After that date, they began to receive variable remunerations out of which the penal administration kept their "expenses for board and lodging" and a food allowance for their families.

15. According to Roland Gaucher, *"L'Opposition en U.R.S.S."* (Albin Michel, 1967), more than *ten thousand* manuscripts came to the editorial staffs of reviews and Soviet publishing houses in the weeks that followed the appearance of Solzhenitsyn's book.

16. The decoration for Bedrich Geminder who had left no family was received by the party, or more precisely, by the cell of the secretariat of the Central Committee of which he had been the head, and which, in 1952, had casually sent him to the gallows.

2

Revolt

The Intellectuals' Bridge — Pen and Sword — Operation
Sparrow — Boomerang — The Communist Revolt — A Socialist Victory — Caesar the Magnificent — Guard in a Cemetery

[The Intellectuals' Bridge]

On the road from Prague to Slapy, the celebrated resort on the
Vltava, an imposing gray bridge unites the two banks of the
river. Quite beautiful, it is useless and impracticable; it leads
nowhere. It is the "Intellectuals' Bridge," a marvelous chef
d'oeuvre of the absurd. Hundreds of men lost their health and
others their lives that the state might strike terror in the heart
of the intelligentsia's resistance.[1] A story circulates to the
effect that as one approached the bridge a persistent murmur
was audible. The voices of the builders of the bridge repeat in
an endless litany as they pass bricks to each other: "Thank you,
Mr. Engineer." "Not at all, Mr. Doctor."

The Prague thaw at first appeared to be a triumph of the
bullied intellectual over the informer and the Stalinist cop;

symbolically, only after the Writers' Congress did the regime seem to totter. Justice, a judicious stage manager, permitted the turbulent young novelists of the Lucerna grand ballroom to avenge in the eyes of the people the galley slaves of the useless bridge.

The Czech and Slovak nations venerate their intellectuals as do no others in Europe. From Jan Hus the reformer to Thomas Masaryk the father of the reborn fatherland, the great men of Czechoslovakia have been priests, teachers, artists. The village and town squares in Bohemia, Moravia, and Slovakia are occupied not by equestrian statues of generals but by images in stone and bronze of poets, historians, and linguists. Three centuries of Germanic oppression for the Czechs, five of forced Magyar rule for the Slovaks, could not quell the national spirit of peoples who made a fortress of their languages. Masaryk wrote in his memoirs: "In my travels around the world, Komensky's Testament, along with the Kralice Bible, was my daily national and political reminder." [2] Bohemia, when it lost its national independence in 1620 and was subjected to a double process of germanization and catholicization, engaged in a bitter struggle to preserve its national tongue. At the end of the eighteenth century, the bastardized tongue preserved in the provinces became once more a literary language. In the nineteenth century, the time of national renaissance, the first newspapers in Bohemia were literary journals. In fact, all Czech papers began as literary pamphlets.

This phenomenon is not confined to Czechoslovakia. In the absence of political life, culture and particularly literature slyly took precedence in eighteenth-century France and, to a degree, everywhere in nineteenth century Central Europe; Dostoevski's and Tolstoy's books expressed opposition to tsarist Russia far more effectively than did the duma. Culture did not resume its conventional role until politics was restored its rights. However, the political aspect of literature has played such an exceptional part in Czechoslovakia that it deserves description in detail.

More than anywhere else, writers rallied around the Czech regime in 1948. The salon communism cultivated in Prague before the war and the Munich complex threw the intellectuals into the arms of the party. Czechoslovakia is practically the only country in the East from which talented writers have not chosen exile during the last twenty years. However, the trials broke the spell: those writers who did not go to prison and those who were not totally corrupted by party propaganda went underground, chose silence, or took refuge in useless tasks. Their hour came, in 1956, after the Twentieth Congress of the Soviet Communist party, so they imagined. Khrushchev's denunciation of Stalinism set the intellectual world of all the Eastern countries bubbling; it stirred most of all in Hungary and Poland. The Czechs seemed to have had some difficulty in throwing off their torpor: "We are reproached for not having moved," Anton Liehm explained to me. He was one of the mainsprings of the big literary weekly *Literarni Listy,* "but our situation was very different from that of the Hungarians and the Poles. In Warsaw and Budapest, the movement began with evidences of popular discontent caused by economic depression. The intellectuals swelled the grumbling of the workers. In Prague, we had no audience then. Czechoslovakia was still relatively prosperous. It was still benefiting from its economic lead over the other countries of the East, from its past riches, which were not yet wholly destroyed by Stalinist economics. We weren't taken seriously. To the people, we were so many Cassandras. The majority of the population believed themselves living better than in 1948 without understanding that production had not grown larger, that the products were simply better distributed. Those in power had become very nonchalant about us. If we were preaching to deaf ears, then we weren't dangerous."

The Budapest uprising made the leaders less nonchalant. Had the Hungarian affair never taken place, it is probable that the destiny of Eastern Europe would have been different, that the situation of all the peoples' democracies would today be that of Czechoslovakia, if not even better.

Between 1958 and 1960 economic conditions grew very much worse. The Slovaks demonstrated, demanding the rehabilitation of the "nationalists"; the economic situation returned to the intellectuals their traditional audience, who made it more and more difficult for Novotny to act with severity. The quarrels between the government and the intellectuals between 1960 and the Prague thaw took on an air of farce rather than one of tragedy.

[Pen and Sword]

The story of *Literarni Listy* is a case in point. For years, those in power, and Novotny in particular, were totally opposed to this, the only nonconformist publication in the country. In September 1967 came a test of strength. The paper was removed from the management of the Writers' Union and transferred to the aegis of the ministry of culture. This move precipitated a complete and spontaneous boycott; the publication's circulation fell in one month from 130,000 to 30,000 copies. No worthwhile writer or journalist would lend his byline to the weekly, whose newly appointed head was a retired colonel. This test of strength preceded by very little the Writers' Congress, prelude to the dissolution of the regime.

The manner in which the writers (as well as the artists, movie-makers, and others) moved from submission to open revolt within ten years is very instructive: the Czech intellectuals began by presenting a remarkably united front on technical and professional matters. Novotny, ignoring the history of his own country, did not take seriously the freemasonry of intellectuals. He tried to divide them: Hendrych called the writers together in little groups, flattered them, and promised them the moon. At the first session of their congress in 1967 he was extremely indignant when he recognized several fellows whom the previous evening he had wined and dined. But the success of the writers' revolt arose less from their duplicity than from a phenomenon unique in a Marxist state, the economic independence of those who lived by the pen in Prague and in Bratislava.

In a system in which the state is the only employer and thus enabled to exert the most efficient of all pressures on every citizen, the writers constituted the only private, though collective, enterprise in the country. The Writers' Union, whose luxurious building on the National Boulevard faces the Opera, was extremely rich. It collected a small percentage on the rights of its author members, but more importantly, it collected considerable sums paid by editors for works in the public domain. The literary fund could by disposal of its funds come to the aid of those of its members (writers, journalists, film-makers, and so on) who found themselves in difficulties with those in power. The latter had tried several times to seize the fund. Eduard Goldstuecker, the acting president of the Writers' Union, liked to recall a highly moral anecdote on this subject:

After Khrushchev's big speech on March 8, 1963, in which he made his about-face on the subject of de-Stalinization, Khrushchev met with Novotny. The latter told him about the trouble "his" intellectuals were causing.

"You have to treat them like sparrows. If you had a sparrow in your hand, what would you do, Comrade Novotny?" asked Mr. K.

Deferential and zealous, the Czech leader replied: "I'd squeeze, Comrade, I'd squeeze." Khrushchev shook his head irritably. "If you squeeze, you'll smother him. The sparrow dies; that creates one more scandal because the workers' republic needs its sparrows."

Disconcerted, Novotny plunged on anyway: "Well then, I'd open my hand."

"Tsk, tsk, the sparrow would fly away. No, I'm going to show you." The Ukrainian held a half-closed hand out to Novotny: "You keep the sparrow in one hand, not too tight, not too loose. With the other, you gently pull out one feather, then another, then all the feathers. When the sparrow is altogether naked, you can open your hand; he'll be so cold that he'll nestle down of his own accord."

Operation Sparrow was tried repeatedly, but unsuccessfully.

[Operation Sparrow]

Anton Liehm began to have difficulties in 1963. On behalf of the entire editorial staff of *Literarni Noviny* he had demanded the dismissal of its director, who was considered too dogmatic. Negotiations with the secretariat of the Communist party lasted for months. The party, tired of this, agreed to the director's dismissal but in return demanded the head of the ringleader of the revolt among the editorial staff: Liehm. He said:

"There were endless quarrels. The leadership of the Writers' Union threatened to quit if I was fired. I won a year of delay. Then there was a new attack from the party, Byzantine negotiations. When the situation became unbearable, I put myself out to pasture. I took a leave of absence and my name no longer figured on the masthead. But I still continued to work in my office and the literary fund paid me the equivalent of my salary."

The philosopher Ivan Svitak told me he had played a similar game within the Institute of Philosophy of Charles University, but with less success because of the economic dependency of teachers.

Jiri Mucha, fifty-three years old, writer and scenarist, son of one of the great names of art nouveau (the painter Alphonse Mucha), was able to take up his literary activities again after his release from a concentration camp in 1954:[3] "There were no rules in this game. Out of three of my articles, only one would be passed, but it was often the least mild of the lot. We felt that those in power were losing their footing. Their attempts to win us over and their provocations would simultaneously multiply. In this context, the letter in the *Sunday Times* was catastrophic." [4]

The leaders were not unaware that this letter was a forgery. They quickly and very discreetly arrested the author of the manifesto, a brave history professor, as naïve as he was zealous, named Ivan Pfaff. But Hendrych and the party ideologists continued to pretend it was authentic, in spite of the panic-stricken denials of the Writers' Union, and at the same time officially disregarded it in order to neutralize the document's effect abroad. C.T.K. stated that the manifesto was "a disgraceful lie which grossly defames both the regime and the internal and external policies of Czechoslovakia" at the very moment that the secretariat of the Communist party prepared to launch the biggest witch hunt against the intellectuals since the time of the great trials.

This time no more petty trickery was possible.[5] The *Sunday Times* manifesto made possible not only the action against the *Literarni Noviny* but also preparations to eliminate the influence of the writers. Frantisek Havlicek, a particularly harsh official, was named by Hendrych as head of the ideological section of the party; jurists began to study the best way to liquidate the literary fund and the last vestiges of the writers' independence.

[Boomerang]

The brutality of the party ideologists boomeranged. The writers' ferment became open rebellion: no longer was just their conscience being trampled; their bread and butter were threatened. Moreover, the writers, a majority of whom were party members and as such inherited a mistrustful attitude about all intellectual provocation which came from the West or the émigrés, began to reread the manifesto so abusively attributed to them. At least in terms of vocabulary they found it to their liking. The forgery in mimeographed form began to make the rounds of the salons, then the streets of Prague.

The Writers' Congress, feverishly organized while the ideological commission of the party furnished itself with arms for repression, became the last-chance congress. Everybody knew what was coming.

The man who was and remained their unquestioned leader, Eduard Goldstuecker (president of the Czechoslovakian Writers' Union, vice-rector of Charles University in Prague, and one of the great world experts on Kafka, whose work, long banished from the literary patrimony of his country, he revived),[6] explained to me the limits and the extent of the revolt of the intellectuals.

With his sharp, sallow, tormented face, his universal culture, his humor whose caustic quality was tempered with warmth, this man past fifty was still astonishingly young. A Communist from the earliest period — he joined the party in 1933 — he had known equally well the honors and the prisons of the regime (he had gone directly from his post as ambassador from Prague to Israel to the hell of Ruzyne and the concentration camps). Both impassioned and thoughtful, Goldstuecker was the soul and conscience of the quiet revolution. He told me:

"The role we played was much exaggerated in the West. It

239

was important but secondary. It would have been in vain, completely useless, if the process of regeneration had not been vigorously encouraged inside the Presidium and the Central Committee of the Communist party of Czechoslovakia. This began with an attack of conscience within the party itself set off largely, though not wholly, by the economic deterioration of the country. The clearest-headed elements in the party believed that the great economic reforms which Novotny himself backed could not take place without democratization in depth of the whole society. We, the writers and the intellectuals in general, were the catalysts of this process. But it must be added that the demands of the writers for greater freedom of expression, a battle from the beginning conducted with ups and downs, found more and more attentive audiences in the ranks of the leadership of the C.P., and even among its simple militants, because of the traditional respect that Czechs felt for intellectuals. The anti-intellectual tendencies of Stalinism had never been able to undermine this national tradition."

And Goldstuecker, whom I saw only during the first months of the thaw, when he was tired to the point of exhaustion, described to me the amazing improvised meetings which he and his friends called in the four corners of the country — in factories, machine shops, and mines — to oppose the Novotnyan speechmakers. The latter, making use of the entire arsenal of workers' demagogy, called up the specter of unemployment to be brought about by the progressives, who wished to return the factories to the capitalists and to liquidate the "conquests of the revolution," and were welcomed with shrugs of the shoulders or boos. And let us not underestimate the dangers of this strategy of demagogy. It had always succeeded in the East. It had blocked the slim hope of liberalization in the U.S.S.R. and reversed the strong progressive current in Poland, where the party bosses roused, among other feelings, old anti-Semitic instincts, made workers into police deputies who took things in their own hands, and tracked down, beat up, and sent to prison the students of Warsaw and Poznan.

Demagogy did not work in Czechoslovakia where common sense and the traditional national virtues put a stop to the *politruks*. In March 1968 I was present at a meeting of workers and students in a packed amphitheater in the University of Prague. The students had invited a delegation of "hard noses" from the business committee of the automobile factory of Mlada Boleslav. Quite openly a speaker described the problem of the hierarchy of salaries, which under the pretext of egalitarianism gave metalworkers and miners a salary double that of doctors or university professors. Amid frantic applause from his companions, the workers' spokesman, a metalworker with a thin face, lively yet pathetic in his leather jacket, cried:

> We are not against you, Comrades. We Czech workers, we know that this policy of low salaries for intellectuals has held us back for twenty years, that our factories cannot work without your brains. You are progress and the future. It is fair that you should earn more money than we do. Those who are your enemies are not true workers; they are parasites, party bureaucrats who don't even know how to handle a screwdriver.

[The Communist Revolt]

Not only was the West somewhat misled as to the importance of the role played by the intellectuals in the process of democratization, but it failed to understand that, above all, the process was a revolt of communist intellectuals. The antirevolutionary forces that Moscow was ridiculous enough to denounce for a year were observed by no foreign observer except in an anonymous tract. Although, in the slightly anarchist climate of the beginnings, such a thing would have been easy. But when several noncommunist (but not anticommunist) voices — one of them that of Ivan Svitak, the philosopher "oppositional Marxist" — made themselves heard during the thaw, they were barely tolerated and found themselves isolated from the major support of broadcasting sources and from the great dialogue on "democratization," which remained a family affair among communists. If tactical considerations played a part after June when Moscow and the Stalinist satellites showed their strength, they appeared to be absent during the explosion of the thaw. However, later the attitudes of Goldstuecker and his friends were very different from those attributed to the Prague writers on the fundamental theses of democracy and freedom. In fact they scarcely differed, except in nuances, from those of the new-style apparatchik whom I was to meet in the bleak building of the Central Committee.

The ambiguities arose from the fact that the words freedom and democracy have not the same meaning in the socialist as in the bourgeois state; the structure and the classic means of control of democratic power — majority vote by secret ballot with the free choice of independent candidates — could only seem inappropriate, except inside the Communist party. Only a million and a half citizens of fifteen million Czechoslovakians appeared to enjoy the privilege of a caste which was the sole beneficiary of democracy; democracy inside the party was, in some sense, opposed to our bourgeois democracy.

[A Socialist Victory]

Goldstuecker summed up his position for me as follows: "The socialist revolution has not been defeated. We did not have a Thermidor in January 1968. There is therefore no reason to abolish the leading position of the C.P. We were only pursuing a new phase of that same revolutionary process that attracted us in 1948; we were moving from revolutionary dictatorship to a rule of law and guaranteed liberties. You are blinded by a single scheme of democratic control of power. We have tried to develop an effective control of power from within our own system. Since the beginning, we have attacked all problems; nothing has been taboo. But one thing has never been challenged by public opinion: the socialist character of our society. We have become a classless society; we have passed the stage at which different political parties and antagonistic classes confront one another."

But in the well-upholstered salon of the Writers' Union in which Goldstuecker made his synopsis for me, his own associate Jan Prochazka, vice-president of the Union (member of the Central Committee in 1967), did not share such categorical views; his dissension was another sign of the intellectual freedom which finally reigned in Prague, where the formal aspect of things meant less than a certain atmosphere. Prochazka, a placid blond giant, understood only Czech. A slow speech, a handsome serious face, sad eyes under heavy lids, Prochazka was the favorite target of the *Literaturnaya Gazeta*, because he had greatly "deceived" conservative circles. This novelist's dense, incisive works seemed true hagiographies of "socialist morality"; his short novel, *Green Horizons*, the only one to be translated into English, was an apologia for the collective farm.[7] A Communist, he passed as one of Novotny's intimates — the latter was godfather to one of his children. On this June day, he was skeptical of the reality of a classless society in Czechoslovakia. For him, the possibility of more than one party could not be excluded from future consideration: "In no way can I believe in a democracy without a real opposition, without some effectual opposition with the sanction of elections. No one can base an evaluation of this country's political evolution on a period of a few months or even a year. But if there is no radical change in its structures, our country, after a short romantic fling, will return to the political Middle Ages which it has just left behind."

Like Goldstuecker, he assured me that the credit for the quiet revolution belonged less to the writers than to the progressive political leaders whose new generation, unencumbered by the anti-intellectual prejudices of the old-timers, sought out and found dialogue with the intellectuals, in the great national tradition: "The whole affair began with quiet discussions, very theoretical, very abstract, on the best way to correct the mistakes of our society, to rebuild our disastrous economy, and so on. It was Novotny's and his associates' hysterical campaign against the intellectuals which blew the whole affair up to proportions which it did not have in the beginning."

To move from "intellectuals" in general to the "intellectuals of the party machine" to the professional communists only accentuates the ambiguities of democratic socialism. Not that the good will and sincerity can be doubted, but it must be said that these did take the place of a political program. But the leaders of the Czechoslovakian C.P. were certainly aware of the importance of their experiment: "What is happening here," Josef Smrkovsky, president of the National Assembly, who became the very symbol of progressivism in the heart of the party, said to me, "is important not only for Czechoslovakia and communism, but for all men. To create a socialist society which offers all the individual freedoms plus a maximum of justice has become our task. We must proceed slowly, with pauses, groping. We have no precedent, no example on which to lean." I resisted the temptation, which would have been in bad taste, to ask him to reread the program of social democracy.

Under the elaborate ceilings of the provisional building of the National Assembly on Gorki Square, his harsh-featured, rough-hewn face assumed the look of heads carved by Trnka

— the head of a tricky peasant who will never be worsted in a horse trade. Because he did not want to buy the Stalinist horse with his eyes closed, Smrkovsky, a Communist from the very beginning and national hero of the Prague insurrection against the Germans, spent four years in Gottwald's prisons. Like other progressives of his generation — Goldstuecker, Husak, Pavel — this ranking chief of the progressives wanted at fifty-seven to revive again the ideals of his adolescence, give his virginity to the party by regilding the escutcheon which had been blotted by "the false deviations of the past": "Civil liberties, socialist democracy, will be the new year's gift which our renewed Communist party will offer (after the September congress) to the Czechoslovakian people."

A student, probably about the same age as Smrkovsky was when he joined the party, said to me, answering him indirectly: "Has anyone ever seen an adult people receive its freedom as a gift? Usually it seizes freedom." And his companion parodied the Book of Job: "The party giveth, the party taketh away; blessed be the name of the party."

[Caesar the Magnificent]

Between the twenty-year-old student, indifferent or hostile to the party, and the old-timer, at once its accomplice and victim, came the generation of men who, like Alexander Dubcek, forty-seven years old, were too young or politically too insignificant to have known the prisons and the Stalinist camps. Today they have the reality of power in Czechoslovakia.

The "process" was their business. Their most typical representative seemed to me to be Cestmir Cisar, forty-five years old, a doctor of philosophy, former minister of culture, secretary of the Presidium, ideologist and spokesman of the party. I saw him at length in the office of his predecessor, Hendrych, whose name had been scratched out and replaced in pencil by Cisar's. The style of welcome had not changed; it remained perfectly "orthodox" in that house of the party: the interminable wait in icy corridors, the suspicious examination of the visitor's identification, the watchdog accompanying one on every floor — in short, more precautions than those taken at the White House or the Pentagon. Once inside, a young Madison Avenue executive came forward to meet me, hands held out; round, jovial, dressed with care, perfectly polyglot, "Caesar the Magnificent," as he was called by his student fans, was a public-relations man such as the new team must have dreamed of. The man was warm, sympathetic, and intelligent. He called himself, and no doubt was, a "liberal," but this qualification did not have the same meaning in Prague as in Paris. Cisar was above all a Communist, a party man, and a man of the machine. In 1957, secretary of the C.P. of Pilsen, the great industrial city, Cisar had quelled a revolt of the workers of Skoda with exemplary firmness.

The walls of Prague still bear in chalk and charcoal enthusiastic slogans about him written by the students who made him "their" candidate for the presidency of the Republic. One more ambiguity had served his popularity admirably: Cisar had the good luck to be the last victim of Anton Novotny, with whom he had had a dispute of order which was more administrative than political. Exiled — as ambassador to Bucharest — he tried to wangle the post in Paris, but Novotny answered him with heavy humor: "Well, you'll go to the 'little Paris' of the East, anyway." He returned to Prague in triumph after the thaw. This description is not intended to denigrate a man for whom I felt a real sympathy after our long interview. I only wish to show the complexity and ambiguity which is essential, so to speak, in a dialogue with this militant communist.

Cestmir Cisar described his actual functions to me, which were opposite to those of his predecessor: "Though a responsible ideologist, Hendrych had to see to the smooth functioning of censorship; my role, on the contrary, is to prevent any curbs on the freedom of the press, on freedom of opinion, in this intermediary period until the statutes which will guarantee these liberties are set down and voted upon."

Very good. Cisar expressed to me his concern that the party should no longer interfere directly in cultural and scientific affairs: "There must not be double use of ministries nor should there be supervision in the intellectual sphere." He was still seeking for his method but did not intend that "the party secretary should be the gentleman who must have the last word in all domains." The party machine would be kept within bounds as would governmental bureaucracy. The only department of intelligence within the Central Committee had some twenty-four members; the department of publications, in fact censorship, consisted of more than one hundred civil servants, a number which could be reduced to three or four who were responsible for legislative and administrative questions. The plethoric bureaucracy which busied itself with awards of paper to journals would be suppressed by the introduction of a free market in newsprint. All this would be coordinated with Ota Sik's great economic reforms, which would eliminate bureaucratic parasitism. And Cisar had fiercely ironic words for that caste of "maniacal bureaucrats who plan everything, down to the chores of housewives, out on paper."

All this was extremely sensible, but when I asked when these reforms would be introduced, his answer was much more vague: "We must proceed in a fashion which corresponds to the morale and the social sentiment of our society . . . step by step, and in a very reasoned way . . . to hurry things would bring on a catastrophe." [8]

Cestmir Cisar admitted, however, that the experiment was a race against time: "I know that the people who have worked for so long at what we call the building of socialism are impa-

tient to see results which correspond to their ideas of democratic humanitarian socialism. But I believe that they are ready
to give us some time because they know that the problems are
so complex that we need time to resolve them."

All the same, Cisar was persuaded that the misunderstandings with Moscow and the sister parties, though persistent,
would ultimately disappear: "What we are doing is something
so new, so extraordinary that they must be given the right to
doubt its outcome." He took exception to the quarrel over
"principles": "Practice shows that it is not the essential principles of socialism which are at stake here; on the contrary, it is
the more or less formal aspects which seem to waken the distrust of our friends."

I willingly granted him that the essential principles, the pri-
mordial dogma of communist states, was not in question; the
exclusive leading role of the party in the guidance of the country was not challenged. If there was to be democracy, it would
be won within the party, from the business cell to the government of all the state machinery, by means of a triumph of the
progressive elements over the conservative elements. The problem of squaring the circle always returns — how to institute
democracy without the secret ballot, an opposition, or political
plurality.

He said, "If we succeed in creating a society in which not
only political parties but all the living forces of the nation —
from the artists' organizations to those of the sportsmen to the
unions, and so on — can take an active part in public affairs,
express their opinions, and directly influence the organizations
of the state, their role can become such that the democratic
experiment of power can move forward without pluralism of
political parties, according to the classic scheme of parliamentary democracy created more than a century ago. It will be
something new, extraordinary." How? My question remained
unanswered. The concrete mechanisms of this new democracy

were under study. I did not have the presumption to speak to this ex-professor of philosophy about the eternal search for utopia, the model states of Plato, Aristotle, or Thomas More, the exalted quest from Babeuf to Lenin by way of Fourier, Saint-Simon, and Marx. He continued:

"If we can just have some time. If we succeed, voices which today call for political pluralism will probably accept our idea of concentrating the mechanism of democracy in a single party, a party which will really create a scientific policy while accepting the fact that it must submit to a real test of support from the masses in elections each time it is necessary. For the time being, all power is concentrated in the hands of the communists. That is the only possible way at present. It is from the C.P. that the necessary drive must come. But we must allow for time, to see what the coexistence of a renovated party and public liberties, exposure to a whole gamut of opinions, has to offer."

I replied that the experiment in progress was attributable less to internal factors than to a geopolitical accident: Prague shared in the heritage of Yalta, because Stalin and the Russian marshals were fervent readers of Clausewitz and Bismarck: "Who holds Bohemia, holds Europe." Cisar reminded me of Smrkovsky's quip: "Liking or not liking the Russians is a matter of personal feeling; our alliance with the U.S.S.R. is a question of geography." [9]

[Guard in a Cemetery]

Who could deny, however, in spite of geopolitics, that the deep inclination of Czechoslovakia is toward the West? That a whole people still have an intense, almost desperate, nostalgia for the bourgeois republic of Benes, when Prague was not at the ends of the earth but in the cultural environs of Paris and London and Berlin.

Several days previously I had gone to Zichov Hill. There I went to the fabulous marble mausoleum where, in imitation of Lenin's in Red Square, lie the mummified bodies of Zapotocky and Gottwald. On the neighboring hill remains only the pedestal of the gigantic statue of Stalin, dismantled in 1957. However, no one had laid a sacrilegious hand on the communist pantheon where the bodies rested, these who bore, much more than the dreary Novotny, scapegoat of democratization, the responsibility for the terrible years. In the immense empty crypt, the only sound was the echo of the heels of an American tourist, alone except for one of those incredible Czech housewives, scarf on her head and cigarette in the corner of her mouth, who passed a lazy dust cloth over the catafalque of the dead gods.

But in the little cemetery at Lany, a small village west of Prague and summer residence of the president of the first Republic, I stood on that same day in an interminable line to pass before the tomb of the Masaryks (Thomas, his wife, and his son Jan, the suicide of the Cernin palace): its three sober blocks of granite had almost disappeared under a mountain of flowers. "Before," the old cemetery guard confided to me, "people came secretly, at night, from Prague. They knew the location of the tomb and threw their flowers over the wall before running off like thieves."

Cisar did not believe that Czechoslovakians really felt nostalgic for the bourgeois Republic. "It's more the nostalgia for something which existed in the nineteenth century, for a civilization of great culture, for a certain way of thinking and living, for the fight for political and social liberty — a combination which formed the very nature of our nation and which manifested itself in the Republic under Masaryk and Benes. We want to correct the mistake of the former communist leaders of this country and bring back to life what is best both in the Czech nature and in the spirit of our times." Cisar thought that adapting the new direction to the scientific and technical revolution would create a modern socialism, would obliterate this nostalgia for the past and allow Prague to preserve that synthesis of West and East which seemed to him to be the mission of his country.

This modern socialism was defined by Cisar as the application of Marxism as a "permanent revolutionary theory": "I am neither a Menshevik nor a Trotskyite partisan in the permanent revolution, and besides I find there is too much tendency to take cover behind manners which are often empty of meaning. I am a Marxist who considers that Marxism is an evolutionary doctrine; no one has a monopoly on its interpretation. In the light of social and other experience of 1900, 1920, 1930, how could anyone interpret the evolving reality of our times? Because it did not understand this, our party lost its character as revolutionary and avant-garde political force. It fell into a stagnation which is the very contradiction of communism. If, as a party, we are capable of giving a response to each new element of life, of the social praxis, then we have the right to call ourselves Marxists. A Marxist is not a guard in a museum."

These were the intellectuals and the ideologists of the Prague thaw. Communists, in some respects intransigent Communists, but men who wanted to be open to dialogue and who thought — naïvely? — that Marxism was also a form of humanism.

The drama of communism, renewed after half a century, is it not still to devour its most promising children? (Even if they are to be posthumously rehabilitated.)

1. It is true that at the same period the Rumanian intellectuals dug the Danube canal, which took fifty thousand victims. By comparison, the Czechs were moderates.
2. The great Czech philosopher and pedagogue Komensky (Comenius), bishop of the Union of Bohemian Brothers, exiled in 1628 after the imperial edict of 1627 decreeing that Catholicism was the only official religion, in 1650 wrote in the *Testament of the Union:* "I believe, before God, that when the storms of rage are past, the government of thine own affairs will return to thee, O Czech people!" The so-called Kralice Bible, translated by the Bohemian Brothers (1579–1593), marked the Czech language's acceptance as the national literary tongue.
3. Jiri Mucha fought in France in 1940 with the Czech division. After that he joined the R.A.F. and followed the Czech fighting men as war correspondent from Tobruk to the Far East, from Italy to Berlin. In 1945, taken in by the radio appeal of the Prague insurgents, he crossed the German lines in a jeep to return to his country. He published a war journal and novels, until his arrest as a "spy" in 1951. He spent three years in prison and in the Jachimov mines.
4. In the first week of September the *Sunday Times* published a "Manifesto of Czech Intellectuals," a thousand words long, which had just been sent to it secretly. The great British weekly made it clear that the signatures were not revealed for obvious reasons of security but that the contents of this document — the most important which had come from the communist world since the books of Sinyavsky and Daniel — as well as its heroic tone left no doubt as to its authenticity. This appeal, addressed to public opinion and to the writers "of the free and democratic world," asked their help in saving the spiritual freedom and the fundamental rights of all independent creators threatened by the terror of state power. It recalled the words of Karel Capek, according to which "each terrorist regime turns first of all against the free intelligentsia and uses its powers of oppression to indoctrinate minds." The signatories insisted on the fact that they were not opposed to socialism and that they were Marxists and communists for the most part. But they wanted Marx's "empire of freedom" and not a reign of terror. They denounced "the flagrant and characteristically fascist witch hunt" and "anti-Semitism and racism" of Czechoslovakia's official policy with regard to Israel. Particularly addressed to leftist intellectuals who protested against what was go-

ing on in Vietnam, Spain, and Greece "but whose tendency is to be blind to what is going on in the countries for which they have such high hopes," they directly called on Arthur Miller, John Steinbeck, Jean Paul Sartre, Jacques Prévert, Bertrand Russell, John Osborne, Heinrich Böll, Günter Grass, Peter Weiss, and Alberto Moravia. In conclusion they adopted as a credo that of President Kennedy, who declared that he was ready to pay any price to assure the survival of freedom.

5. "The party's patience is exhausted," Hendrych was obliged to state in *Rude Pravo* on the day after the *Sunday Times* affair.

6. Goldstuecker has repeatedly explained his position on Kafka, notably in an interview with the French literary critic Claude Roy, to whom he said (*Le Monde,* August 3, 1968): "The history of Kafka's works in Czechoslovakia is complicated by the fact that after the war the socialist camps were cut off from the world; Czechoslovakia was isolated. The dominant political culture condemned Kafka as decadent, anti-realistic, destructive, and incompatible with the construction of socialism. But as Kafka gained prominence in the rest of the world, a battle grew around him, and he thus became a weapon of the cold war. Those who used him in this way saw only one aspect of his work, which they interpreted as a description of man in a totalitarian society, the forerunner of the inhuman bureaucracy which was ruling the socialist party throughout the world. And it happened that Kafka, who would have been quite surprised, was changed into a battlefield scene, a battle of a spiritual Verdun. And he who drew the attention of thousands of readers, the youth in particular, was perhaps not even aware that he had been proclaimed a forbidden fruit and a symbol. Kafka a prophet? He undoubtedly never dreamed of it. But his masochistic quest for the truth of the conditions of life in the present world created an atmosphere with which Czech readers were able to identify, seeing a reflection of their own helplessness in face of the anonymous force which governed their destinies."

7. Artia Publishers (Prague, 1965).

8. In August 1968, eight months after the revolution, neither these projects nor the economic reforms of Ota Sik had yet received any impetus whatsoever.

9. In the era of the atomic bomb and intercontinental missiles the arguments about Czechoslovakia's being the key piece in Soviet strategic troop disposition in Europe have meaning only in terms of one hypothesis: any future conflict in Europe will be conventional. It is possible that while using "global blackmail" against Prague, the Soviet general staff has had some real strategic doubts about this hypothesis.

3

A Lion by the Tail

A Marriage of Reason — The Separation — Charter of Kosice
— Bratislava — Prague — Model for Conciliation

[A Marriage of Reason]

The stylized lion on the coat of arms of the Socialist Republic
of Czechoslovakia has a bifurcated tail.

This zoological peculiarity is reputed to symbolize the union
of the two nations: the Czech and the Slovak. At official cere-
monies, the national anthem surprises the musician's ear in the
country of Dvorak and Smetana. The orchestra plays what is in
effect a division between two tempi, a slow and pathetic largo
followed by a military march; this national anthem is made up
of two, the *Kde Domov Muj* of the Czechs[1] and the *Nad Tatrou sa Blyska* of the Slovaks.[2]

A little after the birth of the new Slavic Republic composed
of the germanicized Bohemia and Moravia and the magyarized
Slovakia, taken from the spoils of the Austro-Hungarian empire, the name for the new state — Czechoslovakia — incited

verbal battles. These have not come to an end in fifty years. The hyphen (Czecho-Slovakia) persistently demanded by Bratislava is refused with no less determination by Prague. Nevertheless, nine out of ten Europeans are persuaded of the existence of an imaginary Czechoslovakian unhyphenated tongue and nation.

Geographically, humanly, Slovakia is at the antipodes of Bohemia-Moravia. Beyond the anecdotal differences — the swarthy Slovak, passionate, drinker of wine, opposed to the blond, placid Czech who loves beer — exist much deeper differences, psychological, cultural, economic.

To the hysterical exaggerations of the Slovak writer Mlynar, who speaks of the "cultural genocide" of his nation by the Czechs — Masaryk in 1918 had to send instructors from Bohemia to reteach Slovakian to a decimated and magyarized Hungarian "colony" — the Czechs replied with an easy conscience; they only wished to see in the "Slovakian question" the issue of economic underdevelopment.

The marriage of reason which Czechs and Slovaks contracted in 1918, in the name of linguistic affinities and memories of a common destiny arising from the Grand Moravian Empire, in the ninth century, was that of ten million overdeveloped Europeans with four million mountaineers. The former were heirs to the rich industrial arsenal of Austro-Hungary (Bohemia was the Ruhr of the monarchy) impregnated with Hussite traditions and lukewarm Catholics; its elite were willing Freemasons and, later, Marxists. The latter inherited only an "Albanian" poverty dispersed by a fanatical clergy who made the Spanish inquisitors look like liberals.

The drama of the republic of Masaryk and Benes was that of all liberal humanist nations between the two world wars. "Purely Czech" values fiercely adhere to a fictitious and centralized universe and a generous Jacobinism in which obligatory lay instruction, social democracy, and the physical culture of the Sokols must eliminate "obscurantist forces." The monopoly of the nationalism was left to the most reactionary elements of a crude population which was just emerging from ten centuries of forced magyarization with an irrepressible will for national affirmation.[3]

[The Separation]

In 1938, the partition of Czechoslovakia did not mean much to the majority of Slovaks who simply followed their shepherds — two sinister colleagues, the priest Andrej Hlinka and bishop Monsignor Tiso. These two created, with Hitler's blessing, the Slovak state which was to distinguish itself by ultra-Nazism. The Slovakian government was the only one among all the puppet governments of occupied Europe to legalize the laws of Nuremberg. The final solution of the Jewish question was applied with zeal.[4] Popular support in the Slovak state was almost unanimous; with more good faith than the Austrians with regard to the Anschluss, the Slovaks welcomed it gladly. "This also is part of our heritage," Mnacko told me bitterly.

When the Slovaks saw that Germany was losing the war, they bought back their compromised honor by an international insurrection without precedent in Central Europe. On August 28, 1944, Hlinka's guards, along with the generals and communist partisans, rose against the Germans, to meet a pitiless repression which created more victims in a few weeks than six years of Nazi occupation in Bohemia did.

Slovakian historians claim, not without reason, that, besides expiating the "original sin" of the Slovakian people, the insurrection of 1944 played a not negligible political role in Benes' last negotiations with the Soviets over the future of his country. Stalin, always impressed by brute force and a great admirer of the Polish and Yugoslav partisans, complained of the passivity of the Czechoslovakians. "The Czechs," Mnacko maintained, "were good at playing statues. A battalion of the Feldgendarmerie were enough to assure order in Bohemia-Moravia. We gave the Germans enough rope to hang themselves." A witticism, to be sure, but symptomatic to the extent that the Slovak bloodbath presented a picture more attractive to the Soviets (themselves plunged into a morass of suffering) of an effective resistance of European peoples to Nazism.[5]

[Charter of Kosice]

In 1945 the provisional Czech government drew up the charter of Kosice in the first Slovak town liberated by the Red Army. This posited the existence of a republic composed for the first time of two equal nations, Bohemia-Moravia and Slovakia, according to the "socialist principle applied to the solution of the national question" and to the claims of the National Slovak Insurrectionist Council:

A federated state, a united, common state, in which each of the nations governed itself but in which at the same time there remained common all that is indispensable to maintain a strong and united state. Slovakia should have its democratic Slovak government and its freely elected parliament, which would decide everything which did not have direct bearing on the common interests of the two nations. A government and a common parliament will decide common business.

The Slovak communists were pleased by a letter from Klement Gottwald to V. M. Molotov, during the first days of the national Slovak uprising in 1944, in which the communist leader, then a refugee in Moscow, spoke of a federative solu-

257

tion to the coexistence of the Czechs and the Slovaks. One of the first figures in the Slovak resistance, Jan Sverman, who died in the underground, had presented this idea at the session of the national Slovak council in the insurgent city of Banska Bystrica: "In Slovakia, the Slovak will be his own master; in Bohemia, the Czech; and our common affairs will be managed in common."

But after a promising beginning, the communist regime succeeded no better than the bourgeois republic in resolving the dangerous national question. The progressive diminution of those autonomous organs of the Slovak executive prescribed in the charter of Kosice liquidated Slovak autonomy. These institutions were to be only formal façades by 1960, when Prague proclaimed the new constitution of which the first article stipulated that "the Czech Socialist Republic is a united state[6] consisting of two sister nations, equal in law, the Czechs and the Slovaks."

Why did the workers' republic prove more anti-Slovak (in the eyes of Bratislava) than the bourgeois republic? If one excepts secular prejudices and the historical superiority complex of the Czechs and the Moravians, two hypotheses attract historians.

From the last free elections, at least formally, the Communist party drew only 30 percent of the votes in Bratislava (against 38 percent in Prague and 43 percent in Brno). The largely rural population of Slovakia voted for the Democratic (Christian) party which won an absolute majority of 62 percent. Discredited, the Slovak Communist party was to some degree punished by its defeat.

Stalinist economy, with its rigid planning, made unbridled centralism the principle of all political action. Slansky's trial made the denunciation of two nationalisms possible, that of the Zionist Jews and that of the Slovaks. Thus the Slovak Communist party, discredited in 1948, became the nation's spokesman. Their struggle for autonomy soon became, in the eyes of the Slovaks, inseparable from the fight for democratization of the regime. It is interesting to note that the conservative elements of the Slovak Communist party played at first the game of autonomy but later that of federalism.

[Bratislava]

Bratislava, a hospitable city, warm, almost meridional, is admirably situated on the banks of the Danube. The food is good, the wines generous, the girls pretty, and friendships spontaneous. Its people commit crimes of passion. In short, the Slovaks are a hotblooded and hotheaded people, capable of the best and the worst, generous or cruel. The city's colorful milling crowds are at first glance very different from Prague's population. In the narrow alleyways of the old city, peasants in local costumes and gypsies add exotic notes. On the banks of the Danube an enormous ruined synagogue, its windows broken, is a reminder of a community which has disappeared forever. On façades, traces of German inscriptions remind one of Pressburg, garrison town of the Hapsburgs, the name of Bratislava at the time of the Austro-Hungarian Empire. One sees little difference in the signs on the shops — the Czech "restaurace" (restaurant) has become a "restauracie."

But the differences between the two languages prove greater than the similarities. I asked Mnacko: "Do Czechs and Slovaks read each other's languages reciprocally?"

"I would say," he replied, "that the Slovaks read Czech; Czech journals and books have a big sale here. But the people of Bohemia and Moravia do not really read Slovakian. They could, no doubt, but in a manner of speaking the Czechs, representatives of a 'great' nation, do not condescend to read the writings of a lesser one. It's more psychological than anything else. As for myself, I can read Czech easily, but I make many mistakes in speaking. Always, when I speak to a Czech, each of us uses his own tongue and we understand each other perfectly. Slovaks and Czechs have had a different history and literature, divergent traditions. Essentially, however, Slovaks think of themselves as a nation, want to be a nation. This is a common phenomenon in the world, for example the French of Quebec, the Scotch, the Welsh. In the last century, had the Slovaks been able to allow themselves to be absorbed, perhaps we would have formed a single nation. But that did not happen, and national sentiment became very strong. Slovaks no longer want to be co-proprietors of Slovakia. We think here that there can be no democracy unless not only citizens but nations, too, have equal rights in this country."

"Can four million Slovaks have the same rights as eleven million Czechs?"

He responded with a question: "Why not? In the United Nations, Zambia has the same rights as the United States of America."

"What do the Slovaks want?"

"In general, not to be considered a minority. They want federation on an equal basis. The difficulty up to now has been that the Czechs think of themselves as 'Czechoslovaks,' in terms of the state, and the Slovaks of themselves in terms of a nation as Slovaks. This has gone on for fifty years. Since the relationship has chiefly profited the inhabitants of Bohemia and Moravia, the most developed part of the country, they have not felt the frustrations which we know here, where we feel like second-class citizens. We must resolve our national question; and this will not be easy. At this very moment similar conflicts paralyze Yugoslavia and Belgium, threaten the unity of the Soviet Union, and so on. Even the Swiss have this problem. These national problems have paradoxically become more acute with integration. Perhaps because people feel so alienated, so alone in today's world, they feel the need to belong to smaller communities, warmer than the state. Tragedy will warp the two nations of this country if we do not find a happy solution."

A human problem, but also, if not at first glance, an economic problem. I went for enlightenment to the other great man of Bratislava, Eugen Loebl, former vice-minister of foreign trade and director of the Bank of Czechoslovakia. I told him of Prague's concern over a demand which seemed impossible to satisfy: the demand of the Slovaks to obtain equalization of economic levels between the two nations by 1980. He told me:

"Whether they ask it or not, it is a necessity. A retarded Slovak economy means a handicapped Czech economy. You cannot have a cart drawn by a race horse and a work horse. Enormous investments have been made here, in steel mills for instance, for political, demagogical, or strategic ends, but they were bad investments which did not really raise the level of the life of the people because these industries were in debt."

"Because the policy of investment was decided in Prague?" I asked.

"It is natural that Prague favor the sectors nearest to central power. We think that investments for Slovakia should be made from Bratislava, those of Bohemia from Prague, those for Moravia from Brno. Each part of the country will try to do its best with its own investments. In the last twenty years that's not the way it has gone. The central government would decide to invest a billion crowns to build a textile factory. Czechs and Slovaks would each vie fiercely to win the investment for their nation. No one tried to find out whether such a factory would be profitable or not to the economy of this or that region. Investments were sought as if they were subsidies; according to the political situation within the party, one or the other side won. Nevertheless, if one is to make, let us say, twenty-billion-crown investments, one must think carefully before deciding how and where to invest. One must stop thinking of the national economy as a system of ration cards. If one receives 'rations' one has a tendency to use them up as soon as one gets them. If one receives money, one can think and select one's purchases according to one's needs."

"Does Slovakia have at her disposal men who would be able to make judicious investments?"

Loebl responded: "Yes, and thanks to the Republic, it must be emphasized. In fifty years, since Masaryk, a sufficiently good bureaucracy has grown up. We are no longer poor and illiterate relations in the Czechoslovakian family. We were, it is true, a retarded nation. But nevertheless we have our universities, our institutes, our elite. This is a great achievement for the Czechoslovakian Republic and perhaps the only great success of this half-century of our history. We are henceforth two equal nations; we should thus have equal chances of development. From an ethical and humanistic point of view, the Slovaks are right to demand equality."

"Will that avoid conflicts in the future?"

"There will probably still be some, as there are in all families, but not, I think, this national tension in which we find ourselves today."

"How is this tension manifested?" I questioned.

"You don't see it when you are a foreigner passing through Bratislava, but it exists in all areas. The Czechs are not loved in Slovakia, and the Slovaks are scorned in Bohemia. This helped Novotny's policy of division, and that of his predecessors, *divide et impera*: the intelligentsia against the workers, the Czechs against the Slovaks, and so on. One never knows how these antagonisms begin, but when they are carefully cultivated they branch out into infinity and poison everyone's existence."

The Slovaks point to a certain number of facts to support

their demand for economic parity. I suggested this to him, and he responded:

"In Slovakia, up to 1970, the annual revenue per inhabitant will be less than that of the Czechs by 3,260 crowns; hence a family income diminished by about 13,000 crowns . . .

"If Czechoslovakia wants to make up for its lag behind Western Europe, its annual national revenue will have to grow by 5 percent, but if Slovakia is to participate equally in the growth of the common revenue, the increase would have to be more than 7 percent . . .

"Czechoslovakia is in large measure dependent on the importation of agricultural products. It imports annually 2,350,-000 tons of cereals. But Slovakia, which has a surplus of agricultural production, partially makes up the currency deficit. This is not sufficiently recognized. Moreover, Slovakian industry remains oriented toward unfinished products, which are then finished in the factories of Bohemia and Moravia . . .

"The underdevelopment of Slovakia forces it to send nearly 100,000 seasonal workers to Bohemia-Moravia . . .

"The effective forces of the diplomatic service and of Czech foreign trade include no more than 450 Slovaks[7] out of ten thousand employed, and those of the central administrative offices of the state scarcely more."

The Slovak Communist party, in its program of action prepared for the Fourteenth Party Congress planned for September 1968, furnished the following statistics:

Slovakia's participation in the growth of the population of Czechoslovakia is relatively large; its population actually makes up 30.9 percent of the entire state, but its contribution to the national revenue is only 20 percent.

The standard of living in Slovakia as compared to that in the Czech regions of Bohemia and Moravia (100 percent) is expressed by the following figures: national revenue per inhabitant, 71 percent; base funds per inhabitant, 70.9 percent; level of individual consumption, 80.5 percent; level of revenue in currency, 75.3 percent. The quota of active inhabitants of productive age in the economy is 90.8 percent in the Czech countries, 83.3 percent in Slovakia — men, 83.1 percent; women, 66.1 percent.

[Prague]

Even more than historical, social, and economic troubles, psychological elements play their part in the deterioration of the relations between the state and the Slovaks. The minority susceptibility of the Slovaks perhaps played a principal role in the genesis of the Prague thaw.

On August 30, 1967, there occurred an event which got no more than ten lines in the papers. President Novotny came to the little town of Martin, in the Tatras of central Slovakia, to dedicate a monument to the glory of the Matiste Slovenska, the awakeners of Slovakia.

This cultural organization, in fact more political than cultural, had united patriots under the Hungarian yoke; ironically, the destinies of the Jews and the Slovaks were once more mingled in this business. The Slovaks' participation in the genocide of the Jews, which Mnacko called "the sin of our fathers," had weighed on their consciences since 1945 and was a principal component of the Slovak complex composed of remorse, frustration, and a bitter feeling of inferiority to the "great" Czech nation.

In the 1950's, the trials of Slansky and Clementis had been those of "bourgeois" nationalisms, the Zionist and the Slovak; they were followed by an anti-Semitic campaign without precedent in Czechoslovakia since the German occupation and by manifestations of anti-Slovak Czech chauvinism.

The treason of the Slovaks after Munich was raised over and over again, emphasizing Prague's unmitigated and obsessive fear of Slovak irredentism. In Eastern Europe, only the Rumanians with their Transylvanian apple of discord have a comparable phobia about dismemberment. Although the Slovaks paid dearly for their follies, Bratislava remained suspect to the successive occupants of the Hradschin.[8] Under Novotny, anti-Slovak sentiments were the source of an entire repertoire of funny stories;[9] the secretary combined with the habitual prejudices of a Czech petit bourgeois a piercing resentment of Slovakia's Communist party.

On that day at the end of August 1967, the Jews and the Slovaks gave trouble to the president as in 1952:

Several days earlier, in a sequel to the war in the Near East, the murder of the Jewish-American leader Charles Jordan by Egyptian agents (protected, it was said, by the Czech security department) had made Prague the target of the international press. The six-day war had already poisoned the spring and a good part of the summer for Mr. Novotny. Mnacko, Slovak novelist and the most famous Czechoslovakian writer of the time, had symbolically chosen to take refuge in Israel and there to begin his crusade against the dictator. At the closing of the ceremony for the Matiste Slovenska in Martin, Novotny gave visible signs of nervousness as young girls in local costume danced folk dances. His short speech was extraordinarily flat:

> Czechoslovakia gives its political, moral, and economic support to all those who must face imperialist aggression, in both Vietnam and the Arab countries. This does not mean that we adopt an anti-Semitic attitude as the West's reactionary press and Israeli propaganda would have the world believe. We reject all kinds of racism and our country respects the equality of rights of all its citizens, which is not the case in the United States.

265

This sally stupefied the Slovaks, who cared nothing about Israel or international politics on this great day of patriotic celebration. The president spoke not a word in praise of the "awakeners" of the Slovak language and culture to whom the day was dedicated. The organizers of the ceremony were subsequently embittered by Mrs. Novotny's refusal of gifts that some young girls offered. She rejected them according to the instructions of her husband, who refused to sign the "golden book": "Send it to the presidential palace," he quipped before disappearing into his Tatra.

This scandal took on proportions of a veritable insult to the Slovak nation when it was learned several days later that precious manuscripts belonging to the first "awakeners" and addressed to the Hradschin came back with the insulting inscription "refused by the addressee." Of course censorship repressed this story in Bratislava as well as in Prague.

Of all Novotny's whims, this unquestionably played an important part in his downfall, disproportionate to the importance of the matter, no doubt, but symbolic.[10] From September 1967 to January 1968, he never stopped making mistakes on the subject of the "sister nation"; his fatal "you talk like a Slovak bourgeois nationalist" thrown at Dubcek in the middle of December's Central Committee session were the same words that Novotny's great friend, attorney-general Josef Urvalek, uttered on November 29, 1952, to Vladimir Clementis, ex-minister of foreign affairs. These words had helped Clementis to power.

Novotny's anti-Slovak phobia finally destroyed him. During the weeks when the Presidium was paralyzed and the dictator had certainly to relinquish his mandate of first secretary, Novotny cleverly accepted Dubcek's candidacy; he was persuaded that the Central Committee would never accept a Slovak as the party leader in Prague. But Dubcek knew how to overcome secular prejudices and to prove that a minority member could be loyal to both his small and his great allegiance, knew how to reconcile the interests of his nation and the state. In the opinion of all the specialists, the national question was better advanced in less than a year of democratic socialism than in twenty years of bureaucratic authoritarianism.

[Model for Conciliation]

The program of action of the Czechoslovakian Communist party has laid the foundation for the federal state without settling the great argument which has, from the beginning of the thaw, set the partisans of the "symmetric" model against those of the "asymmetric" (a federation based strictly on territorial considerations versus one reflecting the "nations").

The problem revolves around the need to conciliate the legitimate national aspirations of the Slovaks with the interests of the Czechoslovakian state and simultaneously to prevent minoritization and domination of eleven million Czechs by four million Slovaks. The Communist party has begun to work out a constitutional arrangement whose complexity reflects that of this, the national question.

According to this project, elaborated by Dubcek, Czechs and Slovaks each have autonomous organizations within the party: congress, Central Committee, Presidium, and president — which title has replaced that of first secretary. The C.P. of Czechoslovakia would head both organizations and deal with problems of the party's foreign policy, the armed forces, the workers' militias, and federal institutions. Decisions "concerning the existence and sovereignty of superior national and territorial interests" would have no force of law unless adopted by an absolute majority of the national organizations in the course of examinations, separate but within the federal central committee.[11]

No doubt the dangers of an excessive policy of federalization were recognized — more in Prague than in Bratislava — for the least disadvantage would be that of superimposing another plethoric bureaucracy upon the Dantesque universe of existing communist bureaucracy. The example of Yugoslav federation was not very reassuring in this respect.

The conflict between the supporters of the symmetrical and those of the asymmetric federation remained unsettled.[12] The territorial basis would permit greater preservation of the national characters and prove a more effective deterrent against Czech assimilation but would be less profitable economically than the principle of nationalities. (In Prague the Byzantine contortions of the Slovak intellectuals attempting to combine the two formulas were followed with either irritation or amusement; it was easy to believe the Slovaks wanted the advantages of federation without any of its inconveniences.) However, on the national aspect was superimposed the problem confronted throughout the world — by the capitalists as well as the socialists — of excessive centralism, of the metropolis versus the provinces: "We've had enough of being the Far East of the Republic; we don't want to have the frontier of Europe in Moravia any more," they said in Bratislava, once "on the outskirts of Vienna." [13]

Edo Fris — Slovak publicist and journalist, former secretary-general of the Central Committee of the C.P., and briefly editor-in-chief of the principal daily of Bratislava, *Pravda* — told me with some justice: "A great part of the Slovak frustrations is less national than 'provincial'; Prague monopolizes the whole substance of the state. If we could limit the excess of centralized power, many obstacles to reconciliation and unity of the two nations would be swept away. We don't care to be the 'ethnic reservation,' the 'national park' of the Czechoslovakian Republic."

Fris also reduced to its true proportions the animosity, according to him much exaggerated by the Western press, that Slovaks felt for Czechs. He was particularly annoyed with certain West German journals which summarily represented the relationship between the two nations as being "an irreconcilable conflict between the *Sklavenvolk*, the Slovak *Untermensch*, and the Czech *Herrenvolk*":

"This same diagnosis also outlined the Irish-British relationship of the past, for example, and even the German-Czech relations during the rule of Hitler. It even described one nation as more 'progressive' than the other: After the line of demarcation between conservative and progressive is established, all schematism must be avoided. Among the most obstinate partisans of political conservatism, of the psychology of servility, and of the glorification of the regime of central power, one finds, one still finds, a good number of Slovak politicians. On the contrary, not only Czech Marxist youth but also the political militants, differing in age and situation, sometimes recognize at a high level the need to overcome all the sequels to protectionism and Czech hegemony in their relations with the Slovaks and to seek to promote the ideology of national equality with an adequate institutional guarantee."

Even before the thaw, Alexander Dubcek, as a Slovak, expressed the intricacy and complementary nature of the process of democratization and that of the solution of the national problem: "We are living at a historical turning point in the passage toward a new kind of socialist society. On the basis of analysis of past and present problems, we must look ahead and make room for everything which is progressive." Of the situation of the party and its methods, among other things, he said:

We must declare war against any element of hegemony or subjectivism and put a stop to any effort which tries to impose party influence within the society by methods which the society will resent insofar as they are hegemonic and sovereign. The party guides the socialist society — this cannot diminish even in the future — and that is the reason why it must entirely embrace its problems. We seek better practical understanding of social processes.

Of the relationships between Slovakia and Czechoslovakia, Dubcek said: "The Republic must prosper in a complex manner if it is truly to prosper. . . . We are not a big enough country to permit ourselves the luxury of having noteworthy economic differences between ethnic regions." [14]

The attitude of the Slovaks during the eight months of democratization often gave rise to very summary interpretations in the Western press; which regarded Bilak, the Stalinist first secretary of the C.P. of Bratislava, as the spokesman of national aspirations when in fact this man had already been discredited and owed his office only to respect for forms and legality. His removal from the September congress left no room for doubt in this matter.[15]

Vladimir Babnic, the editor-in-chief of the Tatrapress Agency in Bratislava, summed up the state of mind of his compatriots for me with the formula: "No democratization without solution of the national problem; no Slovak solution without democratization."

And if perhaps certain Slovak leaders were tempted to profit by the crisis, to snatch some extra concession from Prague, the rising dangers returned them to better sentiments. The Slovaks seemed neither tempted by an independence which would perpetuate their economic underdevelopment nor by their transformation into a Soviet republic. In the actual international context, independence was worth little more than annexation by that powerful neighbor who had in 1945 quite simply seized the easternmost province of Slovakia, sub-Carpathian Ruthenia.

The behavior of the Slovaks at the time of the Soviet aggression furnished, if there was any need of it, supplementary proof of their attachment to Masaryk's state. Yes, the elation of the thaw, the spilling of common blood, and the ordeal of foreign occupation united hearts, something that no federal constitution could have guaranteed. The year 1968, grievous as it was for the two sister nations, at least dissipated fifty years of misunderstandings and offered hope.

Notes for Chapter 3

1. "Where Is My Homeland," the first line of a song taken from *La Kermesse* by Joseph-Kajetan Tyl.
2. "Lightning Flashes Over the Tatras," a patriotic song of 1848.
3. Classical Hungarian historians classified the Slovaks, up to the first world war, first as a "non-nation" and then as a "nonhistorical nation."
4. Seventy thousand persons died in the extermination camps, more than half the Jewish population, the largest proportion in Eastern Europe outside of Poland.
5. Two hundred French prisoners, escaped from the stalags and *oflags* of the region, who had found refuge among the mountaineers, would participate in the uprising under the orders of Captain de Lannurient. A monument commemorates their sacrifice at Strecno.
6. A socialist republic, and no longer a popular one, the forced collectivization of lands by that time having been accomplished.
7. And even then most of the time they were nothing better than porters or chauffeurs, Loebl emphasized, wincing.
8. After the Soviet invasion, Bratislava defended the unity of the Republic as ardently as Prague. The Slovaks in the Presidium did not defer to Moscow as might have been feared, and by their behavior cancelled the U.S.S.R.'s blackmail which threatened, if President Svoboda would not consent to modify the composition of the government and of the party, to detach Slovakia from Prague. It is true that Slovakia would then have known the unenviable fate of becoming an "autonomous Soviet republic."
9. In one of these stories, Mrs. Novotny, desiring to adopt a child, received a baby from the municipal crèche. She unwrapped its swaddling and gave a horrified cry. It was a little Negro. The president in his turn leaned over the baby and declared with satisfaction: "At least I know it isn't a Slovak!"
10. Novotny justified himself to his intimates by saying that he did not intend to encourage any "bourgeois nationalism," neither that of the Slovak Matistes nor the Czech Sokols. This latter organization had in any case been dissolved and forbidden since 1950.
11. This hotly debated point was to receive "corrective mechanism," perhaps in the form of a decision, in the last resort, by the federal Presidium. The Slovaks in fact represented only less than 18 percent of the total effective forces of the party; one can easily imagine the difficulties which could arise in practice, if a decision, the simple

question of national pride, a consideration of prestige, could block it by 9 percent of the Slovak communists who suddenly wished to make their bad temper felt.

12. Almost five hundred thousand Slovaks lived in Bohemia-Moravia. The second Slovak city proved to be Ostrava (eighty thousand) in northern Moravia. It is true that the city of Chicago alone possesses a Slovak population bigger than Bratislava's.
13. An urban tramway linked prewar Bratislava to the Austrian capital.
14. In the Bratislava *Pravda*, December 31, 1968.
15. The congress of the Slovak C.P., meeting again in Bratislava after the Soviet occupation, dismissed him from office on August 29 and replaced him with a progressive, Gustav Husak.

4

Debacle: A Conversation with an Economist

The Face of the Victim — The Facts: Ota Sik Speaks Out — The Conversation with Eugen Loebl

[The Face of the Victim]

A nation was bled white, worn threadbare. In the country, ruined farms and fields lay fallow. In the cities, the absence of construction corresponded to empty display windows and an improbable parade of old jalopies. A proletarianized crowd walked downcast with empty eyes. This was the face of Czechoslovakia before the thaw.

Before World War I, Bohemia-Moravia was the breadbasket and the Ruhr of the Austro-Hungarian Empire; Prague rivaled the prosperity of the capital, Vienna. Under the first republic, the standard of living was comparable to that of France and Belgium.

In 1966 Novotny set up a committee of inquiry to study in detail the reasons for his country's depression. The discoveries of this commission, made up of more than one hundred researchers and headed by the Slovak economist Ivan Sturp, had to be kept secret; its report was presented only to the Presidium and the government. During the thaw it was published in specialized reviews, and its conclusions appeared in the union daily *Prace*. They were stupefying: the standard of living of the salaried Frenchman was more than two and a half times that of the Czechoslovakian (two times higher for the blue-collar worker, six times for the white-collar worker).[1] Sturp believed this anomaly arose from the contrast between Czechoslovakia's "society of production" and France's "society of consumption." Production for production's sake had become "an enormous machine feeding on itself, producing for its own needs without touching the life of the citizens."

In 1938, practicing an intensive agriculture which was one of the best in the world (along with that of the Netherlands and Denmark), Czechoslovakia not only was self-sufficient but exported more than a billion crowns worth of produce. In 1967, to feed itself, it had to import more than 3.5 billion crowns worth of agricultural products, including 2,350,000 tons of cereals.

Before World War II, Czechoslovakia was renowned for the quality of its products, largely exported to the West. At the Brussels exposition, which unhappily coincided with Munich, the workshops of Czechoslovakia's industries won several gold and silver medals. In 1968, the quality norms of Czechoslovakian products were such that the leaders of the exportation trusts themselves recognized that even *after* economic reform the depth of its technological retardation would compel Czechoslovakia to wait three to five years before being ready to furnish to Western markets products of competitive quality.

Although Czechoslovakia ranked third in world production of cement per capita, a Czech could not legally buy a bag of cement or a wheelbarrow full of bricks to build or repair a house. Stripped of paper, which was imported at great cost from Scandinavia, Czechoslovakia continued to export wood pulp from its dangerously impoverished, overexploited forests. In the ultramodern hotel where I always stayed in Prague — it was built several years ago — all sanitary arrangements and pipes had been imported from the United Arab Republic and India because in the 1950's Comecon had decided to move the plumbing and pipe factories to Hungary and to Bulgaria.

Since, finally, in spite of starvation wages and acute penury, the Czechs and Slovaks survived, the black market must have enjoyed a volume at least equal, if not superior, to the transactions of the official economy. Theft and clandestine barter constituted the necessary corrective to the all-powerful but inoperative economic bureaucracy.

The reasons for the country's functional bankruptcy are in fact innumerable; the economic history of this unhappy country was an adventure at least as dramatic as the tragicomedy of Czechoslovakia's twenty years of socialism.

The shameful pillage of the country's natural resources can be illustrated by a single example: in five years, the Soviet Union exhausted fifty years of reserves of uranium ore from Jachimov in Bohemia — the only mine of its kind in Europe. No statistic yet published gives any idea of the damages of this pillage; the Russians are responsible for the "accounting." One of the uranium negotiators with the Russians told me openly: "Sold at its true price, this uranium could have brought our present standard of living up to that of Sweden." [2]

[The Facts: Ota Sik Speaks Out]

In the first two weeks of June, Ota Sik, vice-president of the council of ministers, the father of the economic reform so frequently discussed after January, gave a series of six television broadcasts — one half-hour telecast every two days. They com-

276

prised a complete account of the country's economic situation, sector by sector. They roused certain unease in the party and the government. In the corridors of official buildings it was insinuated that Sik was "avenging" himself: his reforms had barely been instituted. Rumors of his resignation circulated.

Ota Sik made his telecasts freely, but mysteriously enough the press reported only fragments of them. The pamphlet which should have reproduced his talks never materialized. When I asked Jiri Pelikan, the head of television, for recordings of these talks, he told me, after "inquiry," that there were none because Sik had spoken "live." Sik, questioned on the telephone, confirmed the fact that his lectures were improvised and were represented by no notes; he did not feel it opportune to speak to the foreign press. This incident was typical of the climate which was beginning to develop in the last weeks of the thaw. Freedom of information was not in question but lapses of memory, omissions, documents conveniently misplaced, and embarrassed explanations punctuated with sighs replaced the fine frankness of the early days. The orthodox press from Moscow to East Berlin had begun its heavy barrage; reexamination of an economy serving "plan-ism" and Comecon became as sacrilegious as the least observation on the grounds of the Warsaw Pact. Ota Sik became the Kremlin's *bête noire*, as had General Vaclav Prchlik.

However, the archives of the Prague press and the reports of Ceteka — the official press agency — make it possible to reconstruct Ota Sik's statements. (Later, after Sik arrived in Switzerland, having left Czechoslovakia, his economic ideas were published in many countries under the title *The Truth About Czechoslovakian Economy*.) He painted a grim picture of an economy which had for twenty years conformed to Stalinist policy. With concrete examples, Sik revealed the extent of confusion in the Czechoslovakian economy; he gave official confirmation to what all generally well informed circles had suspected for a long time in piecing together scattered fragments of bitter experiences.[3]

Thus, beginning with the Stalinist dogma that absolute priority should be given to heavy industry and to mechanical construction, which continually demand more steel or, in other words, beginning with the heavy metallurgical equipment with which steel is produced, Sik demonstrated this to be a vicious circle which led only to increasingly greater investment in heavy industry: investments destined for heavy industry rose from 35 percent of total investments in 1948 to 44.5 percent in 1963 to 47 percent in 1966. During this period technological retardation was such that the yield was reduced despite the increased investments. (To obtain that increase of national revenue made possible by the investment of 1958, Sik estimated that four times as large an investment would be necessary in 1968.) Moreover, machinery was becoming obsolete — in 1963, 57 percent of the industrial equipment was worn out — and consumption had grown. Ota Sik demonstrated that, if in the United States 186 kilos of steel were needed for production worth one thousand dollars in the metallurgical industry, an identical production in Czechoslovakia would demand 435 kilos of steel. While the ratio of consumption of raw material to value of the finished product diminished in developed countries, it increased in Czechoslovakia; its economy was devouring its own substance.

In the area of construction, the account was just as devastating. In industrial construction, a particularly underequipped branch, the value of the stock of tools per worker was nearly three times less than that of industry and barely more than that of the most neglected area, agriculture. The construction of a new factory required at least three times as long as it would in the West: the atomic center of Trnava, begun in 1958, was never finished, while the building of a similar center was finished in three and a half years in a Western capitalist country. At the end of 1967, total funds frozen in unfinished workshops was estimated at more than 100 billion crowns. The construction of individual dwellings had completely broken down. Czechoslovakia, today at the end of the list of European countries in the number of dwellings built, has constructed less than 100,000 units in a plan calling for 450,000. On the average, in Prague, in 1938, it required 1,392 man hours to finish a dwelling; today it requires 330 more. Technological retardation is so great in all branches of industry that more than 80 percent of materials is handled manually; the proportion is 18 percent in the West.

Agriculture is critical: "Our agricultural production has fallen to an extremely low level, essentially because of the desertion of the rural areas by the young." The number of agriculturalists has fallen from 2,319,000 in 1936 to 1,260,000 in 1964, of which two-thirds have an average age of fifty. According to Sik "the departure of the young agriculturalists has unfortunately not been compensated by an improvement in production techniques." In 1964, the country had only one tractor for 43.5 hectares of arable land. Such statistics are not available after 1964; Ota Sik's discussion suggests that in the following four years the situation became still worse.

Blaming the bureaucrats of the plan, Sik gave examples of bad industrial management. Out of 11,941 factory directors listed in 1963, only 2,822 had taken courses at a university, while 2,265 had barely reached the level of primary instruction; the title of director was too often awarded on the basis of fidelity to the party, or simply friendship.

In his last broadcast, Sik explained to the public the remedies which would enable the Czechoslovakian economy to "attract the West": the introduction of bonuses for the most productive workers, the end of leveling of white-collar workers, an opening up to the West both to obtain loans and to measure Czechoslovakian methods against the most advanced techniques, the loosening of economic bonds with the U.S.S.R. and Comecon. But he was the first to understand that the reorganization of the economic system depended on political reforms in depth and could not be served by a democratic smattering permitting only freedom of speech. Sik's last talk took on the aspect of a testament; he spoke of eliminating blind subordination to a supreme authority and of changing the motivations for progress. Sik's analysis was a singular statement on the national priority of the economic life in a materialist and scientific Marxist society.

[The Conversation with Eugen Loebl]

I wanted to discuss the economic issues and their implications with a man without doubt the greatest economist in the country, Eugen Loebl, director of the state bank at Bratislava. The life of this man, who lived far from the capital and far from power, sums up twenty years of communism in Czechoslovakia.

Arrested in 1949, on no precise charge, with the approval of Slansky, Loebl was held secretly for three years and then judged *with* Slansky, whose codefendant he became in spite of himself. Given a life sentence, Eugen Loebl became a veteran of Stalinist prisons in Czechoslovakia. This great bourgeois, polyglot, and extremely cultivated son of an industrialist from Bratislava was a Communist of long standing — he joined the party in 1931 — but was the first of the Communist leaders to be thrown in prison after the "victorious February" of 1948. A Jewish intellectual and colleague of president Benes, Loebl was passionately attached to the unity of the Czechoslovakian Republic; he was simultaneously accused of Zionism and Slovak separatism. For having struggled against the U.S.S.R.'s deliberate exploitation of the economy of his country, he was condemned to prison for life in 1952 as a saboteur of Czechoslovakian foreign trade.

Eleven years of prisons and concentration camps had not
broken this sexagenarian, who voluntarily retired from active
political life to devote himself to an intensive study of Marxism and our times, a study intensified by the four square
meters of the prison cell to which he was confined for three
years of the most absolute solitude: "I had neither pencil nor
paper. I had to write my books in my head. But when I was
able to set down my ideas, black on white, they poured out by
themselves, like automatic writing." [4]

In the garden of his villa in Novohradska, the residential
section of Bratislava, where I spoke with him in June 1968, his
eyes twinkling with humor behind his thick spectacles, his
round face marked with serenity and benevolence, Eugen
Loebl seemed to have emerged unscathed from a trial about
whose details he was modestly silent.[5] His remarks were interrupted not by bitterness but by bursts of laughter and funny
stories, and they disclosed an astonishing dynamism; he was
preparing a theoretical work and a lecture series while carrying
on the business of his bank. "There are good things about
prison," he said. "It gives you time to think. It shouldn't be
abused, certainly, but it does make you work with a will afterward."

Freed in 1956, Loebl played a role of some importance in
the new direction in Bratislava. "You were the youngest and
the most ardent among us," said the stormy novelist Ladislav
Mnacko, who joined us.

Economist, sociologist, philosopher, Eugen Loebl was for
me the ideal interlocutor, of whom I could ask obvious and
naïve questions about what had been happening in the past
months in Czechoslovakia. What did "new direction" mean
on economic and political levels? Could communism be other
than a totalitarian regime? Was not social equality hell paved

with good intentions, imaginary riches distributed among the ruins of an economy? What did "class struggle" mean in states where discontent and open revolt were the fate of a youth born and educated in the lap of Marxism?

To the one who organized foreign trade in postwar Czechoslovakia, and the one whom everyone considered the most original and strongest contemporary economist (his young disciple Ota Sik, first vice-minister and master thinker in economic matters of the Dubcek team was more conservative than he), I talked of my wanderings in the country, of the spectacle of desolation offered to the best-intentioned observer: the factories, the fields, and the stores of the Republic after twenty years of Soviet colonization.

Loebl protested. Everything could not be blamed on the Russians. If sometimes they had imposed themselves, for the most part they had been willingly and servilely imitated: "At the outset our two economies were essentially different. Until the 1950's Czechoslovakia, a very industrialized country, had always lived on its exports, and the U.S.S.R. had practically no foreign trade (less than 1 percent of its total trade) and lived as an autarky. It was a marriage between the tortoise and the hare.

"The Soviet system looks upon economy as a monolithic enterprise. The Russians say: There are ten thousand capitalists. We will expropriate them and there will be only one, the state. As there is now only one business, it can be administered from one place. Their only interest is in the final balance without any consideration for prices; it is an economy of bookkeepers.

"There is a central brain trust which thinks for all, gives directives to all branches of the economy. At the level of business there is nothing to do but obey. If it is necessary to manufacture three million pairs of shoes at such-and-such a price, it is enough to furnish the enterprise with the material, the funds, and whatever else. Thus business is not interested in the whole economy but only in the single production. It does not care about the quality but about quantity. A plan cannot enter into qualitative details."

"What interest have the Soviets in dislocating and pauperizing the Czechoslovakian economic machine?" I asked.

"They haven't done it with bad intentions. Two factors have played a part: on the one hand, their economic theses are part of their ideological messianism and, on the other, they have applied recipes proven at home without concern for the different structure and level of our population. Rigid planning can sometimes work in retarded economies where there are few standards, but in a scientific economy it is catastrophe. . . . Outside of that, a sort of obsolete glorification of manual labor, anti-intellectual aberration which distinguishes the so-called productive forces from those which are not,[6] has blinded them.

"Thought is the principal source of wealth. If there is no thought at the summit among the leadership of the plan, if thousands of businesses and millions of factories are not given the opportunity to 'think,' the sources of prosperity are destroyed in the egg. In 1948 our economy was already out of breath. In applying Soviet recipes, we brought the roof down."

"Of all the negative factors which, in your opinion, is the most disastrous?" He answered:

"Excessive centralization. In theory, it's a good thing; there should be a headquarters, unconcerned with contingencies of profit and truly 'disinterested,' working in the abstract for the good of the whole collective. In practice, there is not a single example in which this has not proved catastrophic."

"Ota Sik remains a 'plan-ist,' although he envisages the plan in a much more flexible manner . . ."

"Yes," Loebl replied. "I reproached him for this as long ago as 1963; I am still against it. I remain an advocate of free enterprise within our socialist system, on the basis of the theory according to which, in our time, it is not manual labor but intellectual labor which is the source of economic prosperity."

"This is opposite to all the Marxist theses in the matter of economy . . ."

"No doubt. I needed the long night of my detention to see all that is false in this aspect of Marxism. The sum of our economic errors arises from the fact that we have not understood the meaning of intellectual work, of intelligence. We always think of manual labor, and when we speak of leadership of the party, the party workers, we always think of the manual workers. We do not understand that modern socialism can be established only by the intellectuals, only by them. It is a scientific business, requiring the intellectual. We are no longer striking, at the barricades, involved in the romantic struggles of the first industrial societies. In fact, we are already in the postindustrial era. And this new world, this is no longer a matter for strong arms."

"The proletariat has not disappeared," I countered.

"The proletariat remains an immense force, but the future of the proletariat should not be to perpetuate itself no matter what. The proletariat is the only class of society which is interested in taking power not to perpetuate itself but in order to *disappear*. We are moving toward a society in which there will be a growing number of intellectuals. If manual laborers remain, they will be of a new type. They will no longer be concentrated in great factories but dispersed; this can already be seen in the United States. It will be the intellectual or semi-intellectual workers who find themselves concentrated in offices for study, for applied research, and so on. The manual laborers will be in services, the third sector, in little groups who will manipulate automated machines."

"Proletarian power is a nostalgia for the past . . ."

"Precisely. Socialist-societies theory belongs to the past and its axis is the analysis of social conflicts of the past, of the beginnings of industrialization. In socialist societies the most generous hopes for the future and conservative timidity coexist. We take one step forward, one step back. So we have made industries which are good in themselves, built factories, and placed at their heads directors who would have been excellent in the last century, but not today."

"When they aren't just incompetents with valid party cards . . . ," I began, but he interrupted me:

"That was true at one time, but it has been less and less so during this last year. In fact, capitalism and Marxism have nothing to do with this matter; we simply have no one ready to be manager of a modern industry, no one capable of understanding and guiding this machinery which is as complex, as subtle as a modern business. It is to this that I attribute above all the reasons for our economic bankruptcy."

"And the remedy?"

"Independent businesses, a free market, real economic competition, the development of endogenous economic forces which will guide and stimulate the economy better than the dictatorship of the plan."

"By endogenous forces do you mean a return to supply and demand?" I inquired.

"Not only that. The creative imagination is also an endogenous factor. This is not a product one can demand in the market, but on the contrary it is a factor which will arouse a new demand when it appears."

I told Loebl my feelings on what was going on in his country. This seemed to me less a political phenomenon than a crisis of morality and dignity, a cultural conflict of some kind. I told him what I had read on a placard carried by students in the City Hall Square in Prague: "We are not Uzbeks." A people proud of their ancient culture found themselves governed by primitives. A people whose standard of living before

Munich was one of the highest in Europe — almost that of France and Belgium — found itself reduced to beggary. A mistaken and fierce "class struggle" had impoverished everybody without profiting anybody. I reminded him of the Czech proverb: "Who does not steal wrongs his family." Loebl laughed and explained to me that this proverb and a flock of similar ones had not come into their folklore before 1948.

Loebl admitted that this "cultural crisis" was important. The Czechs and the Slovaks had reached the bottom of the abyss. The communists themselves remained plunged in the nightmare of the political trials in the Soviet Union: "We knew that this inhuman caricature could not be the socialist society for which we had fought and suffered."

But for Loebl this moral crisis had been only an accessory factor, an epiphenomenon. It was a phenomenon of another kind which brought the thaw to Prague. And this phenomenon was in essence economic in the largest sense of the term. It was the drama of an intellectually advanced society which could have had access, on demand, to the scientific technological society of the year 2000, if it had not kept its head in the sand. He explained:

"What is actually happening in Czechoslovakia is not liberalization, democratization of a social system and methods of government. Liberalization and democratization are secondary aspects, though spectacular, of a profound intellectual revolution — I underline this word — a revolution of the intelligentsia, a true mutation of our society. The intelligentsia is no longer only one group, the beneficiaries of a certain kind of employment, the heirs of a certain education, but a determining social force, the movers and shapers of the new society. Two hundred years ago, for example, one could have the teachers on the one hand and shoes on the other. The fact that the teacher was good or bad was a thing in itself; the shoes which one bought from the craftsman were without relation-

ship to the existence of good or bad teachers. Today, one cannot buy shoes if one has not also schools, teachers. The teacher
becomes as important in the production of shoes as the factory
worker who makes them. This means that intellectuals are
creators not only of cultural values but also of material
values."

I told him that this phenomenon was not limited to the
socialist society. He admitted this willingly:

"We are present at the emergence of a whole new social
entity, even if the previous one is not aware of it. It is a mana-
gerial revolution like the one which actually took place in the
United States and changed the face of the economy in the
large sense of the term. When a society attains a certain stage
of development, this technological revolution must inevitably
be effected. Galbraith analyzed it perfectly for American society."

"Such a revolution cannot avoid major political consequences. It will inevitably reach the U.S.S.R." And he responded:

"Everything that is happening here will happen elsewhere in
the socialist world. It will not always take the same form.
There will be a continuum of customs and national traditions.
But if a society wants to move toward the future, inevitably it
will know our process, a new role for the intelligentsia, and all
the ensuing political consequences."

"Then you are optimistic for Czechoslovakia."

"No, I do not know if we will emerge victorious from the
crisis this time; I can only hope. It is possible that after our
initial victories, we shall be conquered. But this historical current is irresistible. It is not a question of conflict between
Dubcek and Brezhnev, of the communist regime being more
or less liberal. It is a fundamental revolution, perhaps the
greatest revolution of the human race since 1789. In place of
the manual laborer who undertakes a struggle against nature in

order to wrest his goods from it, nature itself, domesticated by the intellect, will fight for us, offer us her treasures."

"This will not come without dangers . . ."

"Yes, man's alienation and existential problems are linked to this revolution. For, on the one hand, if in our relations with nature we have made amazing progress, if our knowledge progresses to vertiginous heights, on the other, on the level of what I will call man's understanding, *vertù*, interpersonal relations, our progress has been slower. Neither television nor the mass media, instant information with all its miracles, has helped us. Often the reverse. Moreover, we do not yet know how to use our leisure."

"This crisis of civilization affects the capitalist world as well as the socialist societies," I offered. He responded at length:

"That is true. We are in a state of crisis with an impoverished economy while West Germany with a prosperous economy undergoes the same thing. The crisis of our times cannot be reduced to its economic components; it is much more complicated . . .

"In any case, capitalism has won the first round. It has at least known how to resolve its economic problems. The apocalypse foreseen by the Marxists, a new economic 'great crisis,' has not occurred. On the contrary, it is the socialist economies which are foundering, unable to guarantee full employment except at starvation wages, inferior to the allowances we give on our dole.

"But we will win the second round, I am sure. In spite of the mistakes we have made, we will find the primary vocation of socialism which is, before all, humanism. To have forgotten for so many years the role of man is the reason for all our failures. I think that the true rivalry between capitalism and socialism will reveal itself not on the economic level but in the place which is given to man in either society. Which system will tomorrow be able to give man more happiness to stimulate his reasons for living. We have seen that the society of consumption does not make man happy."

"Nor does the society of deprivation . . ."

"I don't say that we ought not catch up, to a certain point, with the Western capitalistic level of life. But a prosperous economy should not be our only goal. We should be able to find something better than Western society, for even if we catch up materially we already know that abundance does not resolve fundamental problems."

"Marxist messianism would thus go on from the utopia of egalitarian justice to the pursuit of happiness . . ."

"In one sense, yes, a society for man, on his scale, to his measure. In America, which represents the worst form of the society of consumption Western-style, they consume in order to produce still more, in order to consume still more. It's a vicious cycle. Production and consumption have lost their basic meaning, and because of this the whole society has lost its meaning."

I retorted that American society, hurried and overcharged, was certainly no Trappist monastery, but that the depressing spectacle of amorphous crowds, miserable and idle, in the communist countries was no more inspiring. I told him of the reflection of a Czech foreman in a factory in Bohemia who freely admitted that his workers' productivity was perhaps inferior by half to that of a Western worker. "They no longer want to work for slogans," he had told me, "for cardboard medals, or for devaluated crowns which won't let them buy what they want. The state pretends to pay them, so they pretend to work."

Loebl was indignant: "Our workers are not basically lazy or negligent. In Czechoslovakia we have a secular tradition of work well done, dedicated, irreproachable. It's the system which has made them as you see them. Not the fact of earning less money than in the West, but bad leadership. If you go to the university and your professors are mediocre, if they do not examine your work, test your knowledge, no matter how gifted you are, you won't accomplish much. This bad leadership has introduced Stakhanovism, 'norms,' and all those methods of constraint which have discouraged the working masses. You work, for example, in a normal rhythm at a rate of ten pieces an hour. You are promised more money if you do fifteen. After a year, you are told that ten is no longer the norm but fifteen; to earn more you must do twenty pieces. For years, the workers were swindled this way. Then they ceased to be dupes and stopped working. Our workers have become lazy just because they are intelligent."

"Will the thaw bring back their zeal?"

"I'm sure of it. They only need a little ray of hope. For six months no one wanted to hear talk about the party, about politics; nobody was interested in politics with the exception of a few intellectuals. All that has changed. Twenty years of Stalinism put their faculties to sleep but did not annihilate them. In the social life great leaps cannot be made. But aptitudes, creative gifts which have been formed in a nation over centuries and centuries of persevering work, cannot be made to disappear."

"So how can they be awakened? It can no longer be done with slogans . . ."

"We don't have a problem with the workers, but with the leaders. What we need is efficient managers.

"Now I come to the problem of the efficiency of the economic machine. For a factory to show a profit in the West, it must have not only good directors and good workers but also an adequate number of the latter. But in the communist societies where the notion of profit plays no part, factories are built to give employment and, moreover, a worker can never be fired nor can an incompetent employee.

"But that will change. A business which does not show a

profit will be closed, and one which shows profits will be enlarged. There will be competition and obedience to the laws of the market. Rivalry between socialism and capitalism will have relevance, for economic efficiency, like a surgical operation, is neither a communist nor a capitalist affair; it is a question of scientific level, of efficiency in management. In the treatment given to man, in the way, for example, the unemployed are treated, will reside the difference between our two systems."

"Let us return, then, to one of the weaknesses of the Marxist economy: the factories created to give work, a plethora of workers."

"No, for we must assure work, but not necessarily jobs. All those who want to work should have the right and the possibility to do so without this implying job security, a definite job."

"What would you do with the unemployed?" I wondered.

"We can take care of this problem. A certain number of unemployed will receive aid."

"That's what we do in the West."

"With this difference always, that if a factory is losing money in the West, the private owners close it immediately. We, on the contrary, in the light of the economic situation, will keep it open for two or three years if necessary, allowing it to function at a loss, over the period of time required to move the workers on to something better. At the same time an attempt will be made to diminish the liability of the factory so maintained. But, I repeat, our immediate problem is that of management. We may not find the managers we need immediately, but if only half of our factories were better run, there could be, let us say, a 2-to-3 percent improvement in production. The people could see that progress was being made."

"The conflict between the dogmatists and the progressives of the C.P., in their search for popular support, is real. The former say — and I've seen the anonymous tracts which are distributed in the factories — we have brought you security.

The new ones want to bring unemployment. Even if security means a fearful mediocrity, the popular masses want it . . ." He interrupted:

"For myself, I would advise abandoning job security. But I would create such an inequality of incomes that this would be a stimulating factor in itself. At this moment, he who has security does not understand how it would be to lose it, because everyone, the good and the mediocre worker alike, is in the same boat. When it is seen that the good worker can earn three, four, and five times more than the bad one, this will create an effective stimulant." [7]

"What's happening with the liberalization of crafts of small trade, small businesses?" I asked.

"I have been particularly active in this area. We are going to do a great deal in this domain. In the little businesses we have the greatest economic reserves, reserves which could be mobilized immediately with a very small investment. The services and goods which these little businesses produce go directly on the market and raise the standard of living. When we begin the operation, the effect will be instantaneous. We have just, for example, created an export company in Prague especially to make use of those little businesses which make handcrafted articles, glassware. For twenty years, clever craftsmen left their tools at home, covered with dust; they hadn't even the desire to try anything. Some of them have just begun, and their merchandise already represents hundreds of thousands of crowns in foreign currency, for export."

"What will be the dimensions of these private businesses?"

"They will be modest, to be sure, not more than one wage-earner to a family. But the contractors would get together and form cooperatives sharing profits among themselves. There would be no limit to their profits. In that case, there would not be any limit to the number of workmen and employees they used either, but these latter would have to be part of the cooperative. They would receive salaries, plus a percentage of the profits."

"But the initiative of a single individual able to have but one worker would be limited to the opening of a little shop or a little craft service?"

"Yes, and we hope thus to find again the craftsmen whom we so desperately need: plumbers, shoemakers, and so on, and to have restaurants and little cafes managed in this way."

"But what will you do about the original sin of Czechoslovakian economy, which explains its actual chaos: the yoke of heavy industry, the orientation of foreign trade exclusively toward the East, the nonconvertibility of money?"

"These are structural problems," he replied, "for which we can only find long-term solutions. What we can do immediately, and this will be some help to us, is to change the proportions. It is not possible to close or reconvert steel mills from one day to the next, but by increasing consumer enterprises strongly, we will have a better balance."

"That takes money. Where will you find it?"

"We have part of this money; for the rest we will find it to borrow. Our merchandise is not of high enough standard, but with the help of credit, we can modernize our production and increase it rapidly enough. We begin at such a low level that an amelioration of 3 or 4 percent will be enough to show change, progress. Political hope must find its equivalent in some sort of material betterment. We have fallen so low that any amelioration will be very much appreciated. I know that these will only be conservative measures. We must be patient. Meantime, we must settle down to the real problems, to the structural reforms, to make up for twenty years of technological arrears."

"And the convertibility of money?"

"It is not an economic problem. It is a problem linked to our price system. Your shirt, for example, costs 100 units in your

country, and your suit 500. There is a certain proportion in
these prices. And this proportion is about the same, whatever
the prices are, in the whole Western economic system. Here,
imagine that the shirt costs 100 units, but the suit is only
worth 80. If we had the same price system as the West, there
would be not the problem of the crown's convertibility but
only that of its exchange. But we cannot have convertible
money as long as our price system is administrative rather than
economic, as yours is."

"The trouble is to some extent the absence of an index, of
economic proportions?"

"We live in an economic ghetto, a very large ghetto which
includes several hundreds of millions of persons but effectively
an isolated bloc not ruled by economic factors."

I began a new topic: "Democratic socialism itself in its
Czechoslovakian version is not ruled by the factors which condition democracy, essentially free and secret elections. We are
returning to our point of departure, the circle is closed . . .
The thaw was born of economic decline, but the economy
cannot recover outside of the political context of democracy."

Loebl took this up: "The problem of democracy is a complex business more than a question of elections. There is no
doubt that the parliamentary democracies of the West are a
more desirable form of government than what we have known.
But is only one kind of democracy possible? If it's a matter of
majority, the majority can be as antidemocratic as dictatorship."

"The majority and respect for the opposition . . ."

"But it remains always the majority, so the respect."

"Also, to be sure, a free press and all that goes with it . . ."

"Yes, but let's go further. I admire parliamentary democracy
when it really plays the game — and I'm thinking particularly
of the British institutions — but more and more in the West,

the parties are monoliths which manipulate both their membership and public opinion. Less and less in the West do you find independent deputies who dare to brave their party machine. The votes scarcely constitute more than a vague indication; the parties make decisions without paying much attention to votes. The problem is to find a new kind of democracy, which I would call an 'anthropocracy' — *anthropos*, the human being, the individual, and not the *demos*, the crowd, the masses. It is in the humanization of socialism more than in its democratization that I see the solution."

"But you must have some criteria. What will yours be if they are not free elections and majority rule?"

"There are spheres in which one must altogether contradict the rule of the majority. Those of fundamental human rights, for example. They must be guaranteed in such a way that no majority could change them. There are, certainly, other areas where the rule of the majority can intervene without threat to the legitimate rights of the citizen. The idea of the democratic majority in the West is always based on notions which arise from antiquity. But the *polis*, the Greek city, did not extend democracy beyond selected members of its patriarchy. Slaves were 'outside the game.' The citizens of the Hellenic democracy were in a position to understand why and for whom they voted. Is that the case of the men of the people in the West? Do they know the why and the how of their vote? We have extended the principle of Greek democracy and created a mechanism by which people vote, but their vote is determined by massive propaganda from one party which is richer than another; by subjective elements — this candidate is an attractive fellow, or speaks better . . ."

"Churchill said that parliamentary democracy is perhaps a very bad system of organizing the political life of a nation, but that he could find no better. And all messianic or utopian systems have finally foundered in an ocean of suffering."

"That does not mean that one could not find another system of government. That is why if the democratization of our system consists of injecting so-called democratic mechanisms into our society, it will not work. Here and there we will meet dead-end paths, where we must choose between socialism and democracy, between justice and liberty; it is not certain that the majority choice will fall on the second half of the alternative."

"If this choice turned out to be possible, I would bet heavily that a vast majority would declare in favor of Western democracy, whatever its inconveniences."

"I'm not so sure. Because the day after the vote we would probably have civil war. There is no political power at the moment other than the C.P. I do not know what there could be in two years, if new powers could emerge, but if there were free and secret elections at this moment, they would create such chaos that we would have lost the benefits of socialism without getting those of democracy in return. That to which we ought to devote ourselves at this moment is democratization within the party. For a year or two at least, I see no other political power which could set in motion here the elements of a certain form of democracy, of any democracy at all. If the C.P. refuses to do so, then there will be no democracy here. If it fails, we would move into an indescribable chaos. After all, for so many years the C.P. has had the absolute monopoly of power. We are no longer in 1948 when, if the bourgeois parties had won, there would not have been chaos. Difficulties, no doubt, and a prerevolutionary situation, but not anarchy in a void. Several weeks ago, in one of the institutes of the academy at Bratislava, I participated in a round-table discussion with the most important personalities of the two Slovak noncommunist parties, Obroda and Svoboda.[8] I was ashamed to be seated at the same table with them. Miserable types. Good-for-nothings. And if there were free elections today, many people, perhaps the majority, would vote for those puppets."

"But who made puppets of them?"

"That's another problem. We are discussing present realities. A majority vote for noncommunist parties would not mean a vote *for* — a program, for men, a platform, and the rest — but a vote *against*, an emotional vote, a vote of resentment and revenge. The very hypothesis in which an international situation would permit such would make it a national suicide to tolerate such elections."

"Then there is no other alternative, for the moment, than the reform of the Communist party?" The Czechoslovakian replied:

"Yes, and it will not be an easy task. These last twenty years have not prepared us for this formidable task, which is the preparation of a real socialist program. Socialism is not only the collective appropriation of the means of production. Nationalization is nothing but another form of property which can coexist with fascism, capitalism, whatever. This is only one of the aspects of a pluridimensional society, dominated by an ethic . . ."

"Our democratic societies in the West are theoretically the same; everyone has equal rights and opportunities," I suggested.

"Yes, but socialist society puts a particular accent on the protection of the weakest, those who are 'less equal' than others. People are not equal in every way, natural gifts, physical and mental qualities, are not equally divided. Society must aid the most handicapped."

"Western society does. But it does not kill the spirit of competition to do so, it doesn't make mediocrity the common denominator in a society which is (apparently) naïvely egalitarian."

"This has been typical of the regime of these last twenty years but I do not believe that it is an integral part of socialism.

Debacle: A Conversation with an Economist

It is still to be proven that the socialist system cannot support the spirit of competition. It's a very primitive way of thinking to believe that only capitalism can have competition, to identify it with the spirit of competition. After 1948, and before the big trials, some among us tried to define the norms of competition in the socialist system. But then it was brutally declared that this was a survival of capitalism and you know what happened . . . But we are no longer at that point. We now admit that a capitalist or a socialist automobile is first of all an automobile and that it should be built in the same way, that the 'management' of the economy is an objective science which should be assumed according to certain rules. If competition is a rational way of approach to economic problems, we would not want to admit all forms of competition — monopolies or understandings with cartels to obtain superprofits at the expense of the consumers — the mechanism of the competition could be adapted to socialism. Even in the capitalist countries, the forms of competition differ from one country to another, depending on the cultural traditions. We have made a serious mistake in assigning to socialism certain attributes. I repeat, an automobile is neither capitalist nor socialist; it is an auto which must be the best made and best adapted to local or foreign markets. And while socialism as a political system has no monopoly on justice, capitalism has none on liberty and democracy. From two basically different socio-economic systems, we are moving together toward a society which will finally be humane. But all the same I believe that we will get there first."

Such were the optimistic ideas of the sage of Bratislava on the eve of the occupation of his country.

The new direction on the economic level had not even begun to be put into practice. Threats, then tanks, kept it from passing from theory into execution. Nevertheless, it made possible some clear and unvarnished observations, a true autopsy of the vices of the classic communist economic system. The same reasons, first and foremost economic, which created the conditions of the Prague thaw will inevitably come into play elsewhere in the Soviet empire.

Notes for Chapter 4

1. The comparison, according to Sturp, should have been favorable to Czechoslovakia, since he estimated that the industrial production of his country was 20 percent superior to that of France per capita, the amount of investments approximately equal, and the military costs of the two countries appeared equal, which seemed improbable to him, since Czechoslovakia had only a conventional army and France maintained a costly atomic striking force. Following his comparative analysis, Sturp noted that the structure of revenues was not very different either and should even have favored his own country, since social allowances outside of salaries, because of family allocations, in particular, were much higher in France than in Czechoslovakia (47 percent of salary against 36.7 percent).
2. The delegation, led by Eugen Loebl, which left to negotiate with Anastas Mikoyan in Moscow in 1947, demanded the prices of the world market. The Russians pretended to accept. Soon after their return, the negotiators found themselves in prison and the Russians paid for the Czech uranium at its cost price plus 10 percent.
3. In Czechoslovakia, as in the other countries of the socialist bloc, concrete economic data are as hard to discover as military secrets. In spite of the abundance of sources of information (Institute of Economics, of State Planning, of Social Planning, of Economic Research at the Academy of Sciences, at Prague, Institute of Research on the Standard of Living in Bratislava), one gets hardly anything but theoretical "papers" and "percentages," without any definite figures.
4. The two first works of Loebl appeared in German in 1967, *Geistige Arbeit* (Dusseldorf and Vienna: Econ Verlag), and 1968, *Die Revolution rehabilitiert ihre Kinder* (Vienna: Europa Verlag).
5. Condemned to prison for life, he learned, in his cell, that his wife was condemned to forced labor in a factory in Bohemia, while his twelve-year-old son was sent to a home for delinquents in Moscow and, two years later, was also put to forced labor.
6. In most of the communist regimes, doctors are considered nonproductive and receive inferior treatment to architects or engineers, who are called productive.
7. The ridiculousness of the leveling of salaries is illustrated by this little story attributed to Ota Sik. An excellent workman earns 3,000 crowns. Singled out by the administration, he becomes a foreman at 2,500 crowns. He is such a brilliant foreman that he is sent to study

to be an engineer. He comes back to his factory with a fine diploma and an assured salary of 2,000 crowns. The illustration is a little heavy-handed, but it illustrates the general tendency well.

8. Parties of the "rebirth" and "freedom," creatures of the National Front in Slovakia.

5

Reflection: Conversations with a Philosopher

The Magic Lantern — A Marxist but Not a Communist — The System and Its Myths — Winter, Spring, and Summer 1968 — A Digression — Antithesis to Summer — A Prospectus for Autumn — Perspective

[The Magic Lantern]

On that sad day of August 24 I thought a great deal about revising this chapter in which I report my numerous interviews with Ivan Svitak. A bulletin from the Agence France Presse came off the teletype. Svitak was in Vienna; in exile but free. His last words to me, after a hasty breakfast at the restaurant of the Magic Lantern theater in Prague on a stormy July day — he was beaming, "My first trip abroad in twenty years" — had been melancholy but optimistic:

"For a long time we will have democratization without real democracy, liberalization without real liberty — a liberty which hands out freedoms piecemeal. As to free and secret elections, it's mad even to think of them, even — even in the long run. The Communist party, however 'progressive' it is, will never renounce its monopoly of power. In which country and under what regime have you ever seen a party in power preparing its own funeral rites? That does not mean we won't have any elbow room at all, but let's not ask for the moon. If Dubcek could only 'hold out,' if we could keep what we have today, neither more nor less, just the few liberties we have now."

[A Marxist but Not a Communist]

At forty-three, long-limbed, nervous, sharp-faced, Professor Ivan Svitak, calling himself "a Marxist but not a communist," had become Dubcek's principal challenger after having been the most immovable and the most persecuted enemy of Novotny's dictatorship.

Cisar, the party ideologist, in irritation and admiration, said of him: "What is he looking for: a stake?" (Jan Hus, the great Czech reformer, was burned at Constance.) Then more gently: "After all, he's a philosopher. His job is to ask questions. It doesn't matter if it's impossible to answer him."

In a word, Svitak stood outside the system, even the improved system. He was a free man. The idol of the Prague students, he founded the Club of Committed Nonparty Members, a political club which had been tolerated since its formation in February 1968 but which as yet had no legal existence. The club could not recruit members, publish a paper or pamphlets, have a telephone number, or establish a bank account.[1] Nevertheless the Club of Committed Nonparty Members constituted a political platform and represented real political opposition. It represented the opposition of the six million Czech citizens who were not members of the Communist party.

The personal and professional life of Ivan Svitak singularly reveals over two decades the communist strangulation of civil liberties and the communist regime's alertness to any form of intellectual liberty or independence, however "peripheral." Svitak was not a politician or a sociologist or an economist; he was only a philosopher whose domain appeared to be as remote as possible from the burning questions of contemporary ideologies. Svitak was a specialist in medieval philosophy. He was only thirteen when the Nazis reached Prague, but, "Our resistance to and hatred of Nazism were unanimous. Above all, our generation learned to recognize all the tortuous and subtle mechanisms of totalitarian oppression. Somewhat naïvely, I believed that we Czechs were completely forewarned against dictatorship. We had learned in a good school."

During 1945 and the liberation, Svitak joined the Social Democratic party and became president of the Socialist Students' Union. In 1948 he joined Fierlinger's socialist splinter group, which after the Prague coup chose to collaborate with the communists: "I was a very ardent socialist, and things were not clear at that time. In view of the bourgeois parties' failures, it seemed to me that collaboration with the communists was the only possible way."

But things were soon made clear. At the end of 1948 Svitak left his party and ceased all political activity; he did not wish to take part in excluding young people of bourgeois families from the university: "This reminded me of the *numerous clausus* against the Jews. I was shocked and horrified by this social racism which combined cruelty with stupidity."

Sickened, young Svitak plunged into intensive study of the beginnings of Greek philosophy and began to teach in 1949.[2] He continued his education, studying the philosophy of the age of enlightenment, and wrote two essays on Montaigne and Voltaire. His troubles began in 1952. Svitak had expressed surprise in a small committee at the fact that there had been no congress of the Communist party since 1949. He was soon questioned by the police, who accused him of an anti-Stalinist attitude. "I defended myself pretty well, but foreign travel was forbidden me. In spite of invitations to different meetings and universities, I was unable to leave Prague between 1948 and 1968."

The Slansky affair marked his complete rupture with the regime and the beginning of his deliberate and open intellectual opposition. In 1954 he wrote a work on religion in the contemporary state. The book was censored: "For a very odd reason. I approved the idea of the separation of church and state as it existed in all modern countries. But Czechoslovakia, a socialist republic, ruled by historical materialism, in which atheism and religious persecution had had free rein for twenty years, had not — and still has not — actualized the separation of church and state. This situation made corruption of the church easier for the political powers."

In 1956 Svitak became the *bête noire* of the regime. With his gentle scholar's naïveté, he took seriously the about-face of the Twentieth Congress of the Soviet C.P. Taking advantage of this brave flare-up of liberalism he published an essay on socialism and democracy in *Literarni Noviny*, journal of the Writers' Union. Events in Hungary swept away any liberal illusions. His new paper, a purely theoretical work, *The Art of Philosophy*, was banned by the censor. Charged with revisionism, Svitak was expelled from the Institute of Philosophy, which he had founded two years before, under the aegis of the Academy of Sciences.

"It is true that I was not altogether 'innocent.' The Institute brought together a whole phalanx of philosophers like Karel Kosic, Kalivoda, Richter, Ivan Dubcik, and others,[3] and we composed a critique, though it was very abstract, of the political situation of the country. It was so esoteric that it must have discouraged the inevitable police informers."

Svitak returned to the Institute a year later and then left it again, according to a regime in which the screws were loosened only to be turned again. For five years he could not publish a line. In 1963 he was authorized to publish an article on Albert Camus. In 1964, on the other hand, with Koucky (ambassador from Czechoslovakia to Moscow) as minister of culture, Svitak was finally expelled from Charles University. He was deprived of all means of earning a living. Koucky, who persecuted him with a passionate hatred, arranged to cut off all his resources and wanted to put him in prison under the terms of the "law against vagrancy and prostitution."

"I finally was authorized to work as an extra in the studios at Barandov." Svitak has tender memories of the "small parts" that kept him from starvation for three years. He was not very gifted, so the film-makers who protected him cast him in silent roles as a soldier on guard in historical films.

Between roles this incorrigible challenger sent letters of protest abroad; he was called up three times before the Prague prosecutor who threatened him with arrest. The last time was next to the real thing. Svitak, who had slipped an article to the Austrian press, had the honor of putting Novotny himself into a rage; in the midst of a council of his ministers, the latter shouted: "Get rid of this madman!" But the matter came to nothing; it coincided with Moscow's Sinyavsky-Daniel trial, whose international repercussions were so unfavorable that the prudent Czechs preferred to avoid a similar trial.

After January 1967, Svitak returned to the university — without his full prerogatives as professor — and resumed his literary collaborations. A few days after the Soviet tanks invaded his country, he fled by way of Austria to the United States, where he teaches at a large university.

The following pages are a synthesis of several interviews which I had with Svitak during the eight months of the Prague thaw. At my request, the philosopher himself reworked these interviews into a consecutive manuscript. The headings more or less correspond to the principal questions asked. An approach to Svitak's thought is not easy. Nor was it easy for this free spirit to remain immune to illusion in the general elation, to illuminate the contradictions of democratic socialism.

[The System and Its Myths]

Totalitarian dictatorships downgrade human lives because they are considered only as tools of power, only as means serving the ends pursued by the state, the political party, the social class, or the leader. The degradation of man as an individual is the greater in the proportion that the dictatorships are effective in the execution of their programs. Human beings considered as tools of the state are much more desperately ready to revolt when they are conscious that man, used in this way, little by little loses all human value, and, as a result, also loses that individual conscience which distinguishes him from animals or stones. Revolt is born out of the absurdity of the human condition.

The European or world revolution for civil rights which began with a series of student revolts in the West and East represents, above all, revolt against the absurd alienation of man in an industrial society. It is revolt against dictatorship, against false values of power or consumption. Attempts to explain the incomprehensible wave of violence in the Western democracies were as vain as those which attempt to find an explanation for the calm and silent revolt going on in Czechoslovakia after twenty years of harsh dictatorship. The most important message of this thaw in Prague, and in Paris, is an entirely new motivation in political action: protest against the fate of the human being in an industrialized society.

The new line of action is applied anthropology — that is to say, practical philosophy in the interests of human existence, an attempt to resolve the crisis of our present condition and to preserve existing values. The young and middle-aged intellectuals are the principal motive forces; they are those who have not responded to the call of materialism or power and who are trying to realize and to affirm the rights of man. The process of transformation which upset the economic aspect of the industrialized countries precipitated a new revolutionary process, the movement in favor of the rights of man and a revolt against absurd alienation in the midst of prosperity. Recognition of this new revolt is necessary to an understanding of the events in Czechoslovakia; without such the Czech thaw would appear to us, at worst, as a series of individual changes and, at best, as a defeat of dictatorship.

The second condition necessary to an understanding of the changes in Czechoslovakia is a knowledge of the characteristic problems encountered en route to limited socialism and is defined by the varying tendencies of revolutionary and democratic socialism. There is fundamental agreement on the concept of socialist society as a society of accelerated production and consumption, as the owner of the principal means of production. But, on the other hand, a fundamental disagreement characterizes the manner in which one may realize this concept. To what extent have the party of the political movement and the government the right to sacrifice civil liberties and democratic control of power to the program of economic development? To what extent are civil rights to be granted and respected? Therein lies the schism dividing the socialist tendencies, the governments, and the nations.

The position of the citizen in the structure of political life and power is of great importance. It is this which reveals the fundamental character of either the democratic or the totalitarian concept of socialism — the extent to which it respects the individuality of man and according to which his liberty is its object, or, to the contrary, the degree to which interests of the individual are secondary to power, to the economy, or to the political interests of society. Such are the values of European society and such is its concept of the raison d'être of man in the world and the universe that this dimension of the religious, the ideological, and the philosophic, which has troubled man since the beginning of time, hides behind the problems of civil rights.

In the course of the last fifty years, the socialist movement has offered three basic ways of overcoming capitalist society: revolution by force and monopoly of power by the Communist party (U.S.S.R.-China); parliamentary reform effected within the democratic process (England-Sweden); the way followed by the democracies of the peoples of the East, with its enormous variations and its attempts to join democratic principles with socialist principles. This last method has succeeded in Yugoslavia and Rumania and failed in Hungary and Poland. But in order to evaluate the events in Czechoslovakia one must realize that neither its communists nor its noncommunists were trying to stir up an anticommunist revolt or an anti-Soviet coup; all were trying to find a way of life which would unite fundamental values of European socialism with their own economic ends.

The third condition rests on respect for the characteristics and history of Czechoslovakia. If today it is part of the Eastern bloc, yesterday it shared for a thousand years the experiences of the nations of Europe, especially Germany and Austria. Czechoslovakia has always been an independent kingdom, even under the Hapsburg domination, and it was the first to introduce the Hussite reformation in the fifteenth century. It suffered the great defeat of conversion to Catholicism after the Thirty Years' War; it revived again toward the end of the century of enlightenment. A nation cannot forget its history and return to oblivion, any more than one can forget how to read and write.

After 1848, the Czech nation had the most developed economy in Austria. In 1878, a social democratic party of a Marxist orientation was established; it became a decisive political force because it was supported by the workers' movement. Even before the first world war this party was powerful enough to elect the independent philosopher T. G. Masaryk to the parliament of Vienna in the course of the first parliamentary elections in 1905.

After the fragmentation of the Austro-Hungarian monarchy, an independent state was finally born. And its great liberal democrat Masaryk preserved the democratic spirit in that part of the world which had already succumbed to fascism. This state endured many difficulties, above all an economic crisis and national differences. This prosperous and democratic state was the first victim of Hitler's aggression in the autumn of 1938 when the powers of the West signed the Munich agreement. Munich in 1938 represented to the Czechs a cruel experience, bitter and unforgettable; they clearly understood that they had been betrayed by their democratic allies. Without this disastrous experience, which was followed by occupation, no Czech government could have reached out in so clear and irrevocable a manner toward the Soviet Union for a guarantee of its national existence as did the president of liberated Czechoslovakia and chief victim of Munich, Dr. Eduard Benes.

The Nazi occupation represented the first phase in the elimination of the defenses of the Czechoslovakian intelligentsia, largely during the Hendrych period in 1942; this elimination continued during the Slovakian revolt in 1944 and finally during the Russian army's liberation of the country. In spite of the political context, the liberators were received with great enthusiasm in the unforgettable spring of 1945. After the experiences of Munich, even noncommunist politicians believed an alliance with the Soviet Union sensible, believed it a permanent guarantee of the independence of our country. Even today, we should not accept as correct the idea that the Czech Republic was then an occupied country which accepted its Soviet orientation by necessity and under pressure.

The period of a little less than three years between 1945 and 1948, a period of working toward the creation of a socialist democracy, was marked by the fruitful policy of the National Front, the noncommunist majority and the strong communist minority, and by the happy beginnings of the nationalization of heavy industry and the land. During this period new institutions were created in which democratic traditions were structurally united with attempts at a revolutionary transformation of the social system. This carefully considered attempt was terminated in February 1948 by events which represented both victory and defeat for the working class. We cannot doubt this paradoxical truth. The events of the month of February 1948 do not add up to a simple coup d'etat by the communists but are an indication of a direction based on the great prestige of the communist and socialist program and on the effective majority of the nation which consented to radical changes. The communists were not "putschists" but revolutionaries who succeeded in isolating so perfectly their adversaries that at the critical moment they found themselves supported not only by the guns of the militia but also by a very real majority. The noncommunist parties were incapable of presenting an effective program of political opposition; they literally scuttled Czechoslovakian parliamentary democracy.

The dark years that followed were not what the instigators of the events of February had hoped; during these years, absolute power came to signify total submission to Stalin. The years of the cold war stopped all political activity and paralyzed those representatives of the Communist party who wished to continue the experiments of the democratic past independently. There were 130,000 political prisoners, of whom 3,000 were communists; innumerable convicts in the forced labor

311

camps and apathetic masses without any rights were all victims of that monopolistic power which, in the beginning, had achieved some good results in the industrialization of the country.

Although the 1950's, or more exactly the period from 1948 to 1955, brought one of the severest political repressions, the new regime still had the confidence of the working class and of a majority of the people. The ordeals created by the totalitarian state were not considered as a terrifying burden imposed on the people, but more as a result of the introduction of socialism which inevitably suffered mistakes and violence on the way to its noble goal, in which the people firmly believed. The political trials alone disturbed this illusion.

In 1956, after the Twentieth Congress, in which the actions of the Communist party of the U.S.S.R. were unmasked, and in spite of the events in Hungary, the illusions persisted. And we must note that the U.S.S.R.'s liberation from the Stalinist nightmare sustained among the majority of the Czechoslovakians a renewal of confidence in the Communist party and the Soviet Union. The idea that Czechoslovakia would also be rid of the yoke of Stalinism was so wholly naïve that it permitted its Stalinist leadership to control the wave of criticism. The repercussions from the Twenty-Second Congress in 1963 were less violent and reached only Slovakia, which no longer constituted a real political threat. But the very real store of illusions and trust was being wasted; the government was exploiting its stability. When the economic crisis reached its nadir in 1968 it fused an explosive situation in which the disillusionments of the past were united with the real differences and subsequently with new illusions.

Slovakia played, and still plays, a special and independent role in the historical development of today's state. For nearly a thousand years four million Slovaks shared a history which differs somewhat from that of the Czechs, because the Slovaks belonged to the Hungarian part of the empire. Slovakia was attached to the Czech crown only during certain periods. This mountainous country was not industrialized; its working class was not very important. The country was still agrarian when it joined the socialist movement in the 1950's. When the Slovaks united with liberated Czechoslovakia after 1918, they were considered only a branch of the "nonexistent" Czechoslovakian nation and were cruelly exploited, because they could not defend themselves as well as the populations of the "historic" countries, Bohemia and Moravia. The Slovaks felt deceived — and justly so. The position of Slovakia as independent state during World War II and the establishment of the nationalist program of independence by Hitler's Germany created additional difficulties.

After 1945, Slovakia was rapidly industrialized. Its national confidence rose again with the evident improvement in the economy, the birth of an important working class, and the disappearance of the erroneous theory of economic "Czechoslovakism." It was also strengthened by the many attempts to emphasize the national independence of Slovakia in the structure of the political institutions which it inherited from the reign of Czechoslovakism. This line of action, which dominated Slovak policy after 1945, repeatedly collided with the obstacle of the political majority and economic superiority of the Czechs. The Slovakian representatives, either corrupted by the Prague centralizers or subject to economic temptations, found their interest difficult to serve; if representatives refused to be corrupted, they were qualified as bourgeois nationalists and lost their political influence — whether they were put in prison or not.

The relative economic superiority of the Czech countries became less apparent in the 1960's; the fundamental reason for which Slovakia had tolerated the archaic structure of the political institutions disappeared. This structure was theoretically founded on national equality, but in reality it rested on the majority system. The program for independent decision and federalization became imperative when economic crisis undermined industrialization and the consequences were reflected in the shut-down of still new factories. This program was to have been pursued by those representatives of Slovak autonomy who had been sentenced in the course of the scandalous trials of 1954.

When the Slovak communist leaders left prison, they were destined to play an important role. After their rehabilitation, they locked horns with Novotny. During 1963, in Bratislava, there began a fermentation which recalled the crisis which shook the Czech countries in 1956. But as in Prague, it was rapidly stifled. Political tension mounted in Slovakia. Novotny's personal power and the deliberate grossness of this primitive Czech dictator when he met with the Slovaks increasingly provoked this nation which had proved its maturity during its national upheaval, on the one hand, and by its accelerated economic development after 1945, on the other. Slovakia was offended, with reason; it protested against the increasingly ubiquitous tutelage of Prague, which was no longer even as useful as it had been before.

The differences between the young and the old nations, between the historical working class and the new one, initiated inevitable conflicts. The idiotic discourtesy of Novotny toward the national Slovak institutions unleashed an avalanche which has already engulfed the system of personal power and which perhaps will engulf even totalitarian dictatorship — if the forces which have united against Novotny's dictatorship continue to maintain their unity. Certain canny Slovak politicians know very well that the program of democratization would suffer severely if the Czechoslovakian front were divided.

The character of Slovakian history could effect either progressive or regressive developments. The Slovak nation is confronting a test which will decisively determine its future. It is faced with the problem of satisfying both the demands of its program and its national exigencies. If its representatives determine that federalization takes precedence over Czechoslovakia's democratization, or is even independent of that, the Slovak people will have to understand that there will be in fact a Slovak government but that after ten years this will end in the problematic situation that the Czechs find themselves in today. This would be as much a catastrophe for Slovak federalization as for Czech democratization; the nations would be obliged to exchange roles.

Only one federal republic of equal nations — Slovakia, Moravia, Bohemia — can resolve the problem of mutual relations in an intelligent and nonviolent fashion; federation will unite itself with democracy. But the subject of the argument is now nothing less than the principles on which two nations and three administrative units will base their modus vivendi. We may still hope that these nations, which have tried out all systems of government, liberal democracy, monarchy, fascism, and Stalinism, will have heads of state who act with prudence enough to permit Czechoslovakia, in the course of its history as a European country, to continue its interrupted humanist tradition and ultimately to try its experiment with the most important problem, socialist democracy.

[Winter, Spring, and Summer 1968]

We can consider the events of the autumn of 1967 as the prelude to the unique process of Czechoslovakia's transformation. In the course of this prelude, *Literarni Noviny* was suppressed in spite of the protests of Czech authors during the Fifteenth congress of that summer. A peaceful student demonstration was brutally repressed. Finally, in the Presidium, the Communist party was openly attacked. The writers, the students, and the representatives would have found themselves without support if a decisive element had not been added to the discontent and to the latent crisis: the national question of Slovakia.

Although we still do not know what happened after the decisive meetings of the Central Committee of the Communist party of Czechoslovakia in January 1968, it is certain that the initially explosive situation was dissipated, after several days of crisis, by the division of the functions of first secretary of the party and those of president of the Republic. The January plenum introduced that process of democratization which is now in its third phase. To simplify, we will distinguish between the winter, the spring, and the summer phases because they singularly differ in their political situations, their programs, their differences, their methods, and their results.

A governmental crisis threatened during the winter phase (January–March) but died down after the abdication of the president of the Republic, a change in the government, and the change of president in the National Assembly. Only a small circle knew the inner problems: certain members of the Central Committee of the Communist party and some intellectual communist writers who had contributed considerably to the fall of the system of personal power. General Sejna's desertion and the suicide of General Janko acted as catalysts. Regardless of the personal attacks made against Anton Novotny, the program of the Communist party did not then go beyond the limits of interior changes. Collective alibis prevented association of the changes made with the support of the Central Committee, for the latter was made up of a majority of supporters of Novotny.

During the winter, the heads of the reform faction had no ambitions beyond the internal change necessary to economic reform. However, the sudden tolerance of criticism, the attacks on Novotny's system, and the crumbling of the state's security

organization stimulated simultaneously an explosive exaspera-
tion and a movement which vehemently demanded rehabilitation of former political prisoners. Although the leaders of the
reform movement would have liked to stop the avalanche of
criticisms — they admitted it themselves — they were unable
to do so and the permanent result of the first phase remains
with us: real freedom of the press.

The representatives of the armed forces of the Communist
party immediately raised their voices against this freedom.
However, the governmental crisis had meanwhile evolved into
a general crisis of the state. Conditions could no longer be
changed without risking serious uprisings or a civil war. The
process of transformation reached its second phase, that of the
spring, during which the number of active participants in the
progressive movement grew considerably.

Enthusiastic youth, communist journalists, and colleagues in
radio and television brought about real miracles by means of
radio or television programs on the violent debates behind
closed doors, personal rivalries, and discussions on the liberty
of man under socialism. The prisons revealed their secrets; reports on the tortures to which prisoners had been subjected, on
suicides of policemen, and on the mysterious death of Jan
Masaryk caused an atmosphere of suspense and excitement.

The Communist party reacted with a program of democratization, rehabilitation, and federalization. However, Anton Novotny not only remained a member of the Central Committee,
as did a certain number of representatives of the conservative
faction, but was also protected by the militia and even, in case
of emergency, by Soviet tanks. An exchange of visits between
Czech and Soviet statesmen was proof of a search for compromise. The progressives insisted on solving the problem of responsibility for the political trials of the 1950's and the crimes
which followed; on the other hand, the conservatives using
anticommunism as a weapon demanded intervention of the

militia against the radio, television, and press and continued to brandish the threat of direct intervention by the Soviet army.

The meeting of the two factions in the spring reestablished the center and prepared the way for a compromise in the June plenum of the Central Committee of the Communist party. In the course of this Novotny and certain others were expelled, but many of his partisans remained. Moreover, the plenum decided not to admit other political parties and agreed to postpone until the extraordinary session of the congress in September the awarding of leadership to one or the other of the two factions.

Even during the second phase, no fundamental changes modified the structure of the social system. On the contrary, a very problematic institution was revived, the National Front, and this phase ended in compromise. Its only results were the legalization of the suppression of censorship, the program of rehabilitation, and the purging of the security services.

The transformation of governmental crisis into a national crisis affected the whole country without sparing the majority, who were not party members; the neutrals, up to now observers who had watched the communists' debates from a safe distance on television, began spontaneously to create political clubs, committees for defense of the press, leagues for political prisoners, and groups which prepared new cultural and political organizations. The circle of participants grew in such a way that the Communist party was incapable of controlling the transformation process. It limited itself to putting a stop to the worst and denied legal status to the organizations and political clubs which had sprung up.

The decisive spirit of the summer phase began with the scientists who demanded in "Two Thousand Words" a program of purgation to be effected by an alliance of communists and non-party members — that is, without the leadership of the Communist party. The reaction of the Communist party to this appeal was hysterical: the Presidium of the Central Committee of the Communist party, the government, and the parliament cried counterrevolution. Nevertheless, the program was very well received and decisively encouraged by the democrats. Let us not forget that the appeal was published during the maneuvers of the general staff of the Warsaw Pact in Czechoslovakia and that at the same time district conferences of the Communist party were meeting to elect delegates to the Extraordinary Congress.

If the first phase had served to resolve internal conflicts and the second to create a compromise between the factions, the third phase revealed the real conflicts between the Communist party and the nonmembers. The attempt to resolve these conflicts, not by resorting to radical actions but by stabilizing the conditions achieved in the course of the Extraordinary Congress, seemed to offer both a solution and yet another obstacle to the transformation process.

[A Digression]

At the beginning of democratization we had to face a nearly insoluble economic crisis. But before we congratulate ourselves on a victory of democratic socialism, we should analyze certain fundamental tendencies which characterized the political development of the democratization process. There are at least ten tendencies which are easily formulated:

The economic crisis, which first caused a governmental and then national crisis, finally degenerated into a crisis of relations between two nations; this situation was rapidly transformed into a crisis of the political structure of the socialist system, which leads to an attempt to reform the mechanism of power.

The communist functionaries — the intellectuals, the writers, and the journalists, followed by the men of science and the nonparty members — had from the beginning played a decisive role in the development of the critical situation. The growing circle of people interested in the positive result of democratization gave rise to unprecedented political alliances between communists and nonparty members against the machine and the former political powers.

The revolutionary process was not premeditated. The initial goals of the Communist party had been radicalized by the spontaneous movement, which directly influenced the communist movement in favor of the rights of man and civil liberties. The program of internal transformation was first changed into a program of democratization and federalization, then into a program of party purges, and perhaps in the future it will become a program for total civil liberty and law based on democratic elections.

One must be blind not to see the growth of resistance to these changes. This resistance, at the beginning organized through personal intrigues, has been continued by public distribution of pamphlets, anonymous letters, resolutions by the militia, attempts to use the armies of the Warsaw Pact, and open threats against the "counterrevolutionaries." The most dangerous of all these forms of resistance is the silent and intense work of that conservative part of the Communist party machine, feverishly preparing the directives for the coming congress and its delegates.

The differences between the progressives and the conservatives grow sharper and more insurmountable. Previously they were only divergences between individual cliques and were solved by compromise. Now they are open conflicts between political factions.

In its evolution the process of democratization passed visibly from internal changes to changes of structure, but this development is not irrevocable. The mechanisms of the former form of executive power have been barely touched. The abolition of censorship and the law on rehabilitation alone must create the basis for transformation of the state into a legal democracy. We must continue to hope for the developments of true democratization rather than accept mere doctoring of the composition of parliament and of the Central Committee of the Communist party.

The most significant tendency of the liberalization movement was eagerness of the machine of the Communist party to stop the process at the stage achieved. However, the propagation of the idea of democratic socialism, the courage and understanding of several people within the Central Committee of the Communist party, the contributions of writers and journalists — communists for the most part — and finally the support given by the people of this country to democratization have prevented the machine from functioning effectively.

The extension of civil rights, the freedom of the press, and the partial freedom of assembly undoubtedly represent the most remarkable aspects of democratization; no longer can one underestimate the return to elementary respect of the rights of the individual. These real, rather than merely proclaimed, liberties have been severely attacked by the conservative faction of the party. This element has already succeeded in prohibiting that political activity characteristic of social democracy, the range of opinions tolerated within the National Front.

Finally, let us not forget that the process of democratization has not yet touched the towns of the various districts and their industries. The structures of power have as yet undergone transformation only in the central urban organizations. One of the weakest points of democratization is just this limitation to the urban populations and the subsequently insufficient support by the rural class of the new program.

Economic programs, derived from democratization, will create additional problems. The most fundamental will be the adoption and application of self-management — the participation of workers in the administration of production. This barely initiated program will dictate the future, for in the end the attempt to resolve the very real economic crisis is the origin of the political crisis. The democratic conception of socialism could fail if its leaders do not offer the people the same economic guarantees offered by the regime of personal power. The optimists now in power cannot achieve victory simply by resolving the political crisis. In fact, they will gain thereby only the conditions necessary to a system which must extend beyond the political domain to each citizen and his individual economic liberty.

[Antithesis to Summer]

Politics is a means of conciliating opposing aspects of certain social contradictions; it is in grasping the juxtaposition of the opposing forces that one can understand their differences. Only a few months of the democratization movement have revealed at least three fundamental contradictions: the machine's power denies the rights of individuals; the conservative faction of the Communist party opposes the spirit of the people; the economic basis of socialism invalidates its freedom. These contradictions are structural rather than individual and can be reconciled only by democratic processes — never by force, arms, or power. While the members of the Communist party, above all those who belong to the intelligentsia, are entirely aware of this situation, the machine of this same party refuses obstinately to recognize it.

The basic fundamental contradiction resides in the absolute power of the party machine; governmental bodies — the parliament and the courts of justice — play only secondary roles in spite of the fact that the proportion between party members and nonmembers is almost 28 to 2. The machine consciously neglects the opinions of millions of nonparty members. Moreover they openly threaten any opposition from these millions with the weapons of the militia and the demagogy of anticommunism. The dictatorship has changed scenery, actors, and ideology, but the old comedy goes on and is more dangerous because the representatives of the democratization process are advancing Novotny's arguments on the subject of the militia.

The powerful elements of the state and of the party machine are confronting a nationwide movement in favor of civil liberty, which is manifested in forms such as clubs. These new organizations, although practically of no significance from a political point of view, are sustained by motives incompatible with the concept of manipulation. The more the machine limits its attention to resolving merely the conflicts within its inner circle of the power elite, the more it stimulates an urgency within the popular movement, whose partisans become extremists with the realization of the increasingly evident incompatibility between the program of the Communist party machine and their own.

The second fundamental contradiction stems from the conflict between the conservative faction and the democratic system. The party has not yet been able to rid itself of the military bureaucratic structure of its organization; it has been unable to transform itself into a popular party which uses the votes of its electorate rather than military force as its base. Each dictatorship protects itself by censorship and is founded on propaganda. But ultimately ideas and truth rather than power of either a machine or individuals are victorious.

If the Communist party is to transform itself into a popular party, it must renounce the idea that it will be able to create the image of a new state in which it will continue to play the role of elected representative of the people. It must consult the people by means of free elections, respect its opinions, and not confuse the solution of its internal problems with that of the critical issues of the nation. If the Communist party does not renounce the fiction that its members represent the will of the people, the divergence between the only political organization of this state and the people can only continue to widen; democratization will not then be anything more than a trick puppet show with the factions of the only party pulling the strings.

The third divergence — the one least spoken of but perhaps the most serious — exists between the economic activity of the state and the goal of socialism. The state traditionally conceived of as a body of class power now presents itself as a state of all peoples — nonsense already criticized by Marx — and as the personification of a nation. The only device which such a nation bears upon its flag is that of an improvement of the standard of living. The state is an industrial agent but a very bad one, because its technocratic ambitions conflict with the democratic basis of its socialism.

A great majority of the population, including the working class, persists in believing that socialism rests on human liberty, not on the standard of living. The proletariat is no longer hoodwinked by litanies on the invulnerability of the power elite. It understands that every tendency not enlarging of the people's liberties is profoundly reactionary, whether that tendency is called communism, Christianity, or socialism.

We, the partisans of the Czech experiment in socialism and democracy, must openly declare that the worst enemy of communism is the conservative faction of the Communist party. Those who threaten the new liberty can in no manner be associated with socialism, democracy, the European left, or with those ideals of socialism which were and are still synonyms for the greater freedom of mankind.

These contradictions can be resolved. They exist in the framework of a bureaucratic dictatorship and can be overcome if the role of the citizens is enlarged. However, a regime of either the right or the left founded on the defeat of the other would be just as bad, for it would again isolate the masses.

The great doctrinaire Machiavelli trusted only in power, the force of arms, and political assassination, and yet he said: "Do you not know that no force can checkmate the spirit of liberty?" No force will be able to cow the spirit of liberty which has risen in Czechoslovakia during the last months. Failure to develop democratic liberties will be fatal not only to Czechoslovakia and the socialist ideal but to the conservative forces. Lenin, the theoretician of the Soviet state and today "counselor" of the Presidium of the Czech Communist party, said in 1918, in the midst of civil war:

> The people must have the privilege of electing workers who will govern them in a responsible manner. The people must have the right to change them. The people must have the right to know and to control their least movements. The people must have the right to invest whomever they wish without regard for intrigue. The people, yes, the people. No force will be able to quench their spirit of liberty.

[A Prospectus for Autumn]

The actual contradictions of democratization have their origin in the historical process. They can be surmounted, but their resolution cannot be indefinitely postponed. The contradiction between the power machine and democratic rights of citizens can be eliminated by the introduction of civil rights which subject the power machine to democratic control. The contradiction between the conservatives of the party and the people can be surmounted only by true parliamentarianism. Finally, the economic bases of socialism and the program for the freedom of the individual can be reconciled within the context of self-management.

If these contradictions are not resolved, they are inevitably going to prohibit any nonviolent solution of the antagonisms. The extremism of the opposing factions results from the real aggravation of contradictory situations. Extremism can only develop parallel to a conflict and is reduced only by realistic political action, not by the verbal camouflage of "opposition," "pluralist conception," "antisocialist forces."

The contradictions cited are intrinsic to the communist social system. Their resolution will not undermine the economic foundations of socialism but must affect the political structure of society. The growing recognition of civil rights has profoundly affected the structure of the power elite. The members of this, whether they are conservative or progressive, attempt to interpret each criticism directed against the political system as an attack against socialism.

Although formerly the progressives understood very well that the elimination of personal power from the political system did not mean the destruction of socialism, they have purposely forgotten this in order to establish the inviolability of their reformed power. But a democratic political system founded on a socialist economy can in no sense be considered a counterrevolution or an expression of antisocialism tendencies; extension of civil rights could only benefit socialism.

The industrialized societies of both West and East suffer from the fundamental contradictions of democratization, transformation, or any revolutionary process. The spontaneous effort to establish human rights in an industrialized civilization is the essence of any transformation of social and political structures in a fully mature country. However, the forms which this effort takes are as yet ambiguous. Only a realistic solution to man's alienation in industrialized society will permit the human being to participate effectively in history as executive of civil rights and individual freedom. The solutions presently put forth by the political men are only a caricature, reflecting a common attempt to escape tomorrow's society of consumption. Men choose security rather than humanitarian aims. The consumer society seems to evolve parallel to individual ambitions and to the aspirations of his nation, when these two are essentially incongruous; even a Czech will compromise with a politician over lowering the price of salami if this politician is trying to achieve the coveted goal of the consumer society. The future will witness the surprise of the representatives of the "left," when they realize that consumer society does not represent a revolution for human rights. It is only a series of upheavals caused by modern technology.

In almost all industrialized countries, the rights of man are sustained by a very powerful movement for concrete civil liberties which reflect applied anthropology or the study of living human beings rather than humanist ideological postulates. The actual contradictions in Czechoslovakia are not just those between people and concepts of socialism; they are above all contradictions derived from the structure of industrial society, contradictions from which all Europe suffers, contradictions precipitating the transformation of European socialism and the international revolution for the rights of man.

These contradictions demand today a program more elaborate than a simple series of empirical actions by political parties; it must go beyond the horizons of consumer society as it appears to technocratic manipulators, to the orthodox Stalinists of yesterday, and to the revisionists. It must offer a solution to the conflicts in industrial society by showing that it is the avalanche of goods that is engulfing the freedom of man.

It is painful to note that in none of the speeches of these last six months, not even in those given by the most qualified representatives, has any mention been made of a realistic program of humanitarian socialism or human relations. There has only been a spate of words. The neo-Stalinist and the revisionist, the technocrat and the ideologist, the bureaucrat and manipulator, neither see nor conceive of the goals of a socialist program to be applied to humanism; all the efforts to go beyond the established system are considered a priori unacceptable, either utopian or extremist. The "experts" who systematize Marxism pillory all the extremist liberating tendencies of Marx. The development of the liberties of man within socialism and the modern society of consumption is limited to being only a link in the chain of technocratic formulas, promises, and political proclamations.

[Perspective]

The immediate change necessary to the institutions of the existing system make us want to believe that there could be a pluralist political system, but this alternative does not yet exist. Political parties have not permission to return to life. Political leaders have done nothing better than return to the model of the National Front, which had already demonstrated its unsuitability. They have tried to modify political crisis by resorting to measures which perpetuate the mechanisms of manipulation.

Seen from this angle, social democracy does not depend on the electors, the workers, or man, in short, but on the fictitious alliance of institutions, institutions united to sustain a wavering establishment which oppresses the rebellious citizen and prevents free elections. This program is not the praiseworthy work of statesmen who understand that the democratic system cannot be based on institutions, that socialist democracy must find a system of solutions to the conflicts of today's industrial society. Such a method of government cannot be applied while the National Front persists in its present form, for the same reason that we no longer use the abacus in business.

In matters concerning the problems of consumer society, the freedom of man, and socialist democracy, the Czech intelligentsia must complete the ideological tasks which it has left undone. Totally concerned with the expulsion of the president, the criticism of past crimes, and questions of tactics, neither the writers nor the men of science, the philosophers nor the artists, and still less their organizations tried to set in motion any counterprogram for progress to combat that of a society defined by technocracy and consumption. The task of the intellectuals is to challenge the limitations of tomorrow's liberties and to deal immediately with the problems which are to be found beyond the horizon of today's imagination. The approach must be developed from scientific methods; it will consist in the application of science to politics, to society, and to the vision of the future. However, men of science have not yet been allowed to speak.

The weakness of the intellectuals is demonstrated above all by the fact that the future possibilities of the new democracy are not a subject for even theoretical considerations. Skepticism is expanding in those very literary clubs in which the new democracy previously grew. This skepticism is founded on arguments according to which the concept of democracy has grown old; civic society no longer exists and therefore cannot support an economic democracy; the only possible escape from personal difficulties becomes for the writers a more intelligent technocracy or even categorical radicalism.

We must reject these a priori arguments; yesterday they served as justification for personal power. The skeptical reaction of the intellectuals precipitates a conservativism which envisions the future of Czechoslovakia only in terms of national independence and a multiparty system, or in the terms of consumer society and an efficient technocratic government. Our solution and progress lies in neither of these directions.

The plan of action for the future of our nation must begin elsewhere than in the offices of the power-monopoly system; it must take into consideration the three conflicts mentioned above; it must envisage that path which will lead to a free and open society by the year 2000. It will be born in imaginative political brains if the representatives of monopolistic power do not place culture and science under a glass bell. The only true counterrevolution is that which commits the fundamental crime against humanity: the crime against freedom of thought. It is always society which pays for this crime because, in principle, it pays for errors which it could have avoided.

History will demonstrate whether or not Czechs and the Slovaks understood in 1968 that they held in their hands the unique occasion to create a new political system. It is up to us to decide if we will be able to resolve the national problems caused by the economic crisis and, if we *are* able, to accomplish a great national and socialist task which will open new horizons for the European left and for the future of socialism.

We are sure that the Communist party will find a solution to the contradictions of 1968 if people like Indra, Kolder, and Svestka and others do not prohibit it from acting. It is improbable that any easy transition to democratization or process of liberalization will remain merely local in application, for such could express universally human liberty, the rights of man, and equality for all citizens. If the party should continue to operate well within the perspective of a consumer society, executive technocracy, and the horrible alienation of industrialized civilization, we will produce cheap cars for the children of those who are making economies to buy them. Should we burn these cars under the banner of Mao Tse-tung while cursing the inhumanity of this society of prosperity?

Perhaps this is the only argument which will shake the materialistic realism of our politicians, which will force them to have, even if only for a moment, the inconceivable thought that the way in which they envision the solution to the economic and political crisis is not necessarily the only one.

Notes for Chapter 5

1. It was the same with other noncommunist groups hatched in the Prague thaw, such as Club 231, which brought together victims of Stalinism, and the Sokols.
2. This reaction was shared by many intellectuals in the communist world, who retired to the ivory tower of specialized and abstruse studies. The Eastern delegations were always the pride of international congresses on the history of medieval art, numismatics, and the like.
3. All these men were to be among the intellectual instigators of the thaw.

Epilogue

Epilogue

I have returned to Prague on several occasions since the invasion. My trips have coincided with the successive crises marking the slow but implacable disintegration of "socialism with a human face."

What will remain of the spirit of the spring? Which of the men who constituted the progressive bloc within the party and the government will still subsist and in what condition? These men, most of whom I met, were open both to hope and to dialogue; no Westerner, least of all a journalist, can now approach them. How many of the people I spoke with, how many of my friends of that exalting period, are today in exile or social pariahs? How many others will be in prison tomorrow?

Whatever is still to come, however long the long night into which the unfortunate country of Jan Hus and Masaryk,

335

Comenius and Kafka, Ryba and Dvorak, has been plunged, the people of Bohemia, Moravia, and Slovakia will resist their oppressors and will triumph. We have permitted the revival of Munich after an interval of thirty years. May we not have to pay again the terrible price for our criminal indifference.

[March–April 1969]

"Forgive us, Dubcek, but you must be lying to us and we must fight you." Written in whitewash on a gray wall, this slogan was the people's last means of dialogue with their leaders since the Kremlin's restrictions on the press.

I arrived in Prague in March the day after that wild night when 100,000 or perhaps 200,000 people had flooded the streets following the victory of the Czech ice hockey team over the Soviets. They had loosed their hatred by burning red flags and ravaging the Aeroflot offices. Would there be another "August" again this spring?

"We should have let the Russians win that cursed hockey game even if we were the strongest. This is one sports victory which may cost us a lot." These were the thoughts of Jiri Hochmann, the editorial writer for the *Reporter* who had been in the front ranks of the progressive struggle ever since the invasion. He had just learned that his newspaper had once again been suspended. Twenty-four hours later, on Thursday, April 3, Alexander Dubcek, the fallen hero of the Czech resistance, informed his compatriots that they were going to "pay heavily for what happened the night of March 28–29." Czechoslovakia, he said in substance, is reliving the days following the arrival of Soviet troops on August 21. And for the first time he uttered the words which the Soviets had been unable to force him to say in the previous nine months: "Anti-socialist and anti-Soviet counterrevolutionary forces have been at work." He also announced in a tone neither convinced nor convincing that "strict measures will be taken to stabilize the situation."

The ice hockey game took place in Stockholm on the evening of Friday, March 28, under harsh projector lights in a stadium filled to overflowing. At 9:15 the Czech center forward made the team's fourth goal, and the Scandinavian crowd applauded thunderously — an applause not without political overtones. It is also interesting to note that before the match Anatole Tarassov, the captain of the Soviet team, had gravely shaken the hand of his Czechoslovakian counterpart and told him that personally he and his teammates disapproved of the August 21 invasion.

Some 750 miles away, millions of Czechoslovakians, their ears glued to transistor radios, learned of their team's victory. Throughout this formerly federal Republic, Czechs, Moravians, and Slovaks crowded the streets. In a few hours, from Bohemia to the heart of Slovakia, crowds attacked everything that reminded them of their detested occupant. At Mlada Boleslav, where Skoda automobiles are made, a group of young workers broke all eighty-one windows of the Soviet barracks. At Usti nad Labem, a truck and a jeep were overturned and burned. At Liberec, Teplice, Olomouc, Kosice, in one hundred localities in all, Soviet flags were burned, vehicles and sentinels stoned, and vengeful slogans painted on walls and pavements. The Prague demonstrations were the most violent. All the inhabitants of the Golden City seemed to have emptied into the streets. Tricolor flags sprang up everywhere. Tens of thousands of jubilant strollers marched up and down Wenceslas Boulevard carrying shrubbery branches, as on Palm Sunday.

These demonstrations resulted in destruction totaling nearly two million crowns (one million for the Aeroflot offices), the injury of fifty-one policemen, and some forty arrests. Were the demonstrations spontaneous or organized? Had there been a

337

"counterrevolutionary" plot as the Soviets and their backers claim?

Eyewitnesses informed me: "There was a plot, but not in the sense that the occupants understand it. On one hand, the hatred of the Soviets is such that it is hardly necessary to organize and plan mass 'spontaneity'; on the other hand, we clearly saw all types of individuals inciting the crowd. These were not the beatniks, the students, or the young workers who usually animate progressivist demonstrations, but hardy, leather-jacketed fellows who looked like professional provocateurs."

But provocateurs on whose payroll?

Whether unconsciously or fatalistically, a certain cheerfulness animates the streets of Prague. This cheerfulness is not just a reflection of the first rays of spring sunshine playing on the lazy waters of the Vltava and illuminating the baroque domes of the old quarter of the city; Prague has let go. While awaiting the punishment she knows is inevitable, she bitterly savors her brief reprieve, and joyous crowds flock day and night in front of the broken windows and the bare walls of the ransacked Aeroflot agency, which is now guarded by policemen impassive to the jeers.

"4–3; Ossouri." Scribbled on every wall, this slogan unites in one short striking phrase the "two Soviet defeats" of 1969, the ice hockey triumph in Stockholm and the battles on the distant shores of the Amur River. In his evaluation of the Sino-Soviet conflict, the man in the street now attributes all the wrongdoing to the Russians. A new Maoist slogan, "Down with the new tsars of the Kremlin," has been taken up by the people of Prague and Bratislava. The intellectuals are considering with interest the Chinese proposition of a "neutral" belt of Eastern European states to the west of the U.S.S.R. which are no longer bound to the Warsaw Pact.

"March 28 was gayer than any July 14 in France, more festive than the Carnival in Rio," I was told by the wife of a Czech diplomat. "Since the liberation, Prague has never been so joyous. With confetti made of Aeroflot's paperwork, the people of Prague demonstrated not only their disgust for the normalization, but also their lack of fear." This woman did not see any "provocateurs," although she admitted that they are a possibility. "In any event," she said, "they couldn't have led the Czechoslovakian crowds, who even when exultant exhibit a political maturity and an understanding of the irreparable."

A curve charting popular demonstrations shows the ever widening schism between the power and the population, which considers the Russians and the government as one. The curve begins with the mob demonstrations of November on the Republic's fiftieth anniversary, followed by the two imposing, grave, and funereal night vigils by the people of Prague after the immolation of the student Jan Palach. Thereafter, the symbol of Jan Hus was no longer reincarnated in Dubcek but in Palach.

On March 11, 1969, several thousand members of the Communist party, less numerous but more aggressive than the demonstrators of preceding weeks and months, gathered before the gloomy building of the Central Committee on the quays of the Vltava. They had come to protest the actions of the party, which, yielding to Russian pressure, had not sent delegates to the Conference of the League of Yugoslav Communists. Shouts of "Shame, Shame" rising from the crowd were followed by "We're with you, Tito. We need leaders, not flunkies." Beneath the hermetically sealed windows of the Central Committee, some communists openly tore up their party cards. Another bond had been broken between Dubcek and his people, this time the militants of the Communist party. The wave of resignations was as strong as the wave of new and enthusiastic membership during the week of the invasion had been. Students by the hundreds posted their letters of resignation in the hall of Charles University. Each day a new batch of letters replaced those of the preceding one. One student summed up for me the thinking of his classmates: "Disgust is stronger than political skill."

If the Soviets had had any doubts, March 28 dispelled them. It is not that the demonstrations were so spectacular — those of November had been much more dramatic — but their cumulative effect and the pretexts cited for them were too clearly symptomatic.

By March 31 the Russians were sending threatening messages to Prague "on the instructions of comrade Brezhnev." Vladimir Semionov, the vice-minister of foreign affairs, and Marshal Andrei Grechko, both surrounded by "delegations," were sent over. On April 2, the Politburo of the Central Committee of the Czechoslovakian Communist party, after a 72-hour meeting, announced the first group of repressive measures: the strengthening of police power, the reestablishment of censorship, the "temporary suppression" of the party weekly *Politika*, which between two preceding "temporary suppressions" had only been able to put out four issues, and lastly the take-over of some progressive newspapers: the *Listy*, the *Reporter*, and a few others.

"They suppress us today but we will reappear tomorrow," the editor of one of these newspapers stated philosophically. "We have been playing cat and mouse for nine months now. This is becoming the national sport. But they can't do anything to us because the nation recognizes itself in us. With the trinity of the students, the workers, and the intellectuals more solid and united than ever, we are, as Mao would say, like a fish in the water."

And then, there was the other "man on his way up," in the progressive camp: Vlastimil Toman, the young president of the Metalworkers Union (one million members), who clearly threatened to use the power of a general strike of the working classes of the Czech and Slovak countries if "the extremism of the right" became a threat.

Excessive optimism? At the Politburo, Josef Smrkovsky, the president of the National Assembly and the only leader in whom the people still have confidence, was much criticized by his "comrades," who designate him exclusively and expressly in a report as having lacked "vigilance." He was ordered by the Kremlin, which coldly accused him of instigating the March 28 demonstrations, to abstain from all contact with the Soviet authorities.

This order was plainly stated in a letter in the form of a pamphlet addressed to the Politburo by Brezhnev, who was "more ferocious than he was at Cierna," and it was personally handed to Alexander Dubcek by Semionov. This same letter also ordered the complete overhaul of the party and the government by Dubcek and President Svoboda and the establishment of absolute censorship and a police regime on the strict Soviet model. This was said to be Moscow's last warning.

Rumors circulating in Prague when I was leaving were very disquieting. When Marshal Grechko landed unexpectedly at the military airport at Milovice he was awaited, as protocol demands, not by Czech Minister of Defense General Martin Dzur — who had not even been forewarned — but by General Maiorov, the chief of the Soviet occupation troops, and by a string of Czechoslovakian officers who had not requested any permission to see the august visitor and who were obviously more informed than their own minister of defense. Is the collaboration perhaps going to be replaced? A military clan at the service of the occupants, which unlike the other groups will "be able to command respect," will perhaps replace the devalued group of unwavering and disgraced "old communists" and the "realists," who hesitate to bring about the latest "progressive" measure of the party and government.

To live in the Czech style today means gritting one's teeth

without giving too much thought to tomorrow, losing neither sense of humor nor sangfroid. There are different ways of living dangerously. Under the circumstances it is not at all certain that the choice of this defenseless and fundamentally peaceful people is the least heroic.

[May 1969]

Since the summer of 1968, the summer of the tanks, my trips to Prague and Bratislava have recalled perhaps the most unpleasant aspect of my former profession as a doctor: witnessing the slow agony of a patient I have become fond of. From time to time I come by to take his pulse. It beats slowly, ever weakening, but it beats. Czechoslovakian freedom simply will not die.

But it has happened. Exit Dubcek. His picture still hangs in a place of honor next to that of President Svoboda, the last survivor of the Prague spring, but Czechoslovakia has just inherited another opportune man.

No one knows what Gustav Husak's rise to power means. News is rare in the press, which has resumed the dullness and conformity of the Novotny era. But the man in the street is still in the habit of "no longer being afraid." Life goes on in a sort of tranquil despair in which anger has become patient.

One becomes accustomed to Husak's wooden face. Impassive, discreet, and secret, he is called the Russians' man, but he returned from Moscow last April 26 empty-handed. He was to have brought back triumphantly some three hundred million rubles in gold which Brezhnev had promised Dubcek after the invasion and to have announced an initial timetable for the pullout of Soviet troops. Instead he modestly announced that he had only partaken in some important discussions.

In any case the cards had been dealt and Dubcek waited for

his time to come. The Kremlin had not forgiven this man for the "seven days of August" and had daily forced him to make humiliating concessions. His slow erosion created, with the help of a few provocations, the necessary climate for the arrival of the "strong man."

Who is Husak? An ambitious neo-Stalinite? Moscow's majordomo? Or, on the contrary, a "progressivist-realist," as he likes to describe himself, who is trying to preserve what can still be salvaged at the cost of apparent concessions — a Talleyrand of the spring political team? What has he saved after all? The press is permanently muzzled. The last remaining strongholds of freedom of expression, which were *Reporter, Literarni Listy,* and a few other liberal periodicals, have been brutally suppressed. True, there have not yet been any massive arrests and trips abroad are still permitted. But was this not the case during the final years of Novotny's rule?

In Prague as in Bratislava, I questioned a great number of Czechs and Slovaks who knew Husak well. From their testimony emerges the image of an energetic, intelligent, ambitious, and shrewd politician: "the first Machiavelli of our political history," said a friend of mine who was at one time one of Husak's closest collaborators. Husak, a former lawyer from Bratislava who looks much older than fifty-six, is still of delicate health as a result of his long imprisonment under Klement Gottwald. One of his former prison mates told me that when Husak had condoned the crushing in 1956 of the Hungarian uprising by the Russians, the other prisoners wanted to lynch him. And Husak bravely confronted them and spoke of "realism." The Communist world seems to specialize in this type of strong, confused mind.

At Bratislava I heard repeatedly about his anti-Semitism. However, most people do not believe that he will initiate an openly anti-Semitic campaign, as Gomulka did in Poland. Husak, like another Slovak, Alexander Dubcek, wants to become the man of all Czechoslovakia — and perhaps its liberator.

In one of his recent television appearances, Husak became animated only once; at the end of his rather dull and mediocre peroration, he repeated with suspicious stress: "I believe that our country's problems will be solved before a year is up — I repeat, *all* the problems." This was naturally considered an allusion to Russian evacuation and the alternative to Dubcek's tactics. The latter had naïvely believed that Czechoslovakia's internal freedoms could survive the occupation; Husak is obviously convinced that nothing is possible without the restoration of national sovereignty. He is ready to pay any price the Russians demand in order to obtain it.

A progressive journalist, now out of work — there are hundreds of them — told me: "Theoretically, the *enlightened absolutism* of Husak, a member of the January political team, is not comparable to Novotny's neo-Stalinite tyranny. But in practice, the result will be the same, and will probably last many long years."

At this stage Gustav Husak is using intimidation rather than repression. During his trip to Moscow, fourteen university faculties were on strike. At Charles University I spoke with protesting students of the philosophy faculty, where Jan Palach had studied. On the walls hung anti-Husak slogans and innumerable party resignation letters. The atmosphere was one of despair and hysteria. This battle of honor was a struggle known to be lost before it was begun. For the first time state security forces entered the faculty. They requested a list of the striking students, which they did not get, and removed the slogans from the walls. "They were courteous, rather ironical. But they announced that they would be less pleasant the next time."

The front of workers, students, and intellectuals, which was said to be invincible, has crumbled. The workers must devote all their energy to simply living. Prices are climbing; the increase on certain food items is more than 40 percent. If, with the help of the Soviets, Husak solves some of the most pressing economic problems, the working class will become permanently resigned.

The intellectuals, exhausted by the vain struggle with the thousand-headed hydra of censorship, have finally succumbed. I attended the final battle in the *Reporter* and *Literarni Listy* offices. The publishers were composing their final issues, as yet unaware that they would be suppressed. The *Reporter* journalists were hastily writing innocuous copy to fill the 25-page gap made by censorship in the columns of their weekly. Over at *Literarni Listy*, half of the copy had been "whitened." In the offices of this literary weekly, I ran into Ludvik Vaculik — a haggard and exhausted Vaculik who had fought all night to save a few scraps of his newspaper. He spoke to me of the new censors. They have adopted a new style: courteous, eager, full of good advice, but implacable. "After socialism with a human face, we have censorship with a human face," he told me bitterly. This last issue of *Literarni Listy* (240,000 copies), more and more sophisticated and subtly allusive, appeared with its front page devoted to a long article minutely describing, in the manner of Robbe-Grillet or Francis Ponge, a cup of coffee.

Lacking newspapers, the writers have begun work on novels which may never reach publication. Milan Kundera, the author of *The Joke*, tells me he is working on a "typically Czech" novel in which an ardent and pure young poet finally becomes a spy for the secret police.

"It's a work on the ambiguity of revolutionary lyricism, which can give rise to anything at all."

Gustav Husak is neither poet nor novelist, but ambiguity seems to be the principal stuff of which good politics is made in Prague.

[Conclusion]

In one of his last interviews, the great Czech writer Karel Capek spoke of the history of his country as subject to the rhythm of the arctic seasons: several hours of light and then a long, very long, night. Has Prague fallen into its darkness again?

Alexander Dubcek, the man who had become in the eyes of the Czechs and the Slovaks a hero of the stature of Jan Hus and Thomas Masaryk, has been politically emasculated by the *diktat* of Moscow. Will he become a Gomulka? Some twelve years passed before that Polish leader fell from his pedestal. Or will he be a Kadar? Will he commit suicide? Will he finish his life in Siberian exile? Or will he end it, obscure and forgotten, in some insignificant provincial post to which the Party, not wishing to take the risk of making him a martyr, will relegate him?

What will remain tomorrow of the exciting victories of the Prague "thaw"? Yellowed posters? Some piously preserved issues of *Literarni Listy*? Here and now the press is muzzled; the economic machine has fallen back into its old rut; consciences and wills, for a moment awakened, are returning to torpor, to the grayness of everyday life, in a universe of desperate sameness, from Berlin to Vladivostok.

But whether it be the romantic heroism of the Hungarians in 1956, or the patience, maturity, the pathetic "wisdom" of the Czechs and Slovaks in 1968, others will try tomorrow, by other means, using unsuspected tricks and ruses or crazy enterprise. For nothing will make me believe that the citizen of Warsaw, or Leningrad, or Sofia has less desire for liberty than the Arab fellah or the Central African bushman.

The pale second-generation heirs of Stalin are soft and indecisive tyrants (only weakness can explain an aggression whose gravity and consequences we cannot yet measure). They have succeeded only in gaining time. Their fall will be the harder.

While waiting for it, the world in which we live will become still more bitter, more distrustful, more radical. And the world in which freedom is as natural as air and water is slowly shrinking. Are we aware of being the cherished children of the gods?

After the Prague aggression and its revolution strangled by savages, let us at least be convinced by this evidence: the worst of our democracies, these "bourgeois" parliamentary democracies, weak, ugly, vomited up by our children who long for the absolute, is worth a thousand, a hundred thousand, times more than the best of worlds in which utopia depends on bayonets.

Index

Academy of Sciences, Czechoslovakian, 42, 300n, 305
Adenauer, Konrad, 51, 228
Aeroflot offices, Prague, 176, 336, 337, 338
Age of Distortion, The (Loebl), 213
Agence France Presse, 302
Algiers, 138
America. See United States
Amur River, 338
Anschluss, 256
Antonovs, 177
Aragon, Louis, 141
Aristotle, 249
Art of Philosophy, The (Svitak), 305
Athletic Associations of Czechoslovakia, 15
Austria, 306, 309, 310
Austro-Hungarian Empire, 255, 259, 274, 310

Auto-Praga factory, 149, 160n
Axen, H., 165

"B.," Colonel, 62
Babeuf, 249
Babnic, Vladimir, 270
Bank of Czechoslovakia, 261
Banska Bystrica, 69, 145, 258
Barak, Rudolf, 5, 11, 30n
Barandov, 62, 306
Barbirek, Frantisek, 144, 163, 183
Bartolomejska St., Prague, 182
Bavaria, 139, 140
B.B.C., 181
Belgium, 260
Belgrade, 175
Ben Gurion, David, 51
Benes, Eduard, 30n, 55, 221, 249, 250, 255, 256, 280, 310
Benes, Jan, 11
Berchtesgaden, 188
Beria, Lavrenty, 211, 221, 228

Index

Berlin, East, 81
Bessarova, Ladislova, 26, 29
Bilak, Vasil, 30n, 66, 144, 163, 166, 183, 184, 189, 270
Bismarck, 249
Black Lion Bundeswehr, 139
Bohemia, 89, 138, 145, 217, 220, 224, 233, 254, 255, 256, 257, 260, 263–264, 276, 313, 315
Böll, Heinrich, 253n
Bolshevik Central Committee of 1920, 20
Bolshevism, 100n
Boruvka, Josef, 148
Bory (prison), 220
Bratislava, 9, 66, 69, 81, 141, 224, 258, 261, 273n, 281, 314; Dubcek's home, 68; freedom under Dubcek, 70; described, 259; state bank, 280
Bratislava meeting and agreement, 90, 152–154, 156–158, 173, 183, 197, 199, 207; names of delegates, 164–166; text of Communiqué, 164–172
Brezhnev, Leonid, 25, 30n, 80, 81, 94, 96, 133, 137, 145, 151, 152, 157, 165, 180, 187, 189, 287, 340, 341, 342
Brno, 11, 15, 16, 20, 31n, 223, 258, 261
Brodsky (secretary of Club 231), 226
Brussels exposition, 275
Bucharest, 171, 246
Budapest, 27, 81; uprising of 1956, 7, 91, 96, 134, 135, 136, 221, 234, 235
Budin, Stanislas, 160n
Bulgaria, 110, 120, 164, 170, 173, 194, 196, 276; Communist party, 164
"Butcher of Jachimov, The," 227

Camus, Albert, 306
Canossa, 149
Capek, Karel, 53, 252n, 346
Ce Soleil sans chaleur, 230n

Ceausescu, Nicolas, 52, 136, 154, 157
Centrist Socialism party, 30n
Cernik, Oldrich, 13, 17, 23, 30n, 77n, 89, 93, 94, 96, 151, 163, 166, 186, 187, 190, 198
Cernin palace, 86, 250
Ceske-Budejovice, 57
Ceteka press agency (C.T.K.), 77n, 130, 179, 238, 277
Charles Bridge, 78
Charles University, 227, 237, 239, 306, 340, 344
Chelepin, Alexander, 180
Chelest, Pierre, 151, 165, 181
Chervonenko, Stepan, 137, 140, 181–182, 185, 186
Chicago, 273n
China, 309
Chnoupek, Bohus, 179
"Christmas-cake truce," 52
Chudik, Michael, 30n
Churchill, Winston, 51, 295
C.I.A., 73, 231n
Cierna nad Tisou, meeting and agreements, 90, 147–151, 152, 153, 159n, 197, 199
Cisar, Cestmir, 15, 31n, 63, 85, 100n, 150, 245–246, 247, 248–249, 250–251, 303
"Citizens' Appeal, The," 145–146, 154, 159n, 161–164
City Hall Square, 285
City University, 24–25
C.K.C. factory, 67
C.K.D. factory, 185
Clausewitz, 249
Clementis, Vladimir, 264, 266
Club of Committed Nonparty Members, 87, 100n, 160n, 303
Club 231, 160n, 220, 224, 225–226, 332n
Comecon, 85, 86, 93, 152, 156, 189, 276, 280
Comenius. See Komensky
Commission of the Second World War in the Netherlands, 5
Common Market, 155
Communist Democrats, 105

Communist League, Yugoslavia, 23, 339

Communist party, Czechoslovakia, 54, 194, 200, 296, 304; economic and historical commissions, 8, 30n; crisis of recruitment, 16; relation to National Front, 22; reply to Warsaw Five letter, 117–131; and Czecho-Slovak question, 267–268; and thaw, 318; future of, 322–325; 14th Congress Extraordinary (1968), 81, 92, 96, 100, 125, 129, 185, 189, 196–198, 199, 263, 319

CENTRAL COMMITTEE: 15, 24, 42, 54, 56, 57, 72, 91, 316, 339; Novotny becomes secretary of, 6; Oct. 1967 meeting opposes Novotny, 18–22; and pluralism of powers, 26–29; and Sejna affair, 58, 59; Novotny resigns, Dubcek takes over, 61–63; make-up under Dubcek, 80, 81; debates monopoly of power by Communist party, 83–84; adopts Dubcek's program, 87–89; May plenum and resolution, 93; planning under Dubcek, 100; and Warsaw Five letter, 98, 133, 135, 149; and Citizens Appeal, 145–146; and Soviet invasion, 177–178, 182; referred to in Moscow Protocol, 199–208 *passim*; Nov. 1968 resolution, 205–208; role in thaw, 240, 318, 321

POLITBURO: 6, 13, 25–26, 99, 340, 341

PRESIDIUM: 13, 14, 16, 17–18, 61, 63, 91, 146, 319; members in 1967, 30n; meets with Soviet Presidium in Moscow, 143, 144, 147–151, 160; elements supporting Soviet invasion, 183; referred to in

Moscow Protocol, 199–204 *passim*

Communist party, Slovak, 9, 14, 30n, 62, 69, 187, 214, 258, 259, 263, 270, 273n

Communist party, U.S.S.R., 136, 156, 180, 186–187; political school of the Central Committee, 69; 20th Congress, 1956 (de-Stalinization), 7, 230n, 234, 305, 312; 22nd Congress, 312; and Moscow Protocol, 199

Contrat Social, Le, Paris, 230n

Couve de Murville, Maurice, 7

C.T.K. *See* Ceteka

Cuba, 52

"Curious Camera, The," 64

Cutka, Mr. (Cisar's secretary), 24

Cyrankiewicz, Joseph, 165

Czechoslovak Airline Co. (C.S.A.), 211

Czecho-Slovak question, 19–20, 25, 66, 70, 109, 254–271, 312–315

Czechoslovakia: in "iron triangle," 7; Council of Ministers, 8; National Assembly, 42, 80, 84, 96, 160n, 184, 191, 193, 194, 195, 196, 226, 229, 230, 244, 316, 341; importance of to U.S.S.R. and Eastern bloc, 52–53, 85; national character, 53, 153, 255; army, 55, 77n; invaded by U.S.S.R., 175–183; Proclamation on the invasion, 193–196; relation of literature to politics in, 233–236; history through World War II, 233, 254–257, 309–313; coat of arms, 254; national anthem, 254; battle over name, 254; partition of in 1938, 256; language, 259–260; Bank of, 261; economic problems under Communism, 274–280, 282–284; agriculture and industry pre–World War II, 275; ice hockey team beats U.S.S.R., 336–337. *See also* Communist party, Czechoslovakia; Czecho-

Index

Czechoslovakia (*continued*)
Slovak question; Slovaks and
Slovakia
Czechoslovakian Christianity, 134

Daniel, Yuli, 228, 252n, 306
Danube River, 21, 259; canal, 252n
Day in the Life of Ivan Deniso-vitch, A (Solzhenitsyn), 228
Democratic (Christian) party, 258
Denmark, 275
Deportation Journal (Mucha), 216
Djakarta, 227
Djilas, Milovan, 23
Dolansky, Jaromir, 30n
Dostoevski, Fyodor, 233
Dragon Is a Dragon, The, 31n
Dresden, 85, 86, 111
Dreyfus affair, 222
Dubcek, Alexander: personal life and earlier career, 68–70, 77, 245; character and appearance, 54, 66–67, 68, 71, 83, 93; as Slovak, 9, 19–20, 70, 266, 267–270; opposes Novotny, 14, 15–18, 18–22, 26, 29; Novotny's dislike of, 30n; popular support for, 54, 66–68, 77n; and Sejna, 59, 60, 72, 75; becomes Central Committee secretary, 62–63, 77; established in power, 66, 67–68, 76, 87–89; tolerance of opposition, 71, 75, 79–81, 85, 182, 222, 228–229; and "pluralism of powers," 83–84; Dresden meeting, 85–86; secret Moscow visit, 89, 94; Cierna meeting, 90, 152; Bratislava meeting, 90, 152–154, 166; and Warsaw Five letter, 98, 132–133, 135–137, 138; Moscow meeting and Protocol, 143, 144, 147–151, 188, 190; dismisses Prchlik, 144; and Soviet invasion, 160n, 177–178, 184, 187; and Svitak, 303; comments on hockey game, 336; exit of, 190, 191, 342, 346; mentioned, 23, 30n, 52, 82, 96,

100n, 108, 139, 145, 158, 159, 163, 186, 198, 287, 339, 341, 343, 344
Dubcek, Anna, 68
Dubcek, Julius, 70
Dubcek, Steve, 68–69
Dubcik, Ivan, 305
Dubnica, 69
Dvorak, Antonin, 254, 336
Dzur, Lieutenant General Martin, 57, 58, 59, 60, 97, 140, 341

Elias, Colonel, 176
England, 79, 309
"Entre Prague et Moscou," 192n
Erivan, 53
Evidence (Svedectvi), 11

"February uprising," 3, 16, 93, 311
Federation of the Democratic Left and Socialists, 6
Feldgendarmerie, 257
Fierlinger (Czech politician), 230n, 304
Fierlinger T.N.P. (Kladno mine), 230n
Fock, E., 165
For Peace and Socialism, 179
Fouquier-Tinville, 27
"4–3; Ossouri," 338
Fourier, 249
France, 54, 233; Communist party, 136
Fris, Edo, 66, 268
Frunze (U.S.S.R.), 69
Fucik Park (Luna Park), 147

Galbraith, J. K., 287
Galuska, Miroslav, 79
Gaucher, Roland, 231n
Geistige Arbeit (Loebl), 300n
Geminder, Bedrich, 231
Germany, 256, 309
Germany, East (Democratic Republic), 7, 85, 97, 110, 115, 120, 141, 164, 170, 173, 194, 196; Communist party, 170
Germany, West (Federal Repub-

lic), 86, 114, 119, 120, 140, 144, 151, 155, 170, 171, 178, 227, 228, 288

Gestapo, 5, 223, 224

Globke (Nazi official), 228

Goldstuecker, Eduard, 31n, 71, 85, 236, 239–240, 242–243, 244, 245, 253n

Gomulka, Wladyslaw, 31n, 52, 54, 157–158, 165, 343

Good Soldier Schweik (Hasek), 143

Gorki Square, Prague, 244

Gottwald, Klement, 4, 6, 56, 67, 142, 227, 229, 245, 250, 257, 343

Grand Moravian Empire, 255

Grass, Günter, 253n

Great Britain. *See* England

Grechko, Marshal Andrei, 138, 340, 341

Green Horizons (Prochazka), 243

Guinea, 52

Hacha, President, 149, 188

Hadju, Vavro, 223

Hapsburgs, 143, 259, 309

Hasek, Jaroslav, 143

Hausberg, Pavel, 179

Havlicek, Dusan, 98

Havlicek, Frantisek, 238

Hendrych, Jiri, 5, 10, 11–12, 14, 19, 21, 30n, 42, 62–63, 236, 238, 245, 247, 253n, 310

Hendrych, Miss, 11

Hilare (Novotny's neighbor), 4

Hitler, 112, 140, 149, 217, 256, 310, 313

Hlinka, Andrej, 256

Hochmann, Jiri, 336

Hodonin, 5

Hoffman, Karel, 179

Honecker, E., 165

Hradschin palace, 5, 7, 10, 18, 27, 52, 184, 266

Hradschin Square, 24, 134

Hungarian Socialist Workers Party, 165

Hungary, 110, 120, 160n, 164,

170, 173, 194, 196, 234, 276, 305, 309, 312

Hus, Jan, 55, 90, 133, 157, 233, 303, 335, 339

Husak, Gustav, 8, 12, 187, 190, 214, 230n, 245, 273n, 342–344, 345

In the Penal Colony (Kafka), 53

Indonesia, 52

Indra, Alois, 144, 183, 184, 185, 189, 276, 330

Institute of Economic Research, Prague, 30on

Institute of Economics, Prague, 30on

Institute of Philosophy, Charles University, 237, 305

Institute of Political and Economic Research, 154

Institute of Research on the Standard of Living, Bratislava, 30on

Institute of Social Planning, Prague, 30on

Institute of State Planning, Prague, 30on

"Intellectuals' Bridge," 232

Interhelpo cooperative farm, 69

International Brigades, 22, 219

Israel, 86, 142, 144, 151, 155, 160n, 170, 239, 265

Italy, 73; Communist party, 136

Izvestia, 141

Jachimov mine and concentration camp, 217–220, 223, 252n, 276; "Butcher of," 227

Janko, General Vladimir, 57, 59, 74, 77n, 316

Japan, 79

Jews, 258, 264, 272n, 304

Jiranek (cartoonist), 145

Jivkov, Todor, 164

Johnson, Lyndon, 180

Joke, The (Kundera), 345

Jordan, Charles, 265

Journalists Union, 42

Jukov, Yuri, 157

Index

"K.," Doctor, 30n
Kadar, Janos, 52, 96, 165
Kafka, Franz, 8, 53, 239, 253n, 336
Kalivoda (philosopher), 305
KAN. *See* Club of Committed Nonparty Members
Kapek (Czech politician), 163
Karlovo Namesti Boulevard, 224
Karlovy Vary, 92, 138, 156, 171
Kaspar (Czech politician), 183
Kde Domov Muj, 254
Kennedy, John F., 30n, 253n
Kermesse, La, 272n
K.G.B., 180, 183
Khrushchev, Nikita, 6, 30n, 228, 234, 236
Kiev, 138
Kirghiz (U.S.S.R.), 69
Kladno (mines and concentration camp), 67, 220, 230n
Klicka, Benjamin, 38
Klima, Ivan, 14
Kliszko, Zenon, 165
Koblenz, Germany, 224
Kohout, Pavel, 10, 14, 145, 154
Kolder, Drahomir, 23, 30n, 31n, 133, 144, 146, 159n, 163, 183, 184, 330
Kolodeje (prison), 214
Komensky, Bishop, 252n, 336
Komensky's Testament, 233
Komoscin, Z., 165
Kosic, Karel, 305
Kosice, 85, 145, 337; Charter of, 257
Kosygin, Alexei, 30n, 92, 97, 151, 152, 165, 180, 187
Koucky (Czech diplomat), 306
Kralice Bible, 233, 250n
Krasnaya Zvezda, 138
Kremlin, 160n, 186, 228
Kriegel, Frantisek, 22, 28, 31n, 85, 87, 150, 160, 163, 183, 187, 188, 191, 192n
Kubadinsky, P., 164
Kulturni Noviny, 77n
Kundera, Milan, 345

"L.T.," 219
Lang, Oscar, 27
Lannurient, Captain de, 272n
Lany, 227, 250
Lastovicka, Buhoslav, 28, 30, 77n
League of Yugoslav Communists, 23, 339
Lenart, Jozef, 28, 30n, 77n, 163, 166
Lenin, 14, 20, 197, 249, 250, 325
Leopoldov (prison), 220
"Letter From a Captain to a General," 154
Liberec, 337
Lieberman, Eugeni, 27
Liehm, Anton, 10, 14, 95, 234, 237
"Lightning Flashes Over the Tatras," 272n
Lioubanka, Caves of, 187
Literarni Listy, 42, 47, 95, 96, 99, 101, 145, 154, 234, 235, 340, 343, 345, 346
Literarni Noviny (earlier name of *Literarni Listy*), 10, 31n, 100n, 237, 238, 305, 315
Literaturnaya Gazeta, 243
Litfund, 45, 50n
Litomerice province, 72, 74
Loebl, Eugen, 213, 214, 216, 261, 262, 272n, 300n; views on Czech economy, 280–299
Loebl, Mrs. Eugen, 224
Lomski, General Bohumir, 56, 75
Lubianka Prison, 211
Lucerna ballroom, 8, 233
Luna Park (Fucik Park), 147
Luxembourg, Rosa, 59
L'vov (U.S.S.R.), 138, 176

McCarthy, Senator Joseph, 64
Machiavelli, 325
Magic Lantern Theater, 302
Maiorov, General, 341
Malaparte, 154
Mala Strana, Prague, 5
Mamula, General Miroslav, 56, 75
Manifesto of Czech Intellectuals, 252n

Manual for the Interrogator, 211
Mao Tse-tung, 330
Martin, 264
Marx, Karl, 197, 249, 324
Marxism, 110, 167, 251, 284, 285, 328
Masaryk, Jan, 250, 317
Masaryk, Thomas G., 5, 68, 70, 98, 233, 250, 255, 262, 271, 310, 335
Matern, H., 165
Matiste Slovenska, 264, 265, 272n
Mauthausen concentration camp, 5, 27
Metalworkers Union, 340
Middle East, 140, 170
Mikoyan, Anastas, 30n
"Military Aspects of the Occupation of Czechoslovakia," 192n
Miller, Arthur, 141, 253n
Milovice, 341
Mirov (prison), 220, 222
Mittag, G., 165
Mitterand, François, 6
Mlada Boleslav, 241, 337
Mlada Fronta, 139
Mlady Svet, 82
Mlynar, Zdenek, 100n, 185, 255
Mnacko, Ladislav, 6, 9, 81, 142, 256, 257, 259, 264, 265, 281
Mollet, Guy, 6
Molnar, Lieutenant Colonel, 182
Molotov, V. M., 257
Monde, Le, 31n, 135, 159n, 160n, 192n, 230n, 253n
Montaigne, 304
Montoire, 149
Montreal exposition, 79
Moravec, Commandant, 57
Moravia, Alberto, 253n
Moravia, 5, 15, 18, 20, 89, 220, 222, 233, 254, 255, 257, 260, 263, 313, 315
More, Thomas, 249
Moscow, 20, 25, 27, 69, 81, 89, 131, 160n, 176, 184, 186
Moscow Protocol, 90, 188–189, 190; text of, 199–205
Mucha, Alphonse, 238

Mucha, Jiri, 216–217, 218–219, 220, 238, 252n
Munich agreement, 56, 85, 90, 170, 188, 265, 310
My 68 (*Us in 68*), 94

"N.," Doctor, 212
"N.," Zdenka, 61
Na Prikope Boulevard, 87
Nabrezi Kijevske Brigade, 17
Nad tatrou sa Blyska, 254
Narodni Boulevard, 76
National Assembly. *See* Czechoslovakia, National Assembly
National Front, 22, 26, 91, 108, 109, 113, 114, 125–128, 150, 160, 183, 192n, 194, 196, 206, 207, 300n, 311, 318, 321, 328, 329
National Museum, Prague, 178
National Slovak Insurrectionist Council, 257
National Socialist Party, 91
NATO, 7, 60, 86, 138, 171, 180
Nazi-Soviet pact, 221
Nazis and Nazism, 304, 310
Near East, 52, 265
Neruda Street, 24
Netherlands, 5, 275
Neues Deutschland, 79
New York World's Fair, 44
Nigrin, Charles, 226
Novohradaska, 281
Novosti Agency, 143
Novotny, Anton: author visits home, 4; appearance and personality, 4, 5; background and earlier career, 5–6; elected President, 1957, 6–7; and economic and historical commissions, 8, 30n; relationship with writers and intellectuals, 8–13, 17–18, 235–237, 244; and Jiri Hendrych, 11–12; speech to military academies, 12; opposition and support within party and army, 18–22, 26–29, 54, 57–60; dislike of Dubcek, 30n; and Slovaks, 70, 262, 264–266, 272,

Index

Novotny, Anton (*continued*)
  314; and Sejna, 57–60, 61, 72,
  74, 75; fall of, 4, 7, 11, 25,
  51–52, 66, 72, 74–75, 80, 317,
  318; resigns as President, 75, 78;
  removed from Central Committee, 61–63; and Cisar, 246; and
  inquiry into depression, 274–
  275; and Svitak, 303, 306; mentioned, 3, 15, 23, 30n, 31n, 80,
  122, 191, 215, 228, 230n, 240,
  250, 316, 317, 318, 323
Novotny, Anton, Jr., 73, 75
Novotny, Mrs., 266, 272n
Nuremberg, 256

Obrana Lidu (Czech army news-
  paper), 58, 60
Obroda (politician), 296
October Revolution, 20, 22, 100n
Olomouc, 337
"Operation Sparrow," 236–237
"L'Opposition en U.S.S.R.," 231n
Osborne, John, 253n
Ossouri, 338
Ostrava, 31n, 273n

Pajetta, Giancarlo, 136
Palach, Jan, 339, 344
Palecek, General Vaclav, 222, 223,
  227
Pankow, 53, 140
Pankrac (prison), 220
Paris, 65, 246
Pasionaria, the Slovak, 20
Pavel, Josef, 92, 150, 185, 217,
  230n, 245
Pavlovsky, Ivan, 185
Pedagogical Institute, Charles Uni-
  versity, 227
Pelikan, Jiri, 64, 134, 159, 230,
  277
Pentagon, 74, 246
Petain, Marshal, 149
Pfaff, Ivan, 238
Piller, Jan, 146, 163, 183
Pilsen, 85, 246
Pioneers, 87, 134
Plato, 249

Podgorny, Nikolai, 165
Poland, 7, 54, 110, 141, 164, 170,
  173, 194, 196, 234, 240, 272n,
  309
Polednak, Deputy, 184, 185
Politika, 23, 340
Ponge, Francis, 345
Ponomarev, B. N., 166
Populist Party (Christian), 30n,
  91
Poznan, 241
Prace, 55, 99, 141, 275
Prague: Communist coup of Feb.
  1948, 3, 55, 56; Novotny's
  birthplace, 5; source of jokes
  about Stalinism, 53; atmosphere
  during thaw, 61, 65, 78–79, 87;
  reaction to Warsaw Five letter,
  135; and Soviet occupation, 81,
  178, 179; Communist showing
  in last free elections, 258; former
  prosperity of, 274; demonstra-
  tions after ice hockey game,
  337; University of, 241
Prague TV, 222
Pravda, Bratislava, 31n, 66, 268,
  273n
Pravda, Moscow, 79, 97, 138, 157,
  160n
Prchlik, General Vaclav, 59–62,
  139, 144, 150, 154, 159n, 181,
  277
Pressburg, 259
Prévert, Jacques, 253n
Pribam (T.N.P.), 220
Printemps de Prague, Le, 231n
Prochazka, Jan, 54, 94, 243
"Proclamation to the Czechoslo-
  vakian People . . . ," 193–196
Psarov, 18

Radio Kosice, 181
Radio Prague, 137
R.A.F., 252n
Red Army, 138, 141, 178–179,
  257
Red Square, Moscow, 250
"Report of the Central Committee
  of the Czechoslovakian Com-

munist Party on Violation of Party Principles . . . in the Era of the Cult of Personality," 215

Reporter, The, 160n, 336, 340, 343, 345

Revolution rehabilitiert Ihre Kinder, Die (Loebl), 230n, 300n

Richter (philosopher), 305

Rigo, Emil, 163, 183

Robbe-Grillet, 345

Rochet, Waldeck, 136, 137

Rome, 74

Roy, Claude, 253n

Rude Pravo, 65, 72, 79, 82, 144, 154, 156, 253n

Rumania, 120, 136, 155, 265, 309

Russell, Bertrand, 141, 253n

Russia. *See* U.S.S.R.

Ruthenia, 270, 181

Ruzyne (section of Prague), 211

Ruzyne airport, 175–177, 183, 211

Ruzyne (prison), 211, 212–214, 217, 220, 224, 239

Ryba, 336

Rytir, General, 57, 60

Rytn-Tmarydul (T.N.P.), 220

S., Jan, crew chief, 175, 176, 177

Saint-Simon, 249

Salgovic, Viliam, 182

Sartre, Jean Paul, 141, 253n

Schneidarek, Antonin, 154, 155

"Schweik," 61, 73, 94, 134, 220

Sedlakova, Maria (Slovak Pasionaria), 20–22

Sejna, General Jan, 15, 57–60, 62, 72–75, 77, 144, 316

Semionov, Vladimir, 340, 341

Siberia, 219

Sik, Ota, 8, 12, 27, 28, 30n, 31n, 77, 85, 93, 99n, 150, 156, 247, 253n, 282, 283, 300n; report on Czech economy, 276–280

Simon (Czech politician), 163

Simunek, Otakar, 30n, 77n

Sinyavsky, Andrei, 228, 252n, 306

Six Day War, 140

Skoda factories, 69, 73, 85, 246

Slansky trial, 6, 188, 221, 222, 223, 258, 264, 280, 305

Slapy, 232

Slavik, Vaclav, 14

Slovakia and Slovaks, 7, 19, 26, 52, 68, 69, 75, 89, 181, 233, 315; national anthem, 254; history through World War II, 254–258, 260, 312–314; language, 255, 259–260; national character, 255, 260; 1944 uprising, 256, 257, 310; economic problems, 263–264. *See also* Czecho-Slovak question; Czechoslovakia; Communist party, Slovak

Smetana, Bedrich, 254

Smichov Hill, 4

Smrkovsky, Josef, 15, 28, 77n, 84, 94, 148, 159n, 163, 166, 186–188, 198, 229, 230n, 244, 245, 249, 341

Social Democratic party, 91, 113, 304

Socialist party of Illinois, 68–69

Socialist Students' Union, 304

Socialist Unity Party, East Germany, 165

Sofia, 81, 175

Sokolov, 138

Sokols, 83, 256, 272n, 332n

Solzhenitsyn, Alexander, 10, 228, 231n

Souslov, Mikhail A., 136, 151, 152, 165, 180

South America, 79

Spacek, Josef, 15, 147, 163

Stachovsky, Lieutenant Colonel, 176

Stakhanovism, 290

Stalin, 70, 142, 221, 228, 249, 250, 311

Stalinists and Stalinism, 6, 7, 80, 81, 82, 142, 153, 226, 228, 234, 240, 312, 332n

Starevicz, A., 165

S.T.B., 180, 182, 184, 185

Steiger (cartoonist), 145

Steinbeck, John, 253n

Index

Stern, Jan, 55, 99
Stockholm, 337, 338
Stoph, Willy, 165
Strahov Hill, 24, 31n
Strecno, 272n
Stur, Ludjovit, 77
Sturp, Ivan, 274, 300n
Sudeten Germans, 140
Sulek, Miroslav, 179
Sunday Times, London, 238, 252n, 253n
Svedectvi (Evidence), 11
Sverman, Jan, 258
Svestka, Oldrich, 72, 144, 146, 163, 183, 330
Svitak, Ivan, 71, 237, 242, 302–306; political/philosophical views of, 306–331
Svoboda, Alois, 23
Svoboda, President Ludvik, 82, 87, 100n, 149, 151, 166, 184, 185, 198, 220, 272, 341, 342; and Moscow Protocols, 186–190
Svoboda, Mrs., 187, 192n
Sweden, 97, 309
Switzerland, 260, 277
Syria, 140

Tarassov, Anatole, 337
Tass Agency, 139, 172–174
Taste for Power, The (Mnacko), 6
Tatra Mountains, 69, 264, 270
Tatu, Michel, 31n, 159n
Technique of a Coup d'Etat (Malaparte), 154
Tel Aviv, 140
Teplice, 337
Testament of the Union (Komensky), 252n
Thirty Years War, 309
Tichy, Mr. (Czech civil servant), 143
Tigrid, Pavel, 11, 186, 189, 225
Times, The, London, 135
Tiso, Monsignor, 256
Tito, 136, 154, 156, 339
T.N.P. (obligatory work camps), 220

Todorov, S., 164
Tolstoy, Leo, 233
Tomasek, Monsignor Frantisek, 134
Toman, Vlastimil, 340
Transylvania, 265
Trencin, 69, 70
Tribuna Ludu, 79
Trnava, 278
Trnka (woodcarver), 4, 244
Truth About the Czechoslovakian Economy, The (Sik), 277
Tuzex stores, 52
"Two Thousand Words," 9, 95–97, 113, 128, 318; text, 101–110
Tyl, Joseph-Kajetan, 272n

Uhrovec, 69
Ukraine, 147
Ulbricht, Walter, 28, 52, 141, 152, 154, 156, 157, 159n, 165, 177
Union of Bohemian Brothers, 252n
United Arab Republic, 276
United Nations, 223, 260; Security Council, 170, 203
United Polish Workers Party, 165
United States, 64, 73, 170, 171, 180, 284, 287, 289, 306
U.S.S.R., 69, 71, 77, 110, 118, 120, 127, 160, 164, 170, 180, 196, 224, 249, 260, 280, 309; and Budapest uprising, 7; attitude to Czech thaw, 78, 80–81, 96–97; economic subjection of Czechoslovakia, 52–53, 93, 94, 276, 282–283; military maneuvers in Czechoslovakia, 93, 97, 139, 141, 157; and Warsaw Five letter, 136–137; and Cierna meeting, 147, 148–151; and Bratislava meeting, 153; invades Czechoslovakia, 173–174, 179, 184; trials of 1930s, 221; post-Stalinism, 228; revolution in technology, 287; ice hockey team defeated by Czechs, 336–

337. *See also* Communist party, U.S.S.R.; Red Army
Urvalek, Josef, 266
Us in 68, 94
Usti nad Labem, 337

Vaclavaske Namesty. *See* Wenceslas Square
Vaculik, Ludvik, 9, 14, 95, 96, 101, 345; text of speech to Writers' Congress, 32–50
Vaculik, Martin, 20, 31n
Valdice (prison), 220
Vienna, 24n, 274, 302, 310
Vietnam, 52, 170, 178, 184
Vlkovice, 15
Vltava River, 5, 145, 178, 232, 338, 339
Vnoukovo (U.S.S.R.), 186
Vodslon, Frantisek, 15, 21, 27, 191
Voltaire, 304
Vyscocany, 185

War With the Newts, The (Capek), 53
Warsaw, 81, 130, 234, 241
"Warsaw Five" letter to Czech C.P., 90, 97–98, 99, 133, 135– 136, 142; text of, 110–116; reply of Czech C.P., 117–131
Warsaw Pact, 7, 74, 85, 93, 138, 139, 151, 171, 180, 189, 194, 197, 203, 277, 319, 320, 338
Weiss, Peter, 253
Wenceslas Boulevard, 337
Wenceslas Square (Vaclavaske Namesty), 65, 145, 146, 178
"Where Is My Homeland?," 272n
Whetten, Lawrence L., 192n
White House, 246
White Mountain, battle of the, 55
Wild Daja (Klicka), 38
World Today, The, 192n
World War II, 178, 275, 313
Writers' Congress (1967), 8, 9– 10, 14, 17, 21, 54, 233, 235, 239, 315; text of Vaculik's speech to, 32–50
Writers' Union, 31n, 40, 41, 45, 141, 235, 236, 237, 238, 239, 243, 305

Yakubovsky, Marshal Ivan, 74, 138, 181
Yalta, 180, 249
Yugoslavia, 23, 73, 136, 260, 309

Zapotocky, Antonin, 6, 250
Zichov Hill, 250